BASIC

PRACTICE

SERIES

ESA

Endangered
Species Act

SECOND EDITION

Sam Kalen
Murray Feldman

AMERICAN BAR ASSOCIATION
Section of Environment,
Energy, and Resources

Printed in the United States of America

16 15 14 13 12   5 4 3 2 1

Library of Congress Cataloging-in-Publication Data

Kalen, Sam.
   Endangered Species Act / Sam Kalen and Murray Feldman.—2nd ed.
      p. cm.—(Basic practice series)
   Rev. ed. of: ESA, Endangered Species Act / Tony A. Sullins. c2001.
   Includes bibliographical references and index.
   ISBN 978-1-61438-557-8 (print : alk. paper)
1.   United States. Endangered Species Act of 1973. 2.   Endangered species—Law and legislation—United States. I. Feldman, Murray D. II. Sullins, Tony A., 1966- ESA, Endangered Species Act. III. Title.
   KF5640.S85 2012
   346.7304'69522—dc23

                                                                        2012034440

Discounts are available for books ordered in bulk. Special consideration is given to state bars, CLE programs, and other bar-related organizations. Inquire at Book Publishing, ABA Publishing, American Bar Association, 321 North Clark Street, Chicago, Illinois 60654-7598.

www.ShopABA.org

Contents

Preface

As our world's population continues to grow, and we place greater pressures on the environment, new species of fish, wildlife, and plants are added to the list of endangered and threatened species established by the Endangered Species Act (ESA). The ESA embodies an important and legally enforceable determination by our country to protect, conserve, and recover these species. But conflict is inevitable. The ESA, its implementing regulations, court decisions, and agency guidance collectively provide a substantial and fairly robust body of law for species protection. Anyone concerned with what can, ought, or must be done to benefit imperiled species should study and appreciate the ESA. Likewise, if for no other reason than the serious nature of the penalties associated with violations of the ESA, anyone engaging in activities that may affect a listed species should proceed with caution and understand what is prohibited, and what is not. Regardless of one's interest in listed species protection, this book provides a basic overview of the major elements of the ESA.

While most seasoned ESA practitioners are already intimately familiar with much of the content of this book, this book may be useful for its ease of access and as a quick reference. The novice may use this book to develop a working knowledge of any common ESA issue. Unfortunately, no basic practice book can address every specific issue that might arise, and this book is no exception. Rather, this book should serve as a valuable starting point for researching most common ESA issues. Any user of this book who has a specific ESA question should consider first consulting the "Frequently Asked Questions" in Appendix A. Likewise, a listing of Key Cases (Appendix B), Glossary, Bibliography, Table of Cases, and Index are provided at the end of the book for quick reference. The main body of the book (Chapters 1 through 11) is separated into several sections and subsections, and provides a more detailed discussion of particular ESA issues, with appropriate citation to case law, statutes, regulations, and secondary authority.

Acknowledgments

The authors thank Leslie Keros for her helpful review, assistance, and guidance in preparing this second edition for publication. And the authors are grateful for the ABA's peer reviewer comments, as well as for the assistance from Dean Hirt and Matthew Stannard, both students at the University of Wyoming College of Law. The authors also thank Tammy Feldman, lecturer at the University of Michigan's Ross School of Business and managing editor of the *Antitrust Law Journal,* for her very thorough and helpful review of the final manuscript citations and format. Finally, Sam Kalen is especially grateful for the support from the Carl Williams Faculty Research Fund, which allowed him the ability to devote the time necessary to work on the manuscript.

About the Authors

Sam Kalen is an Associate Professor of Law at the University of Wyoming College of Law, where he teaches, among other topics, environmental law and energy, and he is Of Counsel at Van Ness Feldman, in Washington, D.C. He has practiced in the environment, energy, and natural resources areas for over 25 years. Throughout his career, he has worked on a number of ESA matters throughout the country, both in counseling clients and in representing parties in court. He has published numerous articles and book chapters on environmental law topics. He is a past vice-chair of the ABA Section of Environment, Energy, and Resources Endangered Species Committee and past Chair of the Public Land and Resources Committee and the Book Publications Committee. He also served in the Solicitor's Office at the Department of the Interior. Mr. Kalen received his J.D. from Washington University School of Law, and his B.A. from Clark University.

Murray Feldman is the administrative partner for the Boise, Idaho, office of Holland & Hart LLP. He represents state and local governments, landowners, and others in ESA litigation and administrative proceedings on species listing, critical habitat designation, consultation, habitat conservation planning, and related issues. He has worked on ESA matters throughout the Pacific Northwest, and in Alaska, Alabama, Nevada, New Mexico, and Michigan, with a variety of species including the polar bear, ribbon seal, Snake River chinook salmon, Moapa dace, Sacramento Mountains thistle, piping plover, and Alabama beach mouse. His practice also includes litigation and regulatory compliance on National Environmental Policy Act, Clean Water Act, public lands, and climate change issues. Mr. Feldman is the author of over 30 published articles and book chapters on environmental law topics. He is a past vice-chair of the ABA Section of Environment, Energy, and Resources Endangered Species Committee and the Public Land

and Resources Committee, and past chair of the Idaho State Bar's Environment and Natural Resources section. He received his J.D. from the University of California, Berkeley (Boalt Hall) School of Law, where he was an associate editor of the Ecology Law Quarterly, and his M.S. degree from the University of Idaho College of Natural Resources.

Abbreviations

ALJ	administrative law judge
APA	Administrative Procedure Act
BA	biological assessment
BLM	Bureau of Land Management
BO	biological opinion
CCA	Candidate Conservation Agreement
CCAA	Candidate Conservation Agreement with Assurances
CFR	Code of Federal Regulations
CITES	Convention on International Trade in Endangered Species of Wild Fauna and Flora
DOI	Department of the Interior
DPS	distinct population segment
EA	environmental assessment
EIS	environmental impact statement
EPA	Environmental Protection Agency
ESA	Endangered Species Act
ESC	Endangered Species Committee
ESU	evolutionarily significant unit
FWS	Fish and Wildlife Service
HCP	habitat conservation plan
ITP	incidental take permit
ITS	incidental take statement
NEPA	National Environmental Policy Act
NMFS	National Marine Fisheries Service
NOAA	National Oceanic and Atmospheric Administration
RPA	reasonable and prudent alternative
RPM	reasonable and prudent measure
SPR	significant portion of its range
SHA	safe harbor agreement
USDA	United States Department of Agriculture
USFS	United States Forest Service

1 Executive Summary

1.1   Overview

The Endangered Species Act (ESA) is perhaps the "most compre-hensive legislation for the preservation of endangered species ever enacted by any nation."[1] Congress's "plain intent" when enacting the ESA "was to halt and reverse the trend toward species extinc-tion, at whatever the cost."[2] Lately the Act has offered the polar bear as an iconic symbol of the efforts to address the Act's con-servation mandate and the regulatory implications of those man-dates. But today, the words "endangered species" are so familiar in American life as to have become a cliché. "Ask [people] in the street what [they think] about the problem of disappearing spe-cies, and [they] may well reply that it would be a pity if the tiger or the blue whale disappeared," yet it is not apparent whether that sentiment is sufficient to cause the same people to alter their lifestyle.[3] Even the name "Endangered Species Act" elicits the strongest of feelings, conjuring up images of the polar bear, the grizzly bear, the gray wolf, spotted owls, or even angry loggers.

This book cannot capture or explore the historical, scien-tific, sociological, political, or psychological underpinnings of the ESA, or even provide a comprehensive survey of wildlife law in the United States.[4] Rather, the purpose of the *Basic Practice*

---

1. Babbitt v. Sweet Home Chapter of Cmtys. for a Great Or., 515 U.S. 687, 698 (1995).
2. Tenn. Valley Auth. v. Hill, 437 U.S. 153, 184 (1978).
3. NORMAN MYERS, THE SINKING ARK: A NEW LOOK AT THE PROBLEM OF DISAPPEARING SPECIES 3 (1979).
4. See MICHAEL J. BEAN & MELANIE J. ROWLAND, THE EVOLUTION OF NATIONAL WILD-LIFE LAW (1997), for a detailed and thorough discussion of federal wildlife law, including the ESA; and for other useful books on the Act, see REBUILDING THE ARK:

1

Series and, in particular, this book, is more modest. The series is designed to introduce the reader to a particular statute and its regulatory program—in this case the ESA—and then offer citations and references that further inform the reader of how the Act and its regulations have been implemented. That the Act will remain a vibrant program warranting continued understanding is underscored, unfortunately, by the fact that climate change "may constitute an important new threat for many" at-risk or vulnerable species.[5]

1.2   Purposes of the Endangered Species Act

By 1973, when the ESA became law, Congress already was acutely aware of the problem of human-induced species extinction.[6] Congress's earlier efforts, the 1966 Endangered Species Preservation Act[7] and the 1969 Endangered Species Conservation Act,[8] had proven insufficient to protect endangered wildlife.[9] Against this backdrop, Congress acted decisively. Finding that "species of fish, wildlife, and plants are of aesthetic, ecological, educational, historical, recreational, and scientific value to the nation and its people,"[10] Congress declared: "The purposes of [the ESA] are to provide a means whereby the ecosystems upon which endangered species and threatened species depend may be conserved, [and] to provide a program for the conservation of such endangered and threatened species."[11] To meet these underlying objectives, Congress established in the ESA a comprehensive suite

---

NEW PERSPECTIVES ON ENDANGERED SPECIES ACT REFORM (Jonathan H. Adler ed., 2011); ENDANGERED SPECIES ACT: LAW, POLICY, AND PERSPECTIVES (Donald C. Baur & Wm. Robert Irvin eds., 2d ed. 2010); KATHRYN A. KOHM, BALANCING ON THE BRINK OF EXTINCTION: THE ENDANGERED SPECIES ACT AND LESSONS FOR THE FUTURE (1991); DANIEL J. ROHLF, THE ENDANGERED SPECIES ACT: A GUIDE TO ITS PROTECTIONS AND IMPLEMENTATION (1989); STANFORD ENVTL. LAW SOC'Y, THE ENDANGERED SPECIES ACT (2001).

    5. HECTOR GALBRAITH & JEFF PRICE, A FRAMEWORK FOR CATEGORIZING THE RELATIVE VULNERABILITY OF THREATENED AND ENDANGERED SPECIES TO CLIMATE CHANGE 1 (Global Change Research Program 2009).

    6. For a discussion about the early concerns animating and surrounding the passage of the Act, see LEWIS REGENSTEIN, THE POLITICS OF EXTINCTION: THE SHOCKING STORY OF THE WORLD'S ENDANGERED WILDLIFE (1975).

    7. Pub. L. No. 89-669, 80 Stat. 926 (1966).

    8. Pub. L. No. 91-135, 83 Stat. 275 (1969).

    9. *See* ROHLF, *supra* note 4, at 21–23.

  10. 16 U.S.C. § 1531(a)(3).

  11. *Id.* § 1531(b).

of affirmative mandates, strict prohibitions, strong recommendations, and limited exceptions.

The U.S. Supreme Court has provided perhaps the most strident and oft-quoted summary of the ESA's breadth.[12] After reviewing the Act and its legislative history, the Court stated that "the plain intent of Congress in enacting this statute was to halt and reverse the trend toward species extinction, whatever the cost," and noted further that this conclusion is reflected "in literally every section of the statute."[13] Although the Court admitted that it might seem "curious to some that the survival of a relatively small number of three-inch fish among all the countless millions of species extant would require the permanent holding up of a virtually completed dam for which Congress has expended more than $100 million," the Court held in *Tennessee Valley Authority v. Hill* that the Act required "precisely that result."[14]

Since the Court's decision in *Hill,* Congress has substantively amended the ESA on four occasions (1978, 1979, 1982, and 1988). The rigidity of the Act's prohibitions has been tempered somewhat through the creation of several exceptions and exemptions[15] and the countervailing Supreme Court statements,[16] but the exceptions and statements have not swallowed the rule. The ESA remains a "powerful tool"[17] for species protection and conservation, and quite possibly warrants the attribution of being the "pit bull"[18] of all environmental and conservation programs. After all, it has served as the fulcrum for driving management decisions

---

12. Tenn. Valley Auth. v. Hill, 437 U.S. 153, 180 (1978).

13. *Id.*

14. *Id.* at 172–73. For an excellent history of the Tellico dam controversy, see KENNETH M. MURCHISON, THE SNAIL DARTER CASE: TVA VERSUS THE ENDANGERED SPECIES ACT (2007).

15. For discussion of the ESA's various exceptions and exemptions, see *infra* chapter 4, sections 4.3 and 4.8; chapter 5, section 5.4.5.4; chapters 6 and 7; and chapter 10, section 10.7.

16. *E.g., Bennett v. Spear,* 520 U.S. 154, 176–77 (1997) (The "obvious purpose of the requirement that each agency 'use the best scientific and commercial data available' is to ensure that the ESA not be implemented haphazardly, on the basis of speculation or surmise. While this no doubt serves to advance the ESA's overall goal of species preservation, we think it readily apparent that another objective (if not indeed the primary one) is to avoid needless economic dislocation produced by agency officials zealously but unintelligently pursuing their environmental objectives.") (quoting 16 U.S.C. § 1536(a)(2)).

17. James C. Kilbourne, *The Endangered Species Act under the Microscope: A Closeup Look from a Litigator's Perspective,* 21 ENVTL. L. 499, 501 (1991).

18. Donald Barry, Address at American Bar Association Section of Natural Resources, Energy, and Environmental Law, Workshop on Endangered Species (Apr. 6, 1990).

on millions of public and private acres, as well as for watersheds and river systems throughout the nation.

1.3   Basic Structure of the ESA

The ESA provides substantive protections to any species listed as endangered or threatened. Key among these protections are the prohibition against any federal agency activity that might jeopardize a listed species or adversely modify or destroy its critical habitat,[19] the prohibition against any activities that would "take" a protected species,[20] the requirement that federal agencies develop programs to conserve and recover listed species,[21] and the obligation imposed on the federal government to cooperate with states and foreign governments to meet the purposes of the Act.[22] The Act explicitly implements two international treaties respecting trade and conservation in wildlife.[23] In some cases, federal agencies may avail themselves of limited exceptions to the Act's mandates,[24] and private parties may obtain a variety of permits allowing limited taking of protected species.[25] Finally, the ESA contains substantial criminal and civil penalties,[26] as well as a liberal citizen-suit provision, encouraging any person to act as a "private attorney general" to enforce the Act.[27]

Each section of the ESA attempts to work in tandem with the others to collectively achieve the Act's overarching conservation objective, although various provisions of the Act affect different people in differing ways and some requirements are relevant only to specific situations. The chapters in this book are organized with that in mind, grouping issues topically when appropriate, while adhering as closely as possible to the underlying organizational structure of the Act itself.

---

19. See infra chapter 5.
20. See infra chapter 4.
21. See infra chapter 3.
22. See infra chapters 8 and 9.
23. See infra chapter 9, section 9.5.
24. See infra chapter 5, section 5.4.5.4, and chapter 7.
25. See infra chapter 6.
26. See infra chapter 4, section 4.7.1.
27. See infra chapter 11.

2 Listing and Critical Habitat Designation

2.1 Overview

Congress described the Endangered Species Act (ESA) section 4[1] listing process as the "keystone" of the Act.[2] The ESA provides substantive protection to species only once they are listed as threatened or endangered pursuant to section 4 of the Act. Congress, therefore, explained, "[T]he protective measures to counter species extinction take effect when a species is listed."[3]

For purposes of the ESA, endangered and threatened species are defined as follows:

> The term "endangered species" means any species which is in danger of extinction throughout all or a significant portion of its range other than a species of the Class Insecta determined by the Secretary to constitute a pest whose protection under the provisions of this Act would present an overwhelming overriding risk to man.[4]
>
> The term "threatened species" means any species which is likely to become an endangered species within the foreseeable future throughout all or a significant portion of its range.[5]

---

1. 16 U.S.C. § 1533.
2. H.R. Rep. No. 97-567, at 10 (1982), *reprinted in* 1982 U.S.C.C.A.N. 2807, 2810. For a detailed review of the listing process, see J.B. Ruhl, *Listing Endangered and Threatened Species, in* Endangered Species Act: Law, Policy, and Perspectives 17 (Donald C. Baur & Wm. Robert Irvin eds., 2010). For a discussion of section 4 generally, see Daniel J. Rohlf, *Section 4 of the Endangered Species Act: Top Ten Issues for the Next Thirty Years,* 34 Envtl. L. 483 (2004).
3. H.R. Rep. No. 97-567, at 10 (1982), *reprinted in* 1982 U.S.C.C.A.N. 2807, 2810.
4. 16 U.S.C. § 1522(6); 50 C.F.R. § 424.02(e). *See* Carlton v. Babbitt, 26 F. Supp. 2d 102, 111 (D.D.C. 1998) (holding that FWS failed to present a defensible case that 26–36 grizzly bears was a "minimal, viable population size" for the bears).
5. 16 U.S.C. § 1532(19); 50 C.F.R. § 424.02(m). The term *foreseeable future* is not defined. *See In re* Polar Bear Endangered Species Act Listing and § 4(d) Rule Litig., 794 F. Supp. 2d 65, 93–96 (D.D.C. 2011) (court accepted a 45-year period),

Section 4 of the ESA vests the Secretary[6] with a "mandatory non-discretionary duty to list qualified species as endangered or threatened."[7] The Secretary may also list any species that so closely resembles in appearance a listed species that enforcement personnel would have difficulty differentiating between the two.[8] Not until recently have the Services been required to articulate any established policy for distinguishing between "endangered" and "threatened" species. But in connection with the listing of the polar bear as threatened, a district court held that the phrase "in danger of extinction" created sufficient ambiguity, prompting the Fish and Wildlife Service (FWS) to articulate a reasoned explanation for the difference between a threatened and endangered species. In a document filed in the polar bear litigation, the FWS emphasized that the distinguishing characteristic between an endangered and threatened species is temporal, and "depends upon the life history and ecology of the species, the nature of the threats, and the species' response to those threats."[9]

The actual lists of species determined to be endangered or threatened under the ESA are published in the Code of Federal Regulations.[10] In addition, the FWS publishes a regular Candidate Notice of Review identifying species that are candidates for

---

appeal docketed, No. 11-5219 (D.C. Cir. Aug. 25, 2011); Ctr. for Biological Diversity v. Lubchenco, 2010 WL 5288188 (N.D. Cal. 2010) (rejecting claim that Service's period for assessing foreseeable future for declining to list the ribbon seal was arbitrary or capricious); W. Watersheds Project v. Foss, 2005 U.S. Dist. LEXIS 45753 (E.D. Pa. Aug. 19, 2005) (definition of "foreseeable future" varies depending upon species); Or. Nat. Res. Council v. Daley, 6 F. Supp. 2d 1139, 1150–51 (D. Or. 1998) (court held that the National Marine Fisheries Service (NMFS) failed to correctly apply the "within the foreseeable future" standard, and that NMFS had wrongly based its listing determination on a finding that coho would not likely become endangered in the interval between NMFS's "not warranted" finding and the adoption of habitat protection measures by the state of Oregon). Most courts have accepted a "more likely than not" understanding of the term "likely" in connection with the "foreseeable future" language. *See* Trout Unlimited v. Lohn, 645 F. Supp. 2d 929 (D. Or. 2007); W. Watersheds Project v. U.S. Forest Serv., 535 F. Supp. 2d 1173 (D. Idaho 2007); *see also In re* Polar Bear Endangered Species Act Listing and § 4(d) Rule Litig., 794 F. Supp. 2d 65, 91–93 (D.D.C. 2011), *appeal pending*.

6. Throughout this book, the terms *Secretary, FWS, NMFS,* and *Service(s)* are used interchangeably, unless otherwise noted. The Secretary of Commerce (delegated to NMFS) is generally responsible for marine species, and the Secretary of the Interior (delegated to FWS) is responsible for all other listings. See 50 C.F.R. §§ 223.102 and 224.101 for species under NMFS jurisdiction.

7. H.R. Rep. No. 97–835, at 20 (1982).

8. 16 U.S.C. § 1533(e).

9. *In re* Polar Bear Endangered Species Act Listing and § 4(d) Rule Litig., 794 F. Supp. 2d 65, 83 (D.D.C. 2011).

10. 50 C.F.R. § 17.11 (fish and wildlife), § 17.2 (plants).

listing.[11] As a matter of policy, and in keeping with an ecosystem-based approach to the ESA, the Secretary will "group" listings on a geographic, taxonomic, or ecosystem basis whenever possible.[12] Although Congress noted that a purpose of the ESA is "to provide a means whereby the ecosystems upon which" the listed species depend will be conserved,[13] for many years the ESA was implemented with quite possibly a more limited focus on a species-by-species basis. Today, we recognize the importance of interrelated, interlocking, and overlapping ecological systems and the role they play toward sustaining the viability of species.[14]

Listing decisions, along with associated critical habitat designations,[15] are vital and often controversial activities that are governed by detailed statutory and regulatory guidelines.

2.2   What Is a Species?

The ESA broadly, if somewhat vaguely, uses the term *species* to define the universe of organisms that may qualify for listing as threatened or endangered; any species of fish, wildlife,[16] or plant[17] is eligible for listing consideration. The Act defines *species* as follows:

> The term "species" includes any subspecies of fish or wildlife or plants, and any distinct population segment of any species of vertebrate fish or wildlife which interbreeds when mature.[18]

---

11.   *See* 76 Fed. Reg. 66,370 (Oct. 26, 2011) (FWS's Candidate Notice of Review). *See* 16 U.S.C. § 1533(b)(3)(c)(iii) (requiring a "regular review of status surveys" with respect to candidate species).

12.   59 Fed. Reg. 34,273, 34,274 (1994).

13.   16 U.S.C. § 1531(b).

14.   *See generally* Bradley C. Karkkainen, *Collaborative Ecosystem Governance: Scale, Complexity, and Dynamism,* 21 Va. Envtl. L.J. 189 (2002).

15.   *See* section 2.8 (discussing critical habitat designation).

16.   The Act defines *fish* and *wildlife* as "any member of the animal kingdom, including without limitation any mammal, fish, bird (including any migratory, non-migratory, or endangered bird for which protection is also afforded by treaty or other international agreement), amphibian, reptile, mollusk, crustacean, arthropod or other invertebrate. . . ." 16 U.S.C. § 1532(8).

17.   *Id.* § 1532(14), defining *plant* as "any member of the plant kingdom."

18.   *Id.* § 1532(16). The term *species* is further qualified through regulation as not including "any species of the class Insecta determined by the Secretary to constitute a pest whose protection under the provisions of the Act would present an overwhelming and overriding risk to man."

Though perhaps not biologically or taxonomically correct, the ESA's definition of *species* implicitly recognizes scientific nomenclature as a starting point for determining eligibility for listing; Congress expressed a working comfort level with "taxonomic categories" at the subspecies level or above.[19] Nowhere in the ESA, however, will one find any rigid adherence to a purely taxonomic definition of *species*.

The Services conclude that because "the Act does not attempt to define 'species' in biological terms,"[20] the term *species* may be applied "according to the best biological knowledge and understanding of evolution, speciation, and genetics."[21] Thus, in establishing the list of endangered or threatened species, the listing agencies may utilize such sources as the *International Code of Zoological Nomenclature,* but only to the extent "practicable."[22]

As discussed in sections 2.2.1 and 2.2.2 below, whether a particular group of vertebrate fish or wildlife is a "distinct population segment" or whether a species is threatened or endangered throughout "all or a significant portion of its range" have provoked attention and controversy.

2.2.1   Distinct Population Segments

In 1978, Congress amended the ESA definition of *species*.[23] The 1978 amendments provide that the term *species* encompasses "*any distinct population segment* of any species of vertebrate fish or wildlife which interbreeds when mature."[24] Congress did not further clarify this amendment, but left it to the listing agencies to fill the definitional void and apply the ESA listing provisions to "distinct population segments" of vertebrate fish and wildlife.

19. H.R. Rep. No. 95-1804, at 17 (1978), *reprinted in* 1978 U.S.C.C.A.N. 9484, 9485.
20. *See* 61 Fed. Reg. 4707, 4710 (1996) (discussing the term *species* in the context of whether "intercrosses" or "hybrids" may be protected under the ESA).
21. *Id.*
22. 50 C.F.R. § 17.11(b).
23. See Karl Gleaves et al., *The Meaning of "Species" Under the Endangered Species Act,* 13 Pub. Land L. Rev. 25, 30–31 (1992), for a detailed discussion of the 1978 amendments to the definition of *species*. *See also* J.B. Ruhl, *supra* note 2. The Act originally defined species to include taxonomic species, subspecies, and "any other group of fish or wildlife of the same species or smaller taxa in common spatial arrangement that interbreed when mature." Pub. L. No. 93-205, 87 Stat. 884 (1973).
24. 16 U.S.C. § 1532(16) (emphasis added).

One year later, in 1979, Congress considered but declined the opportunity to repeal, clarify, or modify its distinct population segment (DPS) language.[25] Instead, in a Senate report discussing the issue, Congress stated: "[T]he committee is aware of the great potential for abuse of this authority and expects the FWS to use the ability to list populations *sparingly* and only when the biological evidence indicates that such action is warranted."[26] Whether a "sparing" use of the authority to list DPSs comports with the agencies' affirmative duty to list any species that otherwise qualifies as endangered or threatened is an unresolved question.[27] Nonetheless, the listing agencies have publicly committed to a sparing use of DPS listing authority[28] and have struggled somewhat to develop a sufficiently predictive policy for applying the DPS listing authority granted by Congress.[29]

The listing agencies have candidly summarized the key challenge in applying ESA coverage to DPSs: "It is uncontested that the term 'distinct population segment' is not mentioned in scientific literature, nor explicitly defined in the ESA."[30] And the Ninth Circuit recently observed that "[t]here is no indication within the text that Congress intended to create a rigid limitation on the agency's discretion to define the statutorily undefined concept" of

---

25. Gleaves, *supra* note 23, at 31–33.
26. S. REP. NO. 96-151 (1979), *reprinted in* CONG. RESEARCH SERV., 97TH CONG., 2D SESS., A LEGISLATIVE HISTORY OF THE ENDANGERED SPECIES ACT OF 1973, at 1396–97 (Comm. Print 1982) (emphasis added).
27. *See* Gleaves, *supra* note 23, at 33, 34.
28. *See* 61 Fed. Reg. 4724, 4722 (1996) (noting that "the services have used this authority relatively rarely, and that of over 300 native vertebrate species listed under the Act, only about 30 are given separate status as DPSs.").
29. *See* Sw. Ctr. for Biological Diversity v. Babbitt, 926 F. Supp. 920, 926–27 (D. Ariz. 1996) (finding that FWS had arbitrarily selected which, among many, draft DPS policies it would follow in a particular case). Because the language appears ambiguous, courts afford the listing agencies deference when interpreting what constitutes a DPS. *See, e.g.,* Ctr. for Biological Diversity v. Lohn, 296 F. Supp. 2d 1223, 1234–36 (W.D. Wash. 2003), *dismissed as moot and ordered remanded by* Ctr. for Biological Diversity v. Lohn, 511 F.3d 960 (9th Cir. 2007).
30. *Id.* at 926. *See also* FWS/NMFS Final Policy Regarding Recognition of Distinct Population Segments Under the Endangered Species Act, 61 Fed. Reg. 4721, 4722 (1996) ("available scientific information provides little specific enlightenment in interpreting the phrase 'distinct population segment'"). The Services occasionally repeat this concern when issuing DPS determinations. *E.g.,* Determination of Nine Distinct Population Segments of Loggerhead Sea Turtles as Endangered or Threatened, 76 Fed. Reg. 58,868 (2011). In one case illustrating the difficulty of reconciling the DPS listing authority with existing scientific nomenclature, a court held that the joint DPS policy, to the extent it limited the DPS to one subspecies, was arbitrary and capricious. Sw. Ctr. for Biological Diversity v. Babbitt, 980 F. Supp. 1080, 1085 (D. Ariz. 1997).

a DPS.[31] The listing agencies, therefore, have developed detailed DPS policy guidance informing their determinations of DPS status. This guidance is embodied in two *Federal Register* publications: the NMFS [National Marine Fisheries Service] 1991 Policy on the Definition of Species under the Endangered Species Act[32] and the 1996 NMFS and FWS Joint Policy Regarding the Recognition of Distinct Vertebrate Population Segments under the Endangered Species Act.[33]

The 1991 NMFS policy is applicable only to species of salmonids native to the Pacific.[34] NMFS has determined that a particular stock of salmon will qualify as a DPS only if that stock "represents an evolutionarily significant unit (ESU) of the biological species."[35] A stock thus qualifies as an ESU if it satisfies two criteria: (1) it must be substantially reproductively isolated from other nonspecific population units and (2) it must represent an important component in the evolutionary legacy of the species.[36]

NMFS applied these criteria in the Columbia River Basin to list different seasonal runs of chinook salmon as separate ESUs.[37] Similarly, NMFS determined that populations of steelhead trout occupying different reaches of the Columbia River also qualify as separate ESUs.[38]

The 1996 joint NMFS/FWS DPS policy[39] provides guidance for determining whether any other (non-Pacific salmonid) group of organisms qualifies as a distinct population segment eligible for listing. The 1996 joint DPS policy lists three "principles"[40] that

---

31. Modesto Irr. Dist. v. Gutierrez, 619 F.3d 1024, 1032 (9th Cir. 2010).

32. 56 Fed. Reg. 58,612–18 (1991). For a more detailed discussion of NMFS's 1991 policy, see Gleaves, *supra* note 23, at 41–44.

33. 61 Fed. Reg. 4721–25 (1996).

34. 56 Fed. Reg. at 58,612. *See also Modesto Irr. Dist.,* 619 F.3d at 1030–31 (noting that NMFS only applies ESU policy to Pacific salmon).

35. 56 Fed. Reg. at 58,618.

36. *Id.*

37. *See, e.g.,* 57 Fed. Reg. 14,653 (Apr. 22, 1992) (listing the Snake River spring/summer chinook salmon and the Snake River fall chinook salmon as two separate species).

38. *See, e.g.,* 62 Fed. Reg. 43,937 (Aug. 18, 1997) (listing the upper Columbia River steelhead); 64 Fed. Reg. 14,517 (Mar. 25, 1999) (listing the middle Columbia River steelhead); 63 Fed. Reg. 13,347 (Mar. 19, 1998) (listing the lower Columbia River steelhead). For a discussion about hatchery-raised fish and their affect on establishing ESUs, see *Trout Unlimited v. Lohn,* 559 F.3d 946 (9th Cir. 2009); *Alsea Valley Alliance v. Evans,* 161 F. Supp. 2d 1154 (D. Or. 2001).

39. 61 Fed. Reg. 4721 (1996).

40. *Id.* at 4725.

will be "considered" in making DPS determinations.[41] These principles are

- *discreteness* of the population segment in relation to the remainder of the species to which it belongs
- *significance* of the population segment to the species to which it belongs
- *conservation status* of the population segment (i.e., whether the DPS is endangered or threatened)[42]

The joint DPS policy provides further guidance with respect to the first two principles, discreteness and significance. A population segment is discrete if it is either (1) markedly separated from other populations of the same taxon as a consequence of physical, physiological, ecological, or behavioral factors or (2) delimited by international governmental boundaries within which significant differences in control of exploitation, management of habitat, conservation status, or regulatory mechanisms exist.[43] Once a population segment has been determined to be discrete, the following factors may be considered to determine whether it is significant to its species:

- persistence of the discrete population segment in an ecological setting unusual or unique for the taxon
- evidence that loss of the discrete population segment would result in a significant gap in the range of a taxon
- evidence that the discrete population segment represents the only surviving natural occurrence of a taxon that may be more abundant elsewhere as an introduced population outside its historic range
- evidence that the discrete population segment differs markedly from other populations of the species in its genetic characteristics[44]

41. *Id.* The policy arguably requires a positive finding on all three elements before a population segment qualifies as a DPS. The second principle will be considered "if" the first principle is satisfied, and the third principle will be considered "if" the first and second principles have been satisfied. *Id.*

42. *Id.*

43. 61 Fed. Reg. at 4724. The Services explicitly noted that only international boundaries, as opposed to state or local boundaries, were appropriate as a focus for a national program; the Services would decline to list entities that are not primarily of conservation interest at a national level. *Id.*

44. 61 Fed. Reg. at 4725. *See, e.g.,* Nw. Ecosystem Alliance v. U.S. Fish & Wildlife Serv., 475 F.3d 1136, 1145 (9th Cir. 2007); W. Watersheds Project v.

Recognizing the flexibility inherent in applying these criteria, the Services caution that it is not possible to describe in any blanket policy all of the classes of information that might influence the biological or ecological importance of determining a discrete or distinct population segment.[45] But at least the Ninth Circuit has indicated that the policy is legally binding and afforded deference to the agencies' interpretation of the Act in the DPS policy.[46] A challenge to a DPS listing, therefore, typically involves determining whether the Secretary acted arbitrarily or capriciously in applying the DPS policy. In a challenge to the listing of the Arizona pygmy-owl as a DPS, for instance, the court affirmed the FWS's discreteness determination for listing the species as a DPS "because the international border divides the [Arizona pygmy-owl from the northwestern Mexico pygmy-owl] and significant differences in conservation status exist between" the two populations.[47] The court was less sanguine, however, with the FWS's "significance" determination, and held that the agency acted arbitrarily in concluding that the loss of the species would create a "significant gap in the range of its taxon or because it differed markedly in its genetic characteristics" from the other population.[48]

Hall, 2007 WL 2790404 (D. Idaho Sept. 24, 2007). When the range of a species arguably is too small, a court might conclude that the Secretary acted arbitrarily in finding "significance." *See* Nat'l Ass'n of Home Builders v. Norton, 340 F.3d 835 (9th Cir. 2003); Nat'l Ass'n of Home Builders v. Kempthorne, No. 02-903 (D. Ariz. Mar. 12, 2007), *aff'd*, 2009 WL 226048 (9th Cir. 2009) (unpublished).

45.   61 Fed. Reg. at 4725.

46.   Nw. Ecosystem Alliance v. U.S. Fish & Wildlife Serv., 475 F.3d 1136, 1143 (9th Cir. 2007) (western gray squirrel). *See also* Coos Cnty. Bd. of Cnty. Comm'rs v. Kempthorne, 531 F.3d 793, 810–12 (9th Cir. 2008) (affirming reliance on DPS policy); Trout Unlimited v. Lohn, 559 F.3d 946 (9th Cir. 2009) (ESU and DPS policies entitled to deference); Nat'l Ass'n of Home Builders v. Norton, 340 F.3d 835, 852 (9th Cir. 2003) ("Having chosen to promulgate the DPS Policy, the FWS must follow that policy.").

47.   Nat'l Ass'n of Home Builders v. Norton, 340 F.3d 835, 842 (9th Cir. 2003).

48.   *Id.* at 852. The Services may not attempt to separate DPS into further discrete categories based on their ranges and protect a DPS in only a significant portion of its range. When the FWS attempted to delist the northern Rocky Mountain gray wolf, a DPS, in a portion of its range, the court held that ESA does not allow the Service to "list a DPS, subdivide it, but then provide the mandated protections to only part of the DPS." Defenders of Wildlife v. Salazar, 729 F. Supp. 2d 1207, 1228 (D. Mont. 2010). *See also* WildEarth Guardians v. Salazar, 2010 WL 3895682 (D. Ariz. 2010) (challenge to determination that a geographic range portion of the DPS of the Gunnison prairie dog should be listed, although precluded due to other priorities).

2.2.2   Throughout All or a Significant Portion of Its Range

When considering whether a species requires listing as either threatened or endangered, the Services must determine whether the species is at risk "throughout all or a significant portion of its range." This "significant portion of its range" (SPR) language has been called "inherently ambiguous."[49] While the Secretary enjoys considerable discretion when applying this standard, the Secretary may not assume that a viable species in a portion of its range obviates the need to list the species.[50] And until recently, the SPR determination has not been overly controversial or even subject to much discussion. Confronted with listing challenges to species, including the Northern Rocky Mountain gray wolf and the Gunnison prairie dog, the Department of the Interior Solicitor issued an opinion in March 2007 suggesting that the FWS enjoys considerable latitude when listing or delisting a species based on geographic considerations.[51] But subsequent litigation questioned the 2007 opinion, which suggested that the Secretary could list a species other than as a DPS in only a part of its geographic range,[52] and the Department of the Interior withdrew the opinion in May 2011.[53]

Therefore, when a species is at risk throughout either all or a significant portion of its range is an area of the law currently developing. Listing cannot be avoided simply because the species is not at risk everywhere,[54] but beyond that proposition remains considerable discretion, and the listing agencies are now attempting to outline a detailed SPR policy. They have proposed a lengthy *Draft Policy on Interpretation of the Phrase "Significant Portion of its Range" in the Endangered Species Act's Definitions*

---

49.   Defenders of Wildlife v. Norton, 258 F.3d 1136 (9th Cir. 2001).

50.   *Id.* Following the Ninth Circuit's decision in *Defenders*, other lower courts invalidated listing decisions. *See* Defenders of Wildlife v. Norton, 386 F. Supp. 2d 553 (Vt. 2005); Defenders of Wildlife v. U.S. Dep't of Interior, 354 F. Supp. 2d 1156 (D. Or. 2005); Defenders of Wildlife v. Norton, 239 F. Supp. 2d 9 (D.D.C. 2002).

51.   Solicitor Opinion M-37013 (Mar. 16, 2007).

52.   *See* Defenders of Wildlife v. Salazar, 729 F. Supp. 2d 1207 (D. Mont. 2010); WildEarth Guardians v. Salazar, 2010 WL 3895682 (D. Ariz. Sept. 30, 2010). When the Service attempted to address the delisting of the DPS of gray wolves in the Rocky Mountain region, those efforts faltered and ultimately precipitated congressional action and a lawsuit challenging Congress's intervention. *See* Alliance for the Wild Rockies v. Salazar, 672 F.3d 1170 (9th Cir. 2012) (rejecting challenge to congressional appropriation rider).

53.   Solicitor Opinion M-37024 (May 4, 2011). A court dismissed as moot the Homebuilders' challenge to the memorandum. Nat'l Ass'n of Homebuilders v. Salazar, 2011 WL 6097988 (D.D.C. 2011).

54.   Defenders of Wildlife v. Norton, 258 F.3d 1136, 1141 (9th Cir. 2001).

of "Endangered Species" and "Threatened Species."[55] If finalized (and not challenged and overturned by a court), the policy will require that a species be protected throughout all of its range if it is either threatened or endangered in a significant portion of its range. And whether a portion of its range is "significant" depends upon "its contribution to the viability of the species" and whether it "is so important that, without that portion, the species would be in danger of extinction."[56] This inquiry is based exclusively upon the "biological importance of the portion to the conservation of the species."[57] The biological question then becomes "whether, *without that portion,* the representation, redundancy, or resiliency of the species . . . would be so impaired that the species would have an increased vulnerability to threats to the point that the overall species would be in danger of extinction (i.e., would be 'endangered')."[58] This inquiry, the Secretary explained, is separate and different from the inquiry into "significance" for purposes of determining whether to list a species as a DPS.[59]

2.3   Listing Criteria and Best Scientific and Commercial Data Available

In the ESA itself, Congress prescribed five criteria for the Secretary to consider when determining whether to list, delist,[60] or reclassify[61] species:

---

55. 76 Fed. Reg. 76,987 (2011) (draft).

56. *Id.*

57. *Id.*

58. *Id.* at 76,994 (emphasis in original). "Range" is further interpreted to consist of "the general geographic area within which the species is currently found and to include those areas used throughout all or part of the species' life cycle, even if not used on a regular basis." *Id.* at 76,996. Lost historical range, while an important factor affecting the status of a species, is not considered a portion of its SPR. The policy purports to explain the issue about historic range considered by the Ninth Circuit in *Defenders of Wildlife v. Norton,* 258, F.3d 1136, 1145 (9th Cir. 2001), and *Tucson Herpetological Soc'y v. Salazar,* 566 F.3d 870, 876 (9th Cir. 2009).

59. 76 Fed. Reg. at 76,994–96. *See* Nw. Ecosystem Alliance v. U.S. Fish & Wildlife Serv., 475 F.3d 1136, 1143 (9th Cir. 2007).

60. *See* 50 C.F.R. § 424.11(d) (providing further that a species may be delisted only for one or more of the following reasons: (1) the species is extinct, (2) the species has recovered to a point where protection is no longer required, or (3) the scientific and commercial data upon which the original listing was made is determined to have been in error).

61. The status of a species under the ESA may be reclassified from "endangered" to "threatened," or vice versa. 16 U.S.C. § 1533(c)(2)(B)(ii)–(iii).

1. The present or threatened destruction, modification, or curtailment of the species' habitat or range;
2. Overutilization for commercial, recreational, scientific, or educational purposes;
3. Disease or predation;
4. The inadequacy of *existing* regulatory mechanisms; and
5. Other natural or man-made factors affecting the species' continued existence.[62]

Any one of these criteria, alone, may yield a supportable determination by the Secretary,[63] but courts have indicated an increasing willingness to closely examine the Secretary's findings with regard to the listing criteria.[64]

Two cases illustrate that any deviation from the five congressionally articulated listing criteria is improper. In *Biodiversity Legal Foundation v. Babbitt*[65] and *Southwest Center for Biological Diversity v. Babbitt*,[66] the U.S. District Court for the District of Columbia determined that the FWS improperly considered the adequacy of proposed future actions designed to ameliorate impacts on the Alexander Archipelago wolf and the Queen Charlotte goshawk, respectively. Because criterion (D) specifically allows only consideration of *existing* regulatory mechanisms,[67] the FWS was directed to reconsider its determinations.

Similarly, the U.S. District Court for the District of Oregon held that NMFS must rely on "current regulatory structure," rather than on any hope that a state will in fact adopt and implement requisite conservation measures sufficient to protect the species.[68] In holding that NMFS improperly had relied upon plans for future

---

62. 16 U.S.C. § 1533(1)(A)–(E); 50 C.F.R. § 424.11(c)(1)–(5) (emphasis added).
63. 16 U.S.C. § 1533(1) (providing that a listing determination may be based on "any" of the five enumerated factors). *See* Sw. Ctr. for Biological Diversity v. Babbitt, 215 F.3d 58, 60 (D.C. Cir. 2000) (list if any of five factors "sufficiently implicated"); *see also* Alaska v. Lubchenco, 825 F. Supp. 2d 209 (D.D.C. 2011) (listing beluga whale); Ctr. for Native Ecosystems v. U.S. Fish & Wildlife Serv., 795 F. Supp. 2d 1199, 1206–07 (D. Colo. 2011). *But see* Friends of Blackwater v. Salazar, 2012 WL 3538236, at *6 (D.C. Cir. Aug. 17, 2012) (indicating that "inadequacy of existing regulatory mechanisms" is to be evaluated in the context of threats to species arising under other listing factors and not independently).
64. *See, e.g.,* N. Spotted Owl v. Hodel, 716 F. Supp. 479 (W.D. Wash. 1988) (holding that FWS had disregarded the expert opinion of its own biologists, and had failed to provide its own or any other expert analysis supporting its decision not to list the spotted owl).
65. 943 F. Supp. 23, 26 (D.D.C. 1996).
66. 939 F. Supp. 49, 52 (D.D.C. 1996).
67. 16 U.S.C. § 1533(1)(D).
68. Or. Nat. Res. Council v. Daley, 6 F. Supp. 2d 1139, 1152 (D. Or. 1998).

conservation actions as the basis for its decision not to list a particular ESU of coho, the court noted that the whole purpose of listing a species as endangered or threatened is to "compel" the changes needed to save the species.[69]

To promote conservation of unlisted species, as well as ensure consistency with respect to consideration of conservation efforts during the listing process, NMFS and FWS published a policy addressing the issue.[70] This policy provides that the two primary considerations in evaluating conservation efforts are (1) the certainty that the conservation effort will be implemented and (2) the certainty that the conservation effort will be effective.[71] Through this policy, the Services seek to encourage voluntary conservation efforts that sufficiently improve a species' status to make listing unnecessary.[72] When considering the adequacy of existing regulatory mechanisms for the delisting of the Yellowstone grizzly bear (a DPS of the North American grizzly bear), the Ninth Circuit suggested that conservation agreements might be acceptable tools to rely upon, but nonetheless avoided the issue by concluding that binding measures incorporated into land management plans (described as legally enforceable) are sufficient.[73]

In addition to providing the considerations upon which a listing decision must be based, Congress also determined what information or data the Secretary may use in making listing determinations. Specifically, Congress directed that the Secretary make listing determinations "solely on the basis of the best scientific and commercial data available."[74]

---

69. *Id.* at 1152. *See also* Friends of Wild Swan, Inc. v. U.S. Fish & Wildlife Serv., 945 F. Supp. 1388, 1398 (D. Or. 1996) (holding that FWS cannot rely upon its own speculations as to the future effects of another agency's management plans to put off listing); Ctr. for Biological Diversity v. Morganweck, 351 F. Supp. 2d 1137 (D. Colo. 2004) (similar decision involving the Yellowstone cutthroat trout).

70. Policy for Evaluation of Conservation Efforts When Making Listing Decisions, 68 Fed. Reg. 15,100 (2003). *See generally* Hadassah M. Reimer & Murray D. Feldman, *Give PECE a Chance: Evaluating Conservation Programs to Avoid Endangered Species Act Listings*, 56 ROCKY MTN. MIN. L. INST. 21-1 (2010).

71. 68 Fed. Reg. at 15,101.

72. *Id.*

73. Greater Yellowstone Coal. v. Servheen, 665 F.3d 1015 (9th Cir. 2011). In *Alaska v. Lubchenco*, 825 F. Supp. 2d 209 (D.D.C. 2011), the court upheld the Service's decision to list the beluga whale, affirming the Service's judgment that the existing conservation efforts lacked sufficient certainty in implementation and effectiveness.

74. 16 U.S.C. § 1533(b)(1)(A); 50 C.F.R. § 424.11(b). *See generally* Michael J. Brennan, David E. Roth, Murray D. Feldman & Andrew Robert Greene, *Square Pegs and Round Holes: Application of the "Best Scientific Data Available" Standard in the Endangered Species Act*, 16 TUL. ENVTL. L.J. 387 (2003).

In the joint listing regulations promulgated by NMFS and FWS, the agencies highlight one particular subset of data that is excluded from the definition of *scientific and commercial data:* economic impact data.[75] In 1982, Congress amended section 4 of the ESA explicitly to overturn the Reagan administration's application, through Executive Order 12,291, of economic impact analysis to ESA listing decisions.[76] In addition to noting that "emotional reasons" and "improper biological data" are not appropriate considerations during the ESA listing process,[77] Congress also "specifically rejected" the application of economic criteria to any determination regarding the status of species.[78] Further, Congress clarified that the term "commercial information" as used in the Act means "trade data"[79] relevant to the trade in a particular species. Section 4's listing criteria, therefore, confirm the conclusion of one commentator who wrote that "the ESA demonstrates a fervent Congressional preference for scientific decision making."[80]

Congress did not illustrate what information satisfies the threshold of "best" scientific or commercial data available. To fill this perceived gap, the Secretary determined through regulation which sources or types of data will be considered in making any revision of the endangered and threatened species lists.[81] For example, the Secretary may review scientific or commercial publications, administrative reports, maps or other graphic materials, information received from experts on the subject, and comments from interested parties.[82] In a 1994 Notice of Policy

---

75. 50 C.F.R. § 424.11(b).

76. *See* H.R. REP. No. 97-567 (1982), *reprinted in* 1982 U.S.C.C.A.N. 2807, 2820 (explicitly addressing Executive Order No. 12,291).

77. H.R. REP. No. 97-567, at 22.

78. *Id. See also* H.R. CONF. REP. No. 97-835, at 20 (1982), *reprinted in* 1982 U.S.C.C.A.N. 2860, 2861 ("economic considerations have no relevance to determination regarding the status of species, and the economic analysis requirements of Executive Order 12291 . . . will not apply to any phase of the listing process"). As discussed in section 2.8.2, economic considerations are relevant to decisions on designating critical habitat.

79. H.R. REP. No. 97-567.

80. Holly Doremus, *Listing Decisions Under the Endangered Species Act: Why Better Science Isn't Always Better Policy*, 75 WASH. U. L.Q. 1029, 1056 (1997). In addition to ensuring that the Secretary limits review to the congressionally authorized listing criteria, courts also will determine whether the source of data is a lawful one. *See* Ala. Tombigbee Rivers Coal. v. Dep't of Interior, 26 F.3d 1103 (11th Cir. 1994) (court enjoined use of scientific report prepared in violation of the Federal Advisory Committee Act), *rejected by* Cargill v. United States, 173 F.3d 323 (5th Cir. 1999).

81. 50 C.F.R. § 424.13.

82. *Id.*

Statement, the Secretary acknowledged the variability in the quality and reliability of information contained in such a wide variety of sources;[83] the challenge, of course, is to identify and utilize the "best"[84] available information in making listing decisions.

To ensure that listing (and other) decisions under the ESA are based on the best available scientific and commercial data, the Services promulgated guidelines directing agency employees to

1. Require that biologists evaluate all scientific and other information that will be used to make any listing decision;
2. Gather and impartially evaluate biological, ecological, and other information that disputes official positions taken by the FWS or NMFS;
3. Ensure that biologists document their evaluation of information that supports or does not support a position being proposed by the agency;
4. Use primary and original sources of information as the basis for listing decisions or recommendations;
5. Adhere to the time frames or "schedules" established by the ESA; and
6. Conduct management-level review of documents developed by the Services to verify and assure the quality of the science used to establish official positions.[85]

In addition, FWS/NMFS policy provides for peer review, by "three appropriate and independent specialists," of pertinent data relating to a species under consideration for listing.[86] The listing

---

83. 59 Fed. Reg. 34,271 (1994).

84. The best "available data" does not mean that FWS must have "conclusive evidence," and in one case FWS was found to have acted arbitrarily and capriciously in requiring conclusive evidence to support listing. Defenders of Wildlife v. Babbitt, 958 F. Supp. 670, 680 (D.D.C. 1997); see also Sw. Ctr. For Biological Diversity v. Babbitt, 215 F.3d 58, 60 (D.C. Cir. 2000) (conclusive evidence not required); Alaska v. Lubchenco, 825 F. Supp. 2d 209 (D.D.C. 2011) (noting that data need not be perfect and deference afforded Service); Ctr. for Biological Diversity v. Lubchenco, 2010 WL 5288188 (N.D. Cal. 2010) (rejecting challenge to best available data); Oceana v. Evans, 384 F. Supp. 2d 203, 219 (D.D.C. 2005) (certainty not required); Conner v. Burford, 848 F.2d 1441, 1454 (9th Cir. 1998), cert. denied, 489 U.S. 1012 (1989) (presently available data). Cf. In re Polar Bear Endangered Species Act Listing and § 4(d) Rule Litig., 794 F. Supp. 2d 65, 110 (D.D.C. 2011) (FWS not acting arbitrarily and capriciously in relying on best available science).

85. 59 Fed. Reg. at 34,271 (1994).

86. 59 Fed. Reg. 34,270 (1994).

agency must include a summary of the opinions of peer reviewers in any final listing rule or withdrawal of a proposed rule.[87]

In the end, the Secretary must base a listing decision on the best available data, even if inconclusive.[88] When the information is inconclusive, the Secretary is simply not legally obliged to find "better data."[89]

2.4   The Petition Process

This listing process can begin in two ways. The Secretary may initiate the section 4 listing process by publishing a proposed rule in accordance with the informal rulemaking procedures under the Administrative Procedure Act (APA). Alternatively, section 4 provides that any "interested person" may submit a written petition to the Secretary, urging the Secretary to list, delist, or reclassify a species.[90] A petition submitted to the Secretary under section 4 of the ESA is considered a petition for informal rulemaking under section 553(e) of the APA,[91] and the Secretary within 30 days must acknowledge receipt of the petition in writing.[92]

---

87. *Id.* at 34,271.

88. Sw. Ctr. for Biological Diversity v. Babbitt, 215 F.3d 58, 61 (D.C. Cir. 2000) (Secretary of the Interior was not obligated to conduct actual counts of Queen Charlotte goshawks, and may base a listing determination on population estimates); Bldg. Indus. Ass'n of Superior Cal. v. Norton, 247 F.3d 1241, 1246 (D.C. Cir. 2001) (best available not best possible science). *But cf.* Tucson Herpetological Soc'y v. Salazar, 566 F.3d 870 (9th Cir. 2009) (data on population size and trends uncertain, and court rejected evidence of persistence of species throughout its current range). "An agency's decision may be based on the best scientific evidence available even if the administrative record contains evidence for and against its decision." Trout Unlimited v. Lohn, 559 F.3d 946, 958 (9th Cir. 2009).

89. *Id. See also* Am. Wildlands v. Kempthorne, 530 F.3d 913, 919 (D.C. Cir. 2008) (independent studies not required).

90. 16 U.S.C. § 1533(b)(3)(A); 50 C.F.R. § 424.14(a). Any person also may petition the Secretary to designate critical habitat or to revise the boundary of designated critical habitat. 50 C.F.R. § 424.10.

91. 16 U.S.C. § 1533(b)(3)(A).

92. 50 C.F.R. § 424.14(a). In 1994, after Congress restricted the FWS's use of funds to list species, the FWS issued a Petition Management Guidance document to address the processing of petitions. 61 Fed. Reg. 36,075 (1996). The Ninth Circuit subsequently held that this guidance document conflicted with the Act. Ctr. for Biological Diversity v. Norton, 254 F.3d 833, 836 (9th Cir. 2001). *See also* Colo. River Cutthroat Trout v. Kempthorne, 448 F. Supp. 2d 170, 177 (D.D.C. 2006) (noting that the court in *American Lands Alliance v. Norton*, 2004 WL 3246687 (D.D.C. June 2, 2004), had issued a nationwide injunction against the guidance).

Regulations promulgated jointly by NMFS and FWS specify the technical requirements of a valid listing petition,[93] as well as the types of substantive information a petition should contain to justify the petitioned-for action. A petition should

- clearly indicate the administrative measure (delisting, listing, etc.) sought;
- give the scientific and common names of the species involved;[94]
- contain a detailed narrative justification for the recommended measure based upon available information, past and present numbers and distribution of the species, and any threats to the species;
- provide information regarding the status of the species overall or throughout a SPR; and
- provide supporting documentation in the form of scientific publications, letters, reports, and the like.[95]

This information provides the basis for the Secretary's first substantive decision following receipt of a valid petition, the so-called 90-day finding.

2.4.1   The 90-Day Finding

To the "maximum extent practicable," the Secretary must make a finding within 90 days of the receipt of a valid petition about

---

93. A valid petition must be clearly identified as a petition, must be dated, and must include the name, signature, address, telephone number, and the business or other affiliation of the petitioner. 50 C.F.R. § 424.14(a).

94. The petitioner may request that a species or subspecies be listed throughout its range, or the petitioner may explicitly request that a DPS be listed. At least one court has held that the Service must at least address the scope of the petition. Friends of the Wild Swan v. Babbitt, 12 F. Supp. 2d 1121, 1134 (D. Or. 1997) (holding that FWS arbitrarily and capriciously made a finding with respect to five DPSs of bull trout, when the petitioner had specifically requested that the entire range of bull trout be listed) (citing Sw. Ctr. for Biological Diversity v. Babbitt, 926 F. Supp. 920, 922 (D. Ariz. 1996) (noting that FWS had properly considered the narrow petition to list a subpopulation of the northern goshawk, and that FWS had expanded consideration to the entire species only when listing of the subpopulation was determined not warranted)). See also Defenders of Wildlife v. Babbitt, 958 F. Supp. 670, 674–75 (D.D.C. 1997) (after deciding that the petitioned-for listing of DPSs of lynx was not warranted, FWS expanded its consideration to the entire lynx population).

95. 50 C.F.R. § 424.14(b)(2)(i)–(iv). The petition also may include information on recommended critical habitat. Id. See generally FWS, Public Advisory: Information to Consider When Submitting a Petition Under the Endangered Species Act, http://www.fws.gov/endangered/esa-library/pdf/petition_guidance_for_internet_final_for_posting_12-7-10.pdf.

whether the petition presents "substantial scientific or commercial information" indicating that the petitioned action may be warranted.[96] Not surprisingly, the phrase "maximum extent practicable" has generated vigorous debate. As one court put it, the phrase is "facially ambiguous," and in fact "the only thing clear about [it] is its ambiguity."[97] The supplemental information accompanying the joint listing regulations states that the 90-day finding may be waived (i.e., determined not to be "practicable") "only if the devotion of staff resources to petition responses would interfere with actions needed to list other species in greater need of protection."[98] The determination of whether other species are in "greater need" of protection must be rooted in a "scientifically based priority system" and may not be based on whether a species is a "higher or lower life form."[99]

If a 90-day finding is practicable, the Secretary must determine either (1) that the petitioned action is not warranted or (2) that the petitioned action may be warranted.[100] Either finding must be published in the *Federal Register*,[101] and a negative finding is subject to judicial review.[102] A positive finding that the petitioned action may be warranted triggers a new time period and a new decision point: "the 12-month finding."

2.4.2   The 12-Month Finding

Having made a 90-day finding that a petitioned action may be warranted, the Secretary then has 12 months from the original receipt of the petition (not from the date of the 90-day finding) to make the next critical determination in the listing process.[103] During this 12-month period, the Secretary must conduct a "review of the status of the species concerned,"[104] and within the 12-month period must make one of the following findings:

---

96. 16 U.S.C. § 1533(b)(3)(A); 50 C.F.R. § 424.14(b). *Substantial information* is defined as "that amount of information that would lead a reasonable person to believe that the measure proposed in the petition may be warranted." 50 C.F.R. § 424.14(b)(1).
97. Biodiversity Legal Found. v. Babbitt, 146 F.3d 1249, 1254 (10th Cir. 1998).
98. 49 Fed. Reg. 38,900 (1984). *See also* H.R. Conf. Rep. No. 97-835, at 21 (1982), *reprinted in* 1982 U.S.C.C.A.N. 2807, 2862.
99. 1982 U.S.C.C.A.N. at 2862.
100. 16 U.S.C. § 1533(b)(3)(A); 50 C.F.R. § 424.14(b)(1).
101. 16 U.S.C. § 1533(b)(3)(A); 50 C.F.R. § 424.14(b)(1).
102. 16 U.S.C. § 1533(b)(3)(C)(ii).
103. 16 U.S.C. § 1533(b)(3)(B); 50 C.F.R. § 424.14(b)(3).
104. 16 U.S.C. § 1533(b)(3)(A); 50 C.F.R. § 424.14(b)(3).

1. That the petitioned action is warranted;
2. That the petitioned action is not warranted; or
3. That the petitioned action is "warranted but precluded," meaning that the promulgation of a rule to implement the action is precluded because of other pending proposals to list, delist, or reclassify; and that expeditious progress is being made to list, delist, or reclassify qualified species.[105]

A determination that the petitioned action is not warranted must be communicated to the petitioner, as well as published in the *Federal Register*,[106] and is also subject to judicial review.[107] A finding that the action is warranted requires the Secretary promptly to publish in the *Federal Register* a general notice and the complete text of the proposed regulation to implement the petitioned action.[108]

Often the most controversial of the three permissible 12-month findings is the finding that the petitioned action is warranted but precluded. A warranted-but-precluded finding may be supported only if (1) the Secretary has determined that the information available indicated that the petitioned action is warranted; (2) the timely promulgation of a rule to implement the petitioned action is precluded by other pending listing decisions; and (3) expeditious progress is being made to list, delist, or reclassify other species.[109]

A petition resulting in a warranted-but-precluded finding is considered automatically resubmitted on the anniversary date of the finding;[110] within 12 months of the warranted-but-precluded

105. 16 U.S.C. § 1533(b)(3)(B)(i)–(iii); 50 C.F.R. § 424.14(b)(3)(i)–(iii). During the 12-month review period, the Secretary also may publish a "notice of review" soliciting information from interested persons regarding the status of the species involved. 50 C.F.R. § 424.15.

106. 16 U.S.C. § 1533(b)(3)(B)(i); 50 C.F.R. § 424.14(b)(3)(i).

107. 16 U.S.C. § 1533(b)(3)(C)(ii).

108. 16 U.S.C. § 1533(b)(3)(B)(ii); 50 C.F.R. § 424.14(b)(3)(ii). See section 2.5 for a discussion of the rulemaking process.

109. 16 U.S.C. § 1533(b)(3)(B)(iii); 50 C.F.R. § 424.14(b)(3)(iii). *See* Biological Diversity v. Kempthorne, 466 F.3d 1098, 1102 (9th Cir. 2006) ("warranted but precluded" finding a narrowly defined circumstance); W. Watersheds Project v. U.S. Fish & Wildlife Serv., 2012 WL 369168 (D. Idaho 2012) (upholding "warranted but precluded" finding for sage grouse). *See generally* K. Molly Smith, *Abuse of the Warranted but Precluded Designation: A Real or Imagined Purgatory?*, 19 SOUTHEASTERN ENVTL. L.J. 119 (2010).

110. 16 U.S.C. § 1533(b)(3)(C)(i). *See* Oliver Houck, *The Endangered Species Act and Its Implementation by the U.S. Departments of Interior and Commerce*, 64 U. COLO. L. REV. 277, 285–87 (1993) (providing a detailed overview of the use

finding, the Secretary must again determine whether the petitioned action is warranted, not warranted, or (once again) warranted but precluded.[111] In 1988, Congress amended the ESA to require the Secretary to develop a system to monitor the status of all species in the warranted-but-precluded category and directed the Secretary to make "prompt use" of the Act's emergency listing authority to prevent significant risks to the well-being of these species.[112]

2.5   Informal Rulemaking Necessary for Listing Species

If the Secretary determines to list, delist, or reclassify any species, whether as a result of the petition process outlined in section 2.4 or on the Secretary's own initiative, the Secretary must adhere to the informal rulemaking procedures outlined in the Act.[113] This rulemaking process begins with publication of a proposed rule in the *Federal Register*[114] and culminates between 90 days[115] and 18 months[116] later in a final rule that either implements or withdraws the proposed listing rule.[117] The following discussion outlines the process from a proposed to a final rule.

2.5.1   Proposed Listing Contents

The Secretary initiates the listing rulemaking process by publishing a "general notice" and the "complete text" of the proposed rule in the *Federal Register*.[118] By regulation, the Secretary must

---

of "warranted but precluded" designations, and describing the 12-month recycling of species as warranted but precluded as a "black hole for unlisted endangered species").

111.   50 C.F.R. § 424.14(b)(4).

112.   16 U.S.C. § 1533(b)(3)(C)(iii).

113.   16 U.S.C. § 1533(b)(4), (6), (8). Except as otherwise provided through these procedural sections, the rulemaking procedures of the Administrative Procedures Act also apply to any listing action. 16 U.S.C. § 1533(b)(4).

114.   16 U.S.C. § 1533(5)(A)(i); 50 C.F.R. § 426.16(c)(1)(i).

115.   16 U.S.C. § 1533(b)(5)(A) (proposed listing may not become effective until at least 90 days after publication of the proposed rule).

116.   *See* section 2.5.3.

117.   16 U.S.C. § 1533(b)(6)(A)(i), (iii); 50 C.F.R. § 426.17(a)(1), (2).

118.   16 U.S.C. § 1533(b)(5)(A)(i); 50 C.F.R. § 424.16(b).

include the following information in the notice of the proposed rule:

1. A summary of the data upon which the proposed rule is based;
2. A showing of the relationship of the data to the proposed rule; and
3. A summary of factors affecting the species.[119]

Persons interested in whether a particular future activity may affect or harm a species proposed for listing should pay particular attention to the "summary of factors affecting the species" section in the proposed listing. This information not only provides insight into the potential restrictions on certain activity, but also may serve as an early starting point for development of measures necessary to permit certain types of "incidental take."[120] Likewise, as discussed elsewhere in this book, candidate species conservation agreements may be fashioned to alleviate the factors negatively affecting the species, and it may be possible *in some cases* to *eliminate the need for* listing altogether.[121]

2.5.2   **Notice and Comment**

In addition to the blanket, constructive notice provided by *Federal Register* publication, the Secretary also must provide "actual notice" of a proposed rule to each relevant "state agency,"[122] as well as to the counties where the species is believed to occur. Any federal agencies, local authorities, and private organizations or individuals "known to be affected" by the rule are entitled to actual notice,[123] as are certain foreign nations[124] and any

---

119.   50 C.F.R. § 424.16(b).

120.   See chapter 6, section 6.2 for a detailed discussion of incidental take permits.

121.   See chapter 6, section 6.5 for a detailed discussion of candidate conservation agreements with assurances.

122.   16 U.S.C. § 1533(b)(5)(A)(ii); 50 C.F.R. § 424.16(c)(1)(ii). *State agency* is defined in the listing regulations as "[a]ny state agency, department, board, commission, or other governmental entity that is responsible for the management and conservation of fish, plant, or wildlife resources within a state." 50 C.F.R. § 424.02(1).

123.   50 C.F.R. § 424.16(c)(1)(iii).

124.   16 U.S.C. § 1533(b)(5)(B); 50 C.F.R. § 424.16(c)(1)(iv).

professional scientific organization the Secretary deems appropriate.[125] Finally, the Secretary must publish a summary of the proposed regulation in a "newspaper of general circulation in each area of the United States in which the species is believed to occur."[126]

After publication of the proposed rule in the *Federal Register,* the Secretary must allow public comment for at least 60 days and may extend or reopen the public comment upon a finding of "good cause."[127] In addition, the Secretary shall "promptly" hold at least one public hearing if any person requests one within 45 days of *Federal Register* publication of the proposed rule.[128]

As mentioned earlier, the procedural requirements of the APA also apply to ESA listing decisions. Therefore, "meaningful" opportunity to participate in the rulemaking process is required, and the opportunity to participate must occur "reasonably close to the time in which the Secretary makes the decision."[129] The public also must be provided access to new information that is "critical to the agency's determination."[130]

2.5.3   The Final Rule

Within 12 months after publication of the proposed listing in the *Federal Register,*[131] the Secretary must take one of the following actions:

---

125.   16 U.S.C. § 1533(b)(5)(C); 50 C.F.R. § 424.16(c)(1)(v).

126.   16 U.S.C. § 1533(b)(5)(D); 50 C.F.R. § 424.16(c)(1)(vi).

127.   50 C.F.R. § 424.16(c)(2). A criminal defendant's failure to comment on a proposed listing of the red-bellied turtle precluded him from later collaterally attacking the validity of the listing by introducing DNA evidence relative to the species determination. United States v. Guthrie, 50 F.3d 936 (11th Cir. 1995).

128.   50 C.F.R. § 424.16(c)(3). At least 15 days' prior notice of the place and time of the hearing also must be published in the *Federal Register. Id.*

129.   Idaho Farm Bureau Fed'n v. Babbitt, 58 F.3d 1392, 1404 (9th Cir. 1995).

130.   *Id.* at 1403 (citing Cmty. Nutrition Inst. v. Block, 749 F.2d 50, 57–58 (D.C. Cir. 1984)).

131.   Congress amended the listing provisions in 1982 to "expedite" the listing process, and thus reduced the allowable time frame for final action on a listing proposal from two years to one year from the date of the proposed listing. H.R. Conf. Rep. No. 97-835 (1982), *reprinted in* 1982 U.S.C.C.A.N. 2807, 2860. The Secretary is entitled to a 12-month period to finalize a proposed listing, even though the Secretary may have belatedly published the proposed rule. Or. Nat. Res. Council v. Kantor, 99 F.3d 334, 338 (9th Cir. 1996) (12-month period to finalize rule begins running on date of publication of proposed listing, not on due date of 12-month finding on petition to list).

1. Publish a final rule implementing the proposed rule;
2. Publish a notice withdrawing the proposed rule, upon a finding that the evidence does not justify the action proposed; or
3. Extend the deadline for a final decision on the proposed listing by no more than six months.[132]

A six-month extension (option 3) is allowed only upon a finding by the Secretary that "there is substantial disagreement regarding the sufficiency or accuracy of the available data relevant to the determination."[133] Before the end of any six-month extension, the Secretary "shall" either publish a final rule or withdraw the proposed rule.[134]

In an instance where the Secretary promulgated a final rule well after the end of the 18-month maximum allowable time frame (seven years in that case), the Ninth Circuit held that the statutory time frames were an "impetus to act rather than a prohibition on action taken after the time expires."[135] In that case, *Idaho Farm Bureau,* the court held that the Secretary's much-delayed listing of the Bruneau hot springsnail was not invalid by virtue of its tardiness. Relying on the legislative history of the ESA and amendments that shortened the listing time frames, the Ninth Circuit held that although a citizen suit would have been possible to *compel* a listing decision within the allowable time frame,[136] "failure of an agency to act within a statutory time frame does not bar subsequent agency action absent a specific indication that Congress intended the time

---

132. 50 C.F.R. § 424.17(a)(1).

133. 16 U.S.C. § 1533(b)(6)(B)(i).

134. The Secretary's duty to finalize or withdraw a proposed rule, within the 12- or 18-month time period specified, has been termed a "mandatory, nondiscretionary duty," excusable only in the face of fiscal impossibility. Envtl. Def. Ctr. v. Babbitt, 73 F.3d 867, 870 (9th Cir. 1995) (court recognized that Secretary could not legally finalize the proposed listing of the red-legged frog because of congressional rescission of appropriated funds), *on remand,* Envtl. Def. Ctr. v. Babbitt, CV-95-2867-R (C.D. Cal. May 6, 1996) (ordering immediate listing of the red-legged frog within two weeks after lifting of the congressional spending moratorium on listing); Sierra Club v. Babbitt, 948 F. Supp. 56 (E.D. Cal. 1996) (lack of funding from Congress excused Secretary's failure to finalize listing of the Peninsular bighorn sheep).

135. Idaho Farm Bureau Fed'n v. Babbitt, 58 F.3d 1392, 1401 (9th Cir. 1985). *See also* Endangered Species Comm. v. Babbitt, 852 F. Supp. 32 (D.D.C. 1994) (violation of Secretary's duty to make supporting data available for public review did not invalidate final listing in light of the equities, the purposes of the ESA, and the relatively small prejudicial effect of lack of availability of data).

136. *Idaho Farm Bureau,* 58 F.3d at 1401.

frame to serve as a bar."[137] The court noted the general rule that a regulation promulgated in violation of the APA is invalid, but held that the Secretary's rule in this case survived, because in some cases "equity demands the regulation . . . be left in place."[138]

A final rule listing, delisting, or reclassifying a species is not effective until 30 days after it is published in the *Federal Register,* unless otherwise provided for "good cause."[139] The final publication of a rule must contain a summary of comments and recommendations received on the proposed rule, a summary of any data upon which the rule is based, and a summary of factors affecting the species.[140] In addition, NMFS and FWS policy requires the listing agencies to identify, at the time the species is listed, specific activities that will, or will not, likely result in a violation of section 9 of the ESA.[141]

Once a species is listed, the Act directs that the Secretary engage in a status review of that species every five years.[142] The purpose of the review is to determine whether the species ought to be delisted or reclassified. Recent litigation suggests that this status review arguably is a mandatory, nondiscretionary duty.[143] But unfortunately the history of the Act does not yet demonstrate that delisting, and to a lesser extent reclassification, is a likely immediate response for many species.[144] In the recent challenge

---

137. *Id.* at 1400.
138. *Id.* at 1405.
139. 50 C.F.R. § 424.18(b)(1). A decision to delist a species or reclassify a species from endangered to threatened follows the same process and requires that the Service consider the same five factors for a listing action. 16 U.S.C. § 1533(a)(1); 50 C.F.R. §§ 424.10, 424.11(a), (c), (d). ESA regulations indicate that a species may be delisted if the petition-submitted information "substantiate[s] that [the species] is neither endangered nor threatened for one or more of the following reasons:" (1) the species is considered to be extinct; (2) the species has recovered to the point where "protection under the Act is no longer required;" or (3) the initial classification of the species as endangered or threatened was in error. *See* 50 C.F.R. § 424.11(d)(1)–(3).
140. 50 C.F.R. § 428.18(a).
141. 59 Fed. Reg. 34,272 (1994). In addition, the final listing rule must list a contact with the Service who will assist the public in determining whether particular activities constitute prohibited actions under section 9. 59 Fed. Reg. at 34,272.
142. 16 U.S.C. § 1533(c)(2); 50 C.F.R. § 424.21. *See also* Nat'l Oceanic & Atmospheric Admin. & U.S. Fish & Wildlife Serv., 5-Year Review Guidance: Procedures for Conducting 5-Year Reviews Under the Endangered Species Act (July 2006).
143. *See, e.g.,* Fla. Home Builders Ass'n v. Kempthorne, 496 F. Supp. 2d 1330 (M.D. Fla. 2007). The decision on the five-year status review, once made, does not appear to be judicially reviewable. *See* Am. Forest Res. Council v. Hall, 533 F. Supp. 2d 84, 90–94 (D.D.C. 2008).
144. *See* Jonathan H. Adler, *The Leaky Ark: The Failure of Endangered Species Regulation on Private Land, in* Rebuilding the Ark: New Perspectives on Endangered Species Act Reform 6, 10 (Jonathan H. Adler ed., 2011).

to the delisting of the Yellowstone grizzly bear, the Ninth Circuit affirmed a lower court's decision vacating the Service's delisting rule, reasoning that the Service failed to explain adequately, in the face of uncertainty and merely parroting adaptive management, why food shortages did not pose a threat to the species.[145]

2.6   Emergency Listings

Since 1982,[146] an important alternative to informal rulemaking has been available to list species, designate critical habitat, or promulgate special rules. The Secretary may promulgate an emergency rule, effective upon publication, implementing one of these actions.[147] The Secretary may invoke these procedures to address "any emergency posing a significant risk to the well-being of any species."[148] The Secretary must merely publish the details of the emergency situation concurrent with publication of the emergency rule in the *Federal Register,*[149] and must give actual notice of the regulation to the state agency in each state where the species is believed to occur.[150] The rule is effective immediately upon publication in the *Federal Register* and remains in effect for up to 240 days.[151]

With respect to candidate species,[152] Congress has directed the Secretary to make "prompt use" of the emergency listing authority.[153] In the only major case construing the ESA's emergency listing procedures, the D.C. Circuit held that Congress unambiguously directed the Secretary to effect emergency listings

---

145.   Greater Yellowstone Coal. v. Servheen, 665 F.3d 1015 (9th Cir. 2011).

146.   Act of Oct. 13, 1982, Pub. L. No. 97-304, § 2(a)(2), 96 Stat. 1411, 1414 (codified at 16 U.S.C. § 1533(b)(7)).

147.   16 U.S.C. § 1533(b)(7); 50 C.F.R. § 424.20.

148.   16 U.S.C. § 1533(b)(7).

149.   *Id. See, e.g.,* 64 Fed. Reg. 19,300 (1999) (emergency rule listing the Sierra Nevada bighorn sheep as endangered due to threat of continual exposure to mountain lion predation).

150.   16 U.S.C. § 1533(b)(7).

151.   16 U.S.C. § 1533(b)(7); 50 C.F.R. § 424.20(a). During the 240-day effective period of the emergency rule, the Secretary may promulgate a formal listing, using formal rulemaking procedures. Alternatively, the Secretary must withdraw the emergency rule if, at any time following promulgation of the rule, he or she determines that substantial evidence does not exist to warrant the rule. 50 C.F.R. § 424.20(b).

152.   See section 2.7 for a discussion of candidate species.

153.   16 U.S.C. § 1533(b)(3)(C)(iii).

"prophylactically," and that Congress intended the Secretary to, in a sense, "shoot first and then ask all of the questions later."[154] The court also held that something less than "substantial evidence" is required to support an emergency listing, and that the ESA contemplates a "somewhat less rigorous process of investigation and explanation for emergency rules than for normal rulemaking."[155] To date, no court has overturned an emergency listing, and whether the emergency listing procedures create an "almost entirely discretionary authority"[156] remains to be seen.

2.7   Candidate Species

Since 1979, the ESA has required the Secretary to establish "a ranking system" to assist in the identification of species that should receive priority review for listing.[157] Congress clarified this mandate in legislative history accompanying the 1982 ESA amendments, noting that species ranking should occur through a "scientifically based priority system," without regard to whether the species is a "higher or lower life form."[158] This candidate list also serves to stimulate public and private efforts to engage in voluntary conservation efforts that might avoid the need to list the species.

In 1983, FWS published notice of its Listing Priority Guidelines,[159] establishing three criteria for prioritizing listing actions: (1) the magnitude of the threat facing the species, (2) the immediacy of the threat facing the species, and (3) the taxonomic distinctiveness of the species.[160] The 1983 guidelines establish priorities *among species,* and more current guidance promulgated by FWS establishes additional criteria to assign priorities to different *types* of listing actions,[161] as follows:

---

154. City of Las Vegas v. Lujan, 891 F.2d 927, 932–33 (D.C. Cir. 1989).
155. *Id.* at 932.
156. *See* Oliver Houck, *supra* note 111, at 296 n.129.
157. Act of Dec. 28, 1979, Pub. L. No. 96-159, § 3(6), 93 Stat. 1225–1226 (1979) (codified at 16 U.S.C. § 1533(h)(3)).
158. H.R. Conf. Rep. No. 835, at 21, *reprinted in* 1982 U.S.C.C.A.N. 2860, 2862.
159. 48 Fed. Reg. 43,098 (1983).
160. *Id.* at 43,103.
161. 64 Fed. Reg. 57,114 (1999). In 1996, the Service eliminated maintaining a separate list for category 2 and category 3 species. 61 Fed. Reg. 64,481 (1996).

1. Highest priority is for processing emergency listing rules;
2. Second priority is for processing final determinations on proposed listings;
3. Third priority is for making determinations regarding current candidate species (either proposing to list a candidate species, or removing the species from the candidate list altogether); and
4. Fourth priority is to process administrative findings on petitions to list or reclassify species.[162]

The listing priority guidelines are intended to serve only as a "guide."[163] At least one court rejected the claim that a listing priority guidance violates the ESA section 4 listing criteria,[164] and courts in particular cases have implicitly recognized the validity of the Secretary's application of the guidelines.[165]

With the number of species being added as candidates for listing by the FWS, the listing process has become hindered by a lack of sufficient agency resources. This in turn has led to litigation, and eventual court decrees or settlements establishing a process for how the FWS will respond to outstanding petitions to list a species as well as render a decision on whether to propose a species for listing. In 2011 petitions to list over 1,200 species were pending, and the FWS had a backlog of numerous species on its candidate list. In a significant settlement, the FWS agreed to make initial or final decisions for hundreds of species in accordance with a schedule established in a pair of settlement agreements.[166]

---

162. *Id.* at 57,118–19. This listing priority guidance eliminates critical habitat designation from the guidance altogether. *Id.* at 57,115.

163. *See* 48 Fed. Reg. 43,098 (1983) (stating that "[t]he priority systems presented must be viewed as guides and should not be looked upon as inflexible frameworks for determining resource allocations").

164. Biodiversity Legal Found. v. Babbitt, 146 F.3d 1249, 1252–53 (10th Cir. 1998) (addressing 1997 Listing Priority Guidance, 61 Fed. Reg. 64,475–81 (1996)).

165. Carlton v. Babbitt, 900 F. Supp. 526, 536 (D.D.C. 1995) (holding that FWS had "provided adequate support for their application of the guidelines to rank the Cabinet/Yaak Grizzly"). *But see* Forest Guardians v. Babbitt, 174 F.3d 1178 (10th Cir. 1999), *amending* 164 F.3d 1261 (10th Cir. 1998) (when faced with a nondiscretionary duty to designate critical habitat, the Secretary must do so "without regard to his preferred priorities").

166. *In re* Endangered Species Act Section 4 Deadline Litig., 277 F.R.D. 1, 80 Fed. R. Serv. 3d 663 (MDL No. 2165, D.D.C. Sept. 9, 2011).

2.8 Critical Habitat

Habitat protection undoubtedly is critical to the recovery and survival of vulnerable species, and the ESA contains several provisions designed to address species' habitat needs. One of those provisions is the designation of critical habitat. For many years, the designation of critical habitat received little attention, and indeed the FWS has suggested that "[f]or almost all species, the Section 7 critical habitat adverse modification and jeopardy standards are the same, resulting in an unnecessary duplicative and expensive regulatory process."[167] But through litigation and continued attention to the critical habitat program, the section 4 designation process has become a prominent component of the Act.

At the time a species is listed, a listing agency "shall [to the] maximum extent prudent and determinable"[168] designate any habitat of the species that is considered to be critical habitat.[169] Critical habitat designations must be based on "the best scientific data available and after taking into consideration the economic impact, the impact on national security, and any other relevant impact" of the designation.[170] This is the singular instance in the ESA where the Secretary is specifically charged with considering the economic impact of a decision under the Act.[171] Also, if the benefits of excluding an area from designation outweigh the benefits of inclusion, an area may be excluded as long as the exclusion does not result in the species' extinction.[172] And whether or how the National Environmental Policy Act might apply to designations remains an open question, with courts reaching differing conclusions.[173]

---

167. 64 Fed. Reg. 57,114, 57,118 (1999). *Cf.* 77 Fed. Reg. 51,503, 51,504 (Aug. 24, 2012) (noting benefits of designation).

168. Forest Guardians v. Babbitt, 174 F.3d 1178, 1192 (10th Cir. 1999), *amending* Forest Guardians v. Babbitt, 164 F.3d 1261 (10th Cir. 1998) (holding that designation of critical habitat is nondiscretionary and that the Secretary's duty to act cannot be excused by a "generalized claim of inadequate resources").

169. 16 U.S.C. § 1533(a)(3); 50 C.F.R. § 424.12(a).

170. 16 U.S.C. § 1533(b)(2); 50 C.F.R. § 424.12(a). The Secretary has claimed broad discretion to determine what other impacts (other than economic and national security) are relevant. *See* Solicitor's Opinion M-37016, The Secretary's Authority to Exclude Areas from Critical Habitat Designation Under Section 4(b)(2) of the Endangered Species Act (Oct. 3, 2008).

171. *See* Bennett v. Spear, 520 U.S. 154, 172 (1997).

172. 16 U.S.C. § 1533(b)(2).

173. *Compare* Douglas Cnty. v. Babbitt, 48 F.3d 1495 (9th Cir. 1996) (NEPA does not apply to critical habitat designations), *cert. denied*, 516 U.S. 1042 (1996), *with* Catron Cnty. Bd. of Comm'rs v. U.S. Fish & Wildlife Serv., 75 F.3d

The ESA defines *critical habitat* as the specific areas containing features essential to the conservation of the species, and that may require "special management considerations or protection."[174] Critical habitat is generally limited to the geographical area *occupied* by the species at the time it is listed, unless areas outside the occupied geographical area are "essential for the conservation of the species."[175] In making the determination as to what areas are essential to conservation of the species or which require special management considerations, the Secretary may consider the following:

- space
- food, water, air, light, minerals, other nutritional or physiological requirements
- cover or shelter
- sites for breeding, reproduction, or rearing of offspring
- habitats protected from disturbance or representative of the historic geographical distribution and ecological distribution of the species[176]

The Secretary must consider "primary constituent elements" such as roost sites, nesting grounds, spawning sites, feeding sites, wetlands, vegetation, soil type, and water quantity or quality.[177] Once determined, the critical habitat must be delineated on a

---

1429 (10th Cir. 1996) (NEPA applies to critical habitat designations), *and* Cape Hatteras Access Pres. Alliance v. U.S. Dep't of the Interior, 344 F. Supp. 2d 108 (D.D.C. 2004) (NEPA applies to critical habitat designations).

174.   16 U.S.C. § 1532(5)(A).

175.   *Id.* § 1532(5)(A)(ii). *See* Otay Mesa Prop., L.P. v. U.S. Dep't of the Interior, 646 F.3d 914 (9th Cir. 2011) (holding insufficient evidence supporting decision that area was "occupied" by the species). *Cf.* Home Builders Ass'n v. U.S. Fish & Wildlife Serv., 660 F.3d 983, 990 (9th Cir. 2010) ("There is no requirement that every area be classified as" occupied or unoccupied). The Ninth Circuit currently suggests that the standard for designating unoccupied habitat is higher than that for occupied habitat. *Id.; see also* Ariz. Cattle Growers' Ass'n v. Salazar, 606 F.3d 1160, 1163 (9th Cir. 2010) (whether a species "occupies" an area is contextual and fact dependent, and a species can occupy an area even if the area merely contains some individuals, where owls used areas with some frequency).

176.   50 C.F.R. § 424.12(b)(1)–(5).

177.   *Id.* § 424.12(b). One court suggests that primary constituent elements must be found on an area for the area to be included in a designation. Cape Hatteras Pres. Alliance v. U.S. Dep't of the Interior, 344 F. Supp. 2d 108, 123 (D.D.C. 2004). *But cf.* Home Builders Ass'n v. U.S. Fish & Wildlife Serv., 616 F.3d 983 (9th Cir. 2010).

map,[178] and critical habitat may not be designated within foreign countries.[179] In May 2012, the Services finalized a rule that alters the pre-existing requirement to publish in the Code of Federal Regulations a textual description of the boundaries for any designated critical habitat.[180]

2.8.1   Prudent and Determinable

The Secretary can avoid designating critical habitat upon a determination that doing so would not be prudent, or when a designation cannot be determined. NMFS and FWS jointly have defined the terms *prudent* and *determinable*. Designation of critical habitat is considered not "prudent" when one or both of the following situations exists:

1. The species is threatened by taking or other human activity, and identification of critical habitat can be expected to increase the degree of such threat to the species.
2. Such designation of critical habitat would not be beneficial to the species.[181]

In a 2008 Solicitor's Opinion, the Department of the Interior further elaborated on the FWS's authority to exclude areas from critical habitat designation.[182] Likewise, critical habitat is not "determinable" when one or both of the following situations exists:

---

178. 50 C.F.R. §§ 424.12(c), 424.18.

179. *Id.* § 424.12(h). *See also* Pub. L. No. 108-136, § 318(a), 117 Stat. 1433 (2003) (codified at 16 U.S.C. § 1533(a)(3)(B)(i) (re designation of Department of Defense lands and adding consideration of national security)).

180. 77 Fed. Reg. 25,611 (May 1, 2012). This change does not affect the designation process. The Services "are making optional the inclusion of any textual description of the boundaries of the designation in the Federal Register for codification in the Code of Federal Regulations. The boundaries of critical habitat as mapped or otherwise described in the Regulation Promulgation section of a rulemaking that is published in the Federal Register will be the official delineation of the designation. The coordinates and/or plot points from which the maps are generated will be included in the administrative record . . . ." *Id.*

181. *Id.* § 424.12(a)(1).

182. Solicitor's Opinion M-37016, The Secretary's Authority to Exclude Areas from Critical Habitat Designation Under Section 4(b)(2) of the Endangered Species Act (Oct. 3, 2008).

1. Information sufficient to perform required analyses of the impacts of the designation is lacking.
2. The biological needs of the species are not sufficiently well known to permit identification of an area as critical habitat.[183]

The agencies initially sought to avoid several critical habitat designations by concluding that the designation would not be prudent, but the trend in the case law suggests that today any attempt to avoid a designation under the not-prudent rationale will be scrutinized carefully by a court.[184]

2.8.2   **Economic Analysis**

The designation of critical habitat is one unique area of the Act where Congress expressly contemplated the consideration of economic impacts.[185] But precisely how that should occur was left open to agency implementation. The Office of Management and Budget suggests that the proper methodology requires comparing the current state of affairs, a baseline, with a postdesignation state of affairs. Another methodology, dubbed the "co-extensive" approach, "would take into account all of the economic impact of the [designation], regardless of whether those impacts are caused co-extensively by any other agency action (such as listing) and even if those

---

183. *Id.* § 424(a)(2).

184. *See* Sierra Club v. U.S. Fish & Wildlife Serv., 245 F.3d 434 (5th Cir. 2001) (invalidated decision not to designate habitat for gulf sturgeon); Nat. Res. Def. Council v. U.S. Dep't of the Interior, 1133 F.3d 1121, 1125–26 (9th Cir. 1997) (FWS's refusal to designate critical habitat for the coastal California gnatcatcher was not supported, and FWS's conclusory statements with regard to increased threats associated with such designation were unsupported by the record. Likewise, the court found unpersuasive the Service's finding that designation of critical habitat on private lands would not benefit the species, nor could critical habitat designation be avoided because another program provided superior protections.); Conservation Council for Haw. v. Babbitt, 2 F. Supp. 2d 1280 (D. Haw. 1998) (Service failed to properly consider evidence concerning the benefit and threat of designating critical habitat; the fact that listed plants were located on private land was insufficient basis for failure to designate critical habitat). A similar hard look might occur when the Service determines that designation is not determinable. *See* Forest Guardians v. Babbitt, 164 F.3d 1261, *amended opinion at* 174 F.3d 1178 (10th Cir. 1998); Ctr. for Biological Diversity v. Evans, 2005 WL 1514102 (N.D. Cal. 2005) (unpublished) (northern right whale).

185. *See* H.R. Rep. No. 97-567, at 12 (1982), *reprinted in* 1982 U.S.C.C.A.N. 2807, 2812 (explaining that the economic analysis required for critical habitat designation offers some "counterpoint" to the listing process). *See also* 77 Fed. Reg. 51,503 (Aug. 24, 2012) (proposed revisions to regulations for impact analyses of critical habitat).

impacts would remain in the absence of the [designation]."[186] The difference between these competing approaches surfaces because of an argument that the listing of the species itself and the accompanying no-jeopardy standard imposes the same economic consequences as a designation. The Ninth Circuit has endorsed the FWS's use of a baseline analysis.[187]

2.8.3   Critical Habitat Designation and Revision

As already discussed, critical habitat designation is an action that should occur concurrently with listing. If, however, the Secretary does not designate critical habitat concurrent with listing a species, the Secretary has 12 months within which to designate critical habitat to the maximum extent prudent.[188] Assuming the Secretary had previously determined not to designate critical habitat for a listed species, regulations implementing ESA section 4 apparently allow any party to petition "independent of any associated listing petition" for critical habitat designation,[189] and the Secretary must promptly conduct a review and take "appropriate action."[190]

Likewise, a person may submit a petition seeking to have designated critical habitat revised, and the Secretary must make a finding, within 90 days of receiving the petition, as to whether the petition revision may be warranted.[191] Within 12 months of a 90-day finding that the petitioned revision may be warranted, the Secretary must publish notice of "how he intends to proceed."[192]

---

186. N.M. Cattle Growers Ass'n v. U.S. Fish & Wildlife Serv., 248 F.3d 1277, 1283 (10th Cir. 2001).
187. Ariz. Cattle Growers Ass'n v. Salazar, 606 F.3d 1160, 1172–74 (9th Cir. 2010); Home Builders Ass'n v. U.S. Fish & Wildlife Serv., 616 F.3d 983, 992–93 (9th Cir. 2010).
188. 16 U.S.C. § 1533(b)(6)(C)(ii); 50 C.F.R. § 424.17(b)(2).
189. 50 C.F.R. § 424.14(d).
190. *Id.* The lack of specificity with regard to the Secretary's obligation upon receipt of a petition to designate critical habitat is probably justified in light of the fact that the Secretary would have, by necessity, already made a determination (either upon listing, or within 12 months thereafter) that critical habitat designation was not prudent and/or determinable.
191. 16 U.S.C. § 1533(b)(3)(D); 50 C.F.R. § 424.14(c)(1).
192. 16 U.S.C. § 1533(b)(3)(D)(ii); 50 C.F.R. § 424.14(c)(1). Options available at this point include publication of a proposed rule designating critical habitat, or a determination that designation of critical habitat is not prudent or determinable. For an example of a critical habitat revision petition decision, see 64 Fed. Reg. 57,399 (Oct. 25, 1999) (NMFS decision to exclude certain areas from designated critical habitat for threatened Snake River spring/summer chinook salmon). *See also* Murray D. Feldman & Michael J. Brennan, *The Growing Importance of Critical Habitat for Species Conservation*, 16 NAT. RES. & ENV'T 88, 93, 134 (2001).

3 Conservation: Section 7(a)(1) and Recovery Planning

3.1   Overview

As the most tangible product or physical manifestation of the Endangered Species Act (ESA), the endangered and threatened species list itself may appear to some to be the goal of the Act. Others may believe that the ESA creates a list of endangered species to further the aim of allowing government regulation of activities affecting species on the list. Professor Houck addresses such perceptions as follows:

> It is not the Act's goal to catalogue [species], to identify their habitats, to review and alter jeopardizing activities, to give developers a difficult time, or perpetuate precarious populations on the brink of extinction. These aspects of the Act are but means to the end of "conserving" these species.[1]

As illustrated in the table at the end of this chapter, the goal of conservation transcends nearly every section of the ESA, and it corresponds with the ultimate goal of the Act to recover species that are in peril.

This chapter discusses two of the mechanisms through which the ESA's conservation mandate may be fulfilled: section 7(a)(1) conservation obligations and section 4(f) recovery plans.

---

1.   Oliver A. Houck, *The Endangered Species Act and Its Implementation by the U.S. Departments of Interior and Commerce*, 64 U. Colo. L. Rev. 277, 344 (1993).

3.2   Section 7(a)(1) Conservation Obligations

Section 7(a)(1) of the ESA directs the Secretaries of Interior and Commerce to review programs administered by their respective departments and to utilize such programs in furtherance of the purposes of the Act.[2] In addition, section 7(a)(1) obligates "all other federal agencies," in consultation with the Secretary of the Interior or Commerce (as appropriate), to "utilize their authorities in furtherance of the purposes of the ESA . . . by carrying out programs for the conservation of [listed species]."[3] Separate and distinct from the ESA section 7(a)(2) consultation and avoidance of jeopardy requirements,[4] section 7(a)(1) suggests independent obligations applicable to all federal agencies. Unfortunately, this obligation is poorly defined, and to date no federal agency has promulgated rules specifically addressing section 7(a)(1).[5] And one should appreciate that section 7(a)(1) and (a)(2) were combined in the original language of the Act, and they only became separated into two provisions (and arguably into independent obligations) after *Tennessee Valley Authority v. Hill*.[6] In fact, the United States occasionally argues that "section 7(a)(1) of the ESA does not require agencies to develop species-specific and location-specific programs for the conservation of listed species."[7] The breadth of section 7(a)(1), therefore, has been established

---

2. 16 U.S.C. § 1536(a)(1). For a very thorough discussion of ESA section 7(a)(1), see J.B. Ruhl, *Section 7(a)(1) of the "New" Endangered Species Act: Rediscovering and Redefining the Untapped Power of Federal Agencies' Duty to Conserve Species,* 25 ENVTL. L. 1107 (1995).
3. 16 U.S.C. § 1536(a)(1).
4. 16 U.S.C. § 1536(a)(2). See chapter 5 for a detailed discussion of ESA section 7(a)(2).
5. Joint regulations promulgated by NMFS and FWS to implement ESA's section 7(a)(2) consultation requirements address the 7(a)(1) conservation mandate peripherally and in the narrow context of federal action likely to adversely affect the listed species. See 50 C.F.R. § 402.14(g)(6) (providing that NMFS or FWS will formulate "discretionary conservation recommendations" that federal action agencies may implement to reduce or mitigate the impacts of federal actions).
6. See Pub. L. No. 93-205, 87 Stat. 892 (1973). Congress redesignated this provision as section 7(a) in 1978, and broke up the sentence with a period. Pub. L. No. 95-632, 92 Stat. 3752 (1978). As the Act was subsequently amended, the provisions then became separated. Pub. L. No. 96-159, 93 Stat. 1226 (1979); Pub. L. No. 97-304, 96 Stat. 1417, 1426 (1982) (as amended).
7. Fla. Key Deer v. Paulison, 522 F.3d 1333, 1141 (11th Cir. 2008). But, for instance, the FWS states that federal agencies "have an affirmative responsibility for species conservation under section 7(a)(1)." 69 Fed. Reg. 24,084, 24,085 (May 3, 2004).

through litigation,[8] resulting in a few general rules but very little in the way of clear guidance.

Whether section 7(a)(1) obligations are mandatory or voluntary has been addressed by the courts, the majority of which have concluded that the section creates some mandatory, affirmative duties on agencies.[9] Courts originally addressed section 7(a)(1) only in the context of agencies acting to carry out other "primary" agency missions; no court had established that an agency must initiate a separate program for the purpose of conserving listed species.[10] For example, courts interpreted section 7(a)(1) to authorize an agency to refuse to execute a new contract,[11] require an agency to implement alternative courses of action when significant conservation benefits may be achieved consistent with an agency's primary mission,[12] require an agency to show that it has minimized harm to listed species, "consistent with other obligations" of the agency,[13] and require an agency at least to consider section 7(a)(1) when undertaking other activities.[14]

In 1998, the Fifth Circuit arguably expanded the section 7(a)(1) ESA conservation obligation. In *Sierra Club v. Glickman,* the court first affirmed that section 7(a)(1) creates an "affirmative duty on each federal agency to conserve each of the species listed pursuant to [the ESA]."[15] The court then went further than prior decisions by requiring that the U.S. Department of Agriculture (USDA)

---

8. *See* J.B. Ruhl, *supra* note 2, at 1125.

9. *See, e.g.,* Tenn. Valley Auth. v. Hill, 437 U.S. 153, 180–85 (1978) (discussing the general conservation mandate of the ESA); Friends of the Wild Swan, Inc. v. U.S. Fish and Wildlife Serv., 945 F. Supp. 1388, 1399 (D. Or. 1996) (suggesting "comprehensive" duty to conserve species); Defenders of Wildlife v. Andrus, 428 F. Supp. 167, 170 (D.D.C. 1977) (FWS's duck-hunting regulation did not adequately address the agency's "affirmative duty" at least to minimize inadvertent killing of listed waterfowl); Pyramid Lake Paiute Tribe of Indians v. U.S. Dep't of Navy, 898 F.2d 1410, 1416–17 (9th Cir. 1990) (recognizing that agencies have "affirmative obligations" under section 7(a)(1)); Connor v. Andrus, 453 F. Supp. 1037, 1041 (W.D. Tex. 1978) (FWS has an "affirmative duty" under section 7(a)(1) to bring listed species to the point where they may be removed from the list).

10. *See generally* J.B. Ruhl, *supra* note 2, at 1135.

11. Carson-Truckee Water Conservancy Dist. v. Clark, 741 F.2d 257, 260–61 (9th Cir. 1984), *cert. denied,* 470 U.S. 1083 (1985) (upholding Bureau of Reclamation decision to refuse a request for a new water contract, even though bureau possessed the discretion to execute such a contract).

12. *Pyramid Lake,* 898 F.2d at 1417.

13. *Defenders of Wildlife,* 428 F. Supp. at 170.

14. Fla. Key Deer v. Stickney, 864 F. Supp. 1222 (S.D. Fla. 1994).

15. 156 F.3d 606, 616 (5th Cir. 1998) (USDA ordered to consult with FWS to develop programs for the conservation of species dependent upon the Edwards Aquifer in central Texas).

"develop" or "adopt" conservation programs for listed species.[16] Although parties invoke *Glickman* and continue to press for an expansive view of section 7(a)(1), the impact of this decision outside the Fifth Circuit remains uncertain.

Subsequent lower court opinions reflect a slightly different view of section 7(a)(1) than that of the Fifth Circuit in *Glickman*. In *Strahan v. Linnon*[17] and *Hawksbill Sea Turtle v. FEMA*,[18] the district courts of Massachusetts and the Virgin Islands, respectively, held that ESA section 7(a)(1) conservation plans are "voluntary measures."[19] Unlike the situation in *Glickman*, however, the defendant agency in each case had taken at least some active steps to fulfill its section 7(a)(1) obligations. The dispositive issue, therefore, was not whether an agency must do something to conserve species, but rather whether what it had done was sufficient. In both cases, the courts concluded that in light of the plaintiffs' failure to specify particular alternative conservation measures that the agency should have implemented, the court would not intrude upon the agency's discretion as to the choice of measures.[20]

Both *Strahan* and *Hawksbill Sea Turtle* illustrate that courts generally are reluctant to set aside an agency's affirmative efforts to implement section 7(a)(1). Instead, the majority of courts emphasize that federal agencies enjoy considerable discretion under section 7(a)(1) and are reluctant to require that federal agencies develop species-specific conservation programs under section 7(a)(1).[21] Even in *Glickman*, had the USDA actually implemented measures specifically designed to address species dependent upon the Edwards Aquifer, the result might have been different. As a general rule, as long as an agency's choice of conservation measures is rational[22] and within the agency's authority

---

16. *Id.* at 618 (noting that mere "incidental benefits" to listed species, arising from other agency programs, are insufficient to fulfill an agency's section 7(a)(1) obligation).

17. 967 F. Supp. 581 (D. Mass. 1997).

18. 11 F. Supp. 2d 529 (D.V.I. 1998).

19. *Strahan*, 967 F. Supp. at 596; *Hawksbill Sea Turtle*, 11 F. Supp. 2d at 542–43.

20. *Strahan*, 967 F. Supp. at 595–96; *Hawksbill Sea Turtle*, 11 F. Supp. 2d at 543.

21. Defenders of Wildlife v. U.S. Fish & Wildlife Serv., 797 F. Supp. 2d 949 (D. Ariz. 2011); Defenders of Wildlife v. U.S. Fish & Wildlife Serv., 354 F. Supp. 2d 1156, 1174 (Or. 2005); Defenders of Wildlife v. Babbitt, 130 F. Supp. 2d 121, 135 (D.C. 2001).

22. Connor v. Andrus, 453 F. Supp. 1037, 1041 (W.D. Tex. 1978) (FWS regulation designed to conserve Mexican duck was rejected because record did not support FWS's determination that the regulation would actually benefit the duck).

to implement,[23] and arguably nothing suggests that some other alternative would provide greater conservation benefits while equally satisfying the agency's primary mission and objectives,[24] agencies enjoy considerable discretion when deciding how to fulfill their section 7(a)(1) obligations.

3.3   Recovery Plans

Although the development of recovery plans was slow in maturing during the ESA's formative years, many now believe that the recovery planning process is critical for the success of the Act and the ability to achieve the ESA's objective.[25] Section 4(f) of the ESA requires the Secretary to develop and implement "recovery plans" for the conservation and survival of each listed species, unless the Secretary finds that a recovery plan will not promote species conservation.[26] To the maximum extent practicable, the Secretary must give priority to the listed species most likely to benefit from recovery plans, such as those in immediate conflict with construction projects or other economic activity.[27] The Secretary is expressly forbidden from prioritizing recovery plans based upon the taxonomic classification of a species.[28] Although no timetable

---

23. Platte River Whooping Crane Critical Habitat Maint. Trust v. FERC, 962 F.2d 27, 34 (D.C. Cir. 1992) (holding that section 7(a)(1) "does not expand the powers conferred on an agency by its enabling act").

24. *See, e.g.,* Pyramid Lake Paiute Tribe of Indians v. U.S. Dep't of Navy, 898 F.2d 1410, 1417 (9th Cir. 1990).

25. *See generally* Federico Cheever, *The Road to Recovery: A New Way of Thinking About the Endangered Species Act,* 23 Ecology L.Q. 1 (1996); Jennifer Jeffers, *Reversing the Trend Towards Species Extinction or Merely Halting It?: Incorporating the Recovery Standard into ESA Section 7 Jeopardy Analyses,* 35 Ecology L.Q. 455 (2008); Daniel J. Rohlf, *Section 4 of the Endangered Species Act: Top Ten Issues for the Next Thirty Years,* 34 Envtl. L. 483, 550 (2004); Jason C. Rylander, *Recovering Endangered Species in Difficult Times: Can the ESA Go Beyond Mere Salvage?,* 42 Envtl. L. Rep. 10017 (2012). *See also* Dale D. Goble, *Recovery, in* Endangered Species Act: Law, Policy, and Perspectives 71 (Donald C. Baur & Wm. Robert Irvin eds., 2010).

26. 16 U.S.C. § 1533(f)(1).

27. 16 U.S.C. § 1533(f)(1)(A). *See* 48 Fed. Reg. 43,098 (1983) (FWS listing and recovery priority guidelines).

28. 16 U.S.C. § 1533(f)(1)(A). Congress expressed concern that about 5 percent of listed species had received up to 45 percent of the available funding for recovery planning, and noted that preferential treatment of "higher life forms" has no basis in the Act. S. Rep. No. 100-240, at 9 (1988), *reprinted in* 1988 U.S.C.C.A.N. 2700, 2708.

is required for development of recovery plans,[29] the Act requires the Secretary to report back to Congress every two years on the status of efforts to develop and implement recovery plans for all listed species.[30]

Recovery plans must be developed and implemented through a public process,[31] and they usually are prepared by a recovery team that includes representatives of state, tribal, or federal agencies, academic institutions, private individuals, and private organizations.[32] Whenever possible, recovery plans will be developed for multiple species, and the Services will seek to minimize the social and economic impacts of recovery activities. To the maximum extent practicable, each recovery plan should include

- a description of site-specific management actions as may be necessary to achieve conservation and survival of the species;
- objective measurable criteria that, if met, would result in the delisting of the species; and
- time and cost estimates to carry out the plan measures, and to achieve intermediate steps toward the goal of recovery.[33]

3.3.1   Discretion of FWS/NMFS in Recovery Plan Preparation and Content

Once the Secretary determines that a recovery plan would promote the conservation of a species, the ESA provides no statutory time limit governing when the Secretary must develop and publish the plan.[34] Unless, therefore, either the Fish and Wildlife

---

29.   NMFS and FWS policy is to finalize recovery plans within two and a half years of a species listing. 50 Fed. Reg. 34,272 (1994).

30.   16 U.S.C. § 1533(f)(3).

31.   *Id.* § 1533(f)(4) (providing for public notice and opportunity for review and comment). In *Friends of Blackwater v. Salazar,* 2012 WL 3538236 (D.C. Cir. Aug. 17, 2012), the court held that recovery plans are nonbinding documents and need not dictate whether a species can be delisted.

32.   50 Fed. Reg. 34,272 (1994).

33.   16 U.S.C. § 1533(f)(1)(B)(i)–(iii). The Services have developed further guidance on the recovery plan process and development, which they update, INTERIM ENDANGERED AND THREATENED SPECIES RECOVERY PLANNING GUIDANCE (version 1.3, June 2010) (latest update).

34.   Or. Nat. Res. Council v. Turner, 863 F. Supp. 1277, 1282 (D. Or. 1994).

Service (FWS) or the National Marine Fisheries Service (NMFS) has "unreasonably" delayed the development of a recovery plan, courts appear unlikely to order recovery plan preparation.[35] And similarly, the contents of a recovery plan are discretionary.[36] Although some courts suggest that the recovery plan requirement "breathes discretion at every pore,"[37] at least one court has held that the Secretary's discretion might be circumscribed by an obligation on the agency to fulfill its statutory commands to the fullest extent feasible or possible.[38] But courts seem unlikely to set aside any reasonable, good-faith effort to prepare recovery plans.

3.3.2 Federal Agency Discretion in Implementing Recovery Plans

Consistent with the discretion afforded the Secretary when developing recovery plans, these plans are not documents carrying the "force of law."[39] As one court noted, a recovery plan "presents a guideline for future goals, but does not mandate any actions,"[40] and courts normally will not "second guess" the Secretary's motives for not following the recovery plan.[41] But an agency's

---

35. *Id.* at 1284 (delay attributable to prioritization of recovery planning efforts was reasonable). For a discussion about the ability to require the agency to implement aspects of the plan, see *Conservation Northwest v. Kempthorne,* 2007 WL 1847143 (W.D. Wash. 2007) (unreported).

36. Morrill v. Lujan, 802 F. Supp. 424, 433 (S.D. Ala. 1992) ("the contents of the plan are discretionary, as evidenced by the language 'to the maximum extent practicable'"); Strahan v. Linnon, 967 F. Supp. 581, 597 (D. Mass. 1997) ("Case law instructs that the . . . content of recovery plans is discretionary[.]"), *aff'd,* 187 F.3d 623 (1st Cir. 1998) (per curiam).

37. *See, e.g.,* Fund for Animals, Inc. v. Rice, 85 F.3d 535, 547 (11th Cir. 1996) (quoting Strickland v. Morton, 519 F.2d 467, 469 (9th Cir. 1975)).

38. Fund for Animals v. Babbitt, 903 F. Supp. 96, 107, 110–12 (D.D.C. 1995) (holding that FWS had not met its ESA section 4(1)(B)(ii) obligation to provide objective, measurable criteria for recovery). *See also* Defenders of Wildlife v. Babbitt, 130 F. Supp. 2d 121, 131–35 (D.D.C. 2001), *later opinion,* Defenders of Wildlife v. Norton, 2003 WL 24122459 (D.D.C. 2003) (reviewing revised BOs following remand). In *Homebuilders Ass'n of Northern California v. U.S. Fish & Wildlife Service,* 616 F.3d 983, 989 (9th Cir. 2010), the Ninth Circuit observed that the "ESA does require a determination of criteria for measuring when a species will be conserved, but that requirement applies to the preparation of a recovery plan."

39. Fund for Animals, Inc. v. Rice, 85 F.3d at 548. The Service has stated that such plans are not regulatory documents but rather guidance. *E.g.,* Friends of Blackwater v. Salazar, 2012 WL 3538236 (D.C. Cir. Aug. 17, 2012).

40. *Or. Nat. Res. Council,* 863 F. Supp. at 1284. The court also stated that "the development and publication of a recovery plan in and of itself would not have afforded the endangered species any additional protection." *Id.*

41. Nat'l Wildlife Fed'n v. Nat'l Park Serv., 669 F. Supp. 384, 389 (D. Wyo. 1987).

deviation from a recovery plan, unless explained, can amount to arbitrary and capricious behavior, otherwise impermissible under the Administrative Procedure Act.[42]

Despite the discretionary nature of recovery planning generally, recovery plans are viewed as an integral component of species conservation, and while early development of recovery plans was slow, the development of such plans has been much more robust during the last two decades. Today, most of the listed wildlife species have recovery plans.[43] The FWS maintains a searchable database of its existing plans,[44] and the NMFS too operates a recovery plan web page.

42. See Defenders of Wildlife v. Hall, 565 F. Supp. 2d 1160, 1170 (D. Mont. 2008). Cf. Friends of Blackwater v. Salazar, 2012 WL 3538236 (D.C. Cir. Aug. 17, 2012) (deviation from plan upheld).

43. The FWS maintains a box score web page for, inter alia, recovery plans. See FWS, Species Reports, http://ecos.fws.gov/tess_public/pub/Boxscore.do.

44. See FWS, Recovery Plans Search, http://www.fws.gov/endangered/species/recovery-plans.html.

ESA's Conservation Directives

ESA Provision	Conservation Directive
Section 2(b)— Purposes	"The purposes of this chapter are to provide a means whereby the ecosystems upon which endangered species and threatened species depend may be conserved." (16 U.S.C. § 1531(b))
Section 2(c)— Policy	"[A]ll federal departments and agencies shall seek to conserve endangered species and threatened species and shall utilize their authorities in furtherance of the purposes of this chapter." (16 U.S.C. § 1531(c))
Section 3(3)— Definitions	"The terms 'conserve,' 'conserving,' and 'conservation' mean to use and the use of all methods and procedures which are necessary to bring any [listed] species to the point at which the measures provided pursuant to the Act are no longer necessary." (16 U.S.C. § 1532(3))
Section 4(f)— Recovery Plans	Recovery plans are developed and implemented expressly for the "conservation and survival" of the listed species. (16 U.S.C. §§ 1533(f)(1), (1)(B)(I))
Section 5— Implementation of Conservation Programs	The Secretaries of Interior and Commerce, and the Secretary of Agriculture (with respect to national forest land), shall establish and implement a program to conserve all species, and shall use land acquisition authority as appropriate. (16 U.S.C. § 1534)
Section 6— Cooperation with States	Provides for management agreements and cooperative agreements with states for the establishment of areas and programs for conservation of listed species. (16 U.S.C. § §1535(b), (c))
Section 7(a)(1)— Federal Agency Conservation Obligations	Federal agencies shall use their authorities in carrying out programs for the conservation of listed species. (16 U.S.C. § 1536(a)(1))

(continued)

ESA's Conservation Directives (*continued*)

Section 8— International Cooperation	The Secretary may provide financial and personnel assistance to, and may encourage bilateral and multilateral agreements with, foreign countries in order to develop, promote, and encourage conservation of fish, wildlife, or plants. (16 U.S.C. § 1537(a), (c))
Section 10— Permits	No permit may be granted under Section 10 that contravenes the purposes and policies of ESA section 2 (which includes conservation). (16 U.S.C. § 1539(d))
Section 10(j)— Reintroductions	The Secretary may authorize release of experimental populations if the Secretary determines that such releases will further the conservation of such species. (16 U.S.C. § 1539(j)(2)(A))

4 Prohibited Acts and Penalties: Sections 9 and 11

4.1 ## Overview

Section 9 of the Endangered Species Act (ESA) reflects Congress's effort to address threats to species comprehensively.[1] It is, in short, a suite of prohibitions that, as noted by J.B. Ruhl, serve as "the central prohibitory ESA provision."[2] Section 9 outlines the ESA's prohibited acts and accompanying consequences that apply to individuals and entities, private as well as public.

Any "person" subject to the jurisdiction of the United States is subject to the prohibitions of section 9.[3] Through a 1988 amendment, Congress clarified that, in addition to individuals, any and all governmental, business, or private entities are subject to section 9; thus, the Act defines *person* broadly to include

> an individual, corporation, partnership, trust, association, or any other private entity; or any officer, employee, agent, department, or instrumentality of the Federal Government, of any State, municipality, or political subdivision of a State, or of any foreign government;

---

1. 16 U.S.C. § 1538.
2. J.B. Ruhl, *Regional Habitat Planning Under the Endangered Species Act: Pushing the Legal and Practical Limits of Species Protection,* 44 Sw. L.J. 1393, 1397 (1991); *see also* Federico Cheever, *An Introduction to the Prohibition Against Takings in Section 9 of the Endangered Species Act of 1973: Learning to Live with a Powerful Species Preservation Law,* 62 U. Colo. L. Rev. 109 (1991); George Cameron Coggins & Irma S. Russell, *Beyond Shooting Snail Darters in Pork Barrels: Endangered Species and Land Use in America,* 70 Geo. L.J. 1433, 1460 (1982) (characterizing ESA as creating "a cocoon of legal protection" for listed species). *See generally* Patrick Parenteau, *The Take Prohibition, in* Endangered Species Act: Law, Policy, and Perspectives 147 (Donald C. Baur & Wm. Robert Irvin eds., 2010); Steven P. Quarles & Thomas R. Lundquist, *Land Use Activities and the Section 9 Take Prohibition, in* Endangered Species Act: Law, Policy, and Perspectives 161 (Donald C. Baur & Wm. Robert Irvin eds., 2010).
3. 16 U.S.C. § 1538.

any State, municipality, or political subdivision of a State; or any other entity subject to the jurisdiction of the United States.[4]

With the exception of the occasional, unsuccessful state claim that the Tenth Amendment prohibits application of section 9 to state governmental entities,[5] the definition of *person* is sufficiently broad to preclude substantial litigation on the issue. The principal issue, therefore, is not "who" section 9 covers, but rather what conduct it prohibits.

4.2   Conduct Prohibited

Section 9's prohibition applies to a wide range of human activities; in limited circumstances, certain inactivity and some omissions are prohibited. Except as explicitly allowed through operation of other provisions of the ESA,[6] section 9 prohibits the following activities with respect to endangered, and in most cases threatened,[7] fish and wildlife:

- importing or exporting endangered species[8]
- "taking" any endangered species within the United States, its territorial sea, or upon the high seas[9]

---

4.   16 U.S.C. § 1532(12). The definition owes its breadth in part to the congressional response to a 1988 Ninth Circuit Court of Appeals decision, which held that municipalities were not "persons" under the ESA. United States v. Rancho Palos Verde, 841 F.2d 329 (9th Cir. 1988).

5.   *See, e.g.,* Strahan v. Coxe, 127 F.3d 155, 163 (1st Cir. 1997), *cert. denied,* 525 U.S. 830 (1998) (holding that "a governmental third party pursuant to whose authority an actor directly exacts a taking of an endangered species may be deemed to have violated the provision of the ESA"); Loggerhead Turtle v. Cnty. Council of Volusia Cnty., 148 F.3d 1231 (11th Cir. 1998) (holding that county could potentially be in violation of section 9 by harming listed turtles through inadequate regulation of beachfront lighting); United States v. Town of Plymouth, 6 F. Supp. 2d 81, 90–91 (D. Mass. 1998) (preliminary injunction was issued enjoining town's permitting of off-road vehicles, based on findings that operation of the vehicles was causing take of endangered piping plovers).

6.   See sections 4.8 and chapters 6, 7, and 10 for a thorough discussion of the exceptions to takings provided in various provisions of the ESA.

7.   *See* section 4.3.

8.   16 U.S.C. § 1538(a)(1)(A). Section 3(10) of the ESA defines *import* as follows:

The term "import" means to land on, bring into, or introduce into, any place subject to the jurisdiction of the United States, whether or not such landing, bringing, or introduction constitutes an importation within the meaning of the customs laws of the United States.

16 U.S.C. § 1532(10).

9.   *Id.* § 1538(a)(1)(B), (C).

- possessing, selling, delivering, carrying, transporting, or shipping any endangered species unlawfully taken, in the course of any commercial activity[10]
- engaging in any activity involving interstate or foreign commerce in endangered species[11]
- violating any regulation of the Secretary pertaining to endangered or threatened species[12]

As discussed more fully in section 4.4 *infra,* section 9(a)(2) of the Act[13] also extends limited protection to listed plants, and section 9(c) of the Act makes unlawful the trade of wildlife in violation of the Convention on International Trade in Endangered Species of Wild Fauna and Flora (CITES).[14] As a final additive, ESA further provides that it is unlawful even to *attempt* to commit a violation of section 9, or to solicit another to commit such a violation or cause such an offense to be committed.[15]

4.3 Threatened Species and Section 4(d) Rules

Congress did not expressly apply section 9(a)(1) prohibitions to threatened species, but rather left it to the discretion of the Secretaries of Interior and Commerce to promulgate regulations deemed "necessary and advisable" to conserve threatened species of fish and wildlife.[16] For a threatened species of fish and wildlife, "the Secretary may by regulation prohibit . . . any act prohibited under Section [9]."[17] To date, the Secretaries of Interior and Commerce have treated threatened species differently.

---

10. 16 U.S.C. § 1538(a)(1)(D). Section 3(2) of the ESA defines *commercial activity* as follows:

> The term "commercial activity" means all activities of industry and trade, including, but not limited to, the buying or selling of commodities and activities conducted for the purpose of facilitating such buying and selling: *provided, however,* that it does not include exhibitions of commodities by museums or similar cultural or historical organizations.

16 U.S.C. § 1532(2). By regulation, the phrase "industry and trade" encompasses only those activities done for "gain or profit." 50 C.F.R. § 17.3.

11. 16 U.S.C. § 1538(a)(1)(E), (F).
12. *Id.* § 1538(a)(1)(G).
13. *Id.* § 1538(a)(2).
14. See chapter 9, section 9.5 for a discussion of CITES.
15. 16 U.S.C. § 1538(g).
16. *Id.* § 1533(d).
17. *Id.*

The Secretary of the Interior has exercised the full extent of discretion under section 4(d) to extend the full range of section 9 prohibitions to all threatened species under the jurisdiction of the Department of the Interior, unless a species is subject to its own individual "4(d) rule."[18] Because section 9 provides the maximum protection available to threatened species, any species-specific section 4(d) rule promulgated by the Fish and Wildlife Service (FWS) generally decreases the protections afforded to the particular threatened species at issue.[19] The Secretary of Interior's blanket application of section 9 prohibitions to all threatened species, except those subject to an individual section 4(d) rule, was upheld by the U.S. Court of Appeals for the D.C. Circuit in 1993.[20] Though the court held the ESA and its legislative history to be ambiguous with respect to whether the Secretary could protect all threatened species in a blanket rule, the court concluded that the regulation was a "reasonable and permissible construction of the ESA."[21]

The Secretary of Commerce implements section 4(d) a bit differently from the Secretary of Interior, extending section 9 prohibitions/protections to threatened species on a case-by-case basis. As a result, the prohibitions outlined in ESA section 9 do not apply to threatened species listed by the National Marine Fisheries Service (NMFS), unless and until NMFS promulgates a 4(d) rule governing a particular threatened species.[22] Section 4(d) emerged in the 1990s as a mechanism for implementing the Act in a more flexible manner, and while a section 4(d) rule generally decreases the protections applicable to threatened species under FWS jurisdiction, a NMFS section 4(d) rule conversely is necessary to afford section 9 protection.[23]

4.4   Plants

Although the ESA provides for listing and protection of endangered or threatened plants, listed plants are not protected to the

18.   50 C.F.R. § 17.31(a).

19.   *See* 50 C.F.R. §§ 17.40–17.48 (section 4(d) rules promulgated by FWS), 17.84 (section 4(d) rules promulgated by FWS to address "experimental populations"). See chapter 10 for a discussion of experimental populations.

20.   Sweet Home Chapter of Cmtys. for a Great Or. v. Babbitt, 1 F.3d 1, 5–8 (D.C. Cir. 1993), *rev'd on other grounds,* 515 U.S. 687, 692 n.5 (1995).

21.   1 F.3d at 8.

22.   *See* 50 C.F.R. pt. 223 (section 4(d) rules promulgated by NMFS).

23.   *See, e.g.,* 65 Fed. Reg. 42,481 (2000) (NMFS 4(d) rule extending certain ESA section 9 protections to several threatened species of salmon and steelhead).

same extent as listed animals, because the section 9(a)(1)(C) prohibition against "take" applies only to listed wildlife. Endangered plants are subject to the protection of a separate prohibition in section 9(a)(2) making it unlawful to

> remove and reduce to possession any such species from areas under Federal jurisdiction; maliciously damage or destroy any such species on any such area; or remove, cut, dig up, or damage or destroy any such species on any other area in knowing violation of any law or regulation of any state or in the course of any violation of a state criminal trespass law.[24]

The phrase "areas under Federal jurisdiction" generated litigation, with the Ninth Circuit concluding that it does not include areas over which Congress has the ability to exercise federal jurisdiction, such as over "waters of the United States" under the Clean Water Act.[25]

Similar to the prohibitions affecting endangered wildlife, endangered plants are subject to a full panoply of protections prohibiting their import, export, and other activities involving interstate or foreign commerce in protected plants.[26] Yet while section 9 prohibits "possession" of endangered wildlife taken in violation of the Act, one may possess an illegally obtained plant without violating section 9.[27] Just as threatened wildlife may be afforded the same protection as endangered wildlife, threatened plants also may be afforded the same protections afforded to endangered plants.[28] FWS, however, has not extended the same blanket protection to threatened plants as it has to threatened wildlife.[29] Rather, the prohibitions against "maliciously" (a term undefined by the ESA and implementing regulations) damaging plants, or damaging or destroying plants in violation of state law or in the course of criminal trespass,[30] remain applicable only to endangered plants, unless provided for in a special regulation regarding a particular threatened plant species.

---

24. 16 U.S.C. § 1538(a)(2)(B).
25. N. Cal. River Watch v. Wilcox, 633 F.3d 766 (9th Cir. 2011).
26. 16 U.S.C. § 1538(a)(2)(A), (C), (D), (E).
27. *Compare* 16 U.S.C. § 1538(a)(1)(D) *with* 16 U.S.C. § 1538(a)(2)(C).
28. 16 U.S.C. §§ 1534(d), 1538(a)(2)(E).
29. *See* 50 C.F.R. § 17.71(a) (1998) (This provision extends the protections outlined in 50 C.F.R. § 17.61 to threatened plants; however, the ESA's statutory (section 9(a)(2)) prohibition against malicious damage or destruction is curiously absent from 50 C.F.R. § 17.61.).
30. The prohibition against taking plants while in the course of violating state trespass law was added to section 9 in a 1988 amendment. S. REP. No. 100-240, at 12–13 (1988), *reprinted in* 1988 U.S.C.C.A.N. 2700, 2711–12.

4.5   Prohibited "Take": What Constitutes Harm

By many accounts, a far-reaching aspect of section 9 is its prohibition against "take" of protected species of fish and wildlife.[31] *Take* is defined broadly in the Act as "to harass, *harm,* pursue, hunt, shoot, wound, kill, trap, capture, or collect, or to attempt to engage in any such conduct."[32] An oft-quoted statement from the ESA's legislative history expresses Congress's intent with regard to the extent of the "take" prohibition; the term *take* is "defined in the broadest possible manner to include every conceivable way in which a person can 'take' or attempt to 'take' any fish or wildlife."[33]

The regulations further define two elements of the "take" definition, the terms *harass* and *harm:*

> *Harass* in the definition of "take" in the Act means an intentional or negligent act or omission which creates the likelihood of injury to wildlife by annoying it to such an extent as to significantly disrupt normal behavioral patterns which include, but are not limited to, breeding, feeding or sheltering.[34]
>
> *Harm* in the definition of "take" in the Act means an act which actually kills or injures wildlife. Such act may include significant habitat modification or degradation where it actually kills or injures wildlife by significantly impairing essential behavioral patterns, including breeding, feeding or sheltering.[35]

These definitions, particularly the definition of *harm,* have produced a significant body of case law, including the 1995 decision of the U.S. Supreme Court in *Babbitt v. Sweet Home.*[36] However, even the most superficial understanding of section 9 jurisprudence requires some familiarity with two earlier opinions from the Ninth Circuit, known as *Palila I* and *Palila II.*

---

31. 16 U.S.C. § 1538(a)(1)(B).

32. 16 U.S.C. § 1532(18) (emphasis added).

33. S. Rep. No. 93-307 (1973), *reprinted in* 1973 U.S.S.C.A.N. 2995. See Cheever, *supra* note 2, at 128–30 for a good overview of the legislative history of section 9.

34. 50 C.F.R. § 17.3. *See, e.g.,* Ctr. for Biological Diversity v. Marina Point Dev. Co., 535 F.3d 1026, 1036–37 (9th Cir. 2008) (alleged harassment of eagles from construction but issue rendered moot by delisting of species); Cold Mountain v. Garber, 375 F.3d 884, 889–90 (9th Cir. 2004) (alleged harassment of bald eagles from helicopters); Fund for Animals v. Fla. Game & Fresh Water Comm'n, 550 F. Supp. 1206 (S.D. Fla. 1982) (alleged harassment from boats).

35. 50 C.F.R. § 17.3. NMFS has promulgated its own "harm" definition, substantially mirroring the FWS definition. 50 C.F.R. § 222.102; *see also* 64 Fed. Reg. 60,727 (1999).

36. 515 U.S. 687 (1995).

4.5.1   *Palila I* and *II:* Habitat Modification May Result in Prohibited Harm

In 1981, the Court of Appeals for the Ninth Circuit affirmed a lower court determination that feral goats and sheep, maintained by the state of Hawaii, were harming the endangered palila bird.[37] The goats and sheep browsed on seedlings of the mumane tree, thereby denying the palila the benefit of the mature mumane trees that would have grown from the seedlings. Because the palila depended on the mumane trees for its survival (food, shelter, and nest sites), the court held that elimination of the goats and sheep was necessary to the bird's survival; thus, the state's maintenance of the goat and sheep herd was a violation of section 9.[38] Commentators agree that the Ninth Circuit's opinion in *Palila I* was a watershed event in section 9 jurisprudence, because habitat modification alone was determined to amount to a prohibited "take."[39] FWS took the *Palila I* opinion seriously and amended the regulatory definition of *harm* to clarify that "habitat modification alone without any attendant death or injury of the protected wildlife" is not a section 9 violation.[40] It is perhaps fitting, then, that another dispute involving the palila bird provided the factual background for application of the new "harm" regulation.

In 1985, the original plaintiffs in *Palila I* again brought suit to allege that the palila bird was being harmed by damage to the critical mumane tree. In this new case, evidence showed that another animal, the mouflon sheep, was also eating mumane tree shoots. Applying the new 1981 definition of *harm*,[41] the Ninth Circuit held that Hawaii's maintenance of the sheep herd violated section 9. Specifically, the court held that the 1981 rule change "did not embody a substantial change" in the definition of *harm*,

---

37. Palila v. Haw. Dep't of Land & Nat. Res. (*Palila I*), 639 F.2d 495 (9th Cir. 1981), aff'g 471 F. Supp. 985 (D. Haw. 1979). *But see* N. Slope Borough v. Andrus, 486 F. Supp. 332, 362 (D.D.C.) (refusing to enjoin offshore oil leasing to protect endangered whale species on the ground that no injunction should issue unless "danger to the protected species is sufficiently imminent or certain"), *aff'd in part, rev'd in part*, 642 F.2d 589 (D.C. Cir. 1980); California v. Watt, 520 F. Supp. 1359 (C.D. Cal. 1981) (mere "threat" to survival of listed species held insufficient to amount to a section 9 violation, without more "immediate injury"), *aff'd in part, rev'd in part*, 683 F.2d 1254 (9th Cir. 1982), *rev'd on other grounds sub nom.* Sec'y of Interior v. California, 464 U.S. 312 (1984).

38. *Palila I*, 639 F.2d at 497.

39. *See, e.g.,* DANIEL J. ROHLF, THE ENDANGERED SPECIES ACT: A GUIDE TO ITS PROTECTIONS AND IMPLEMENTATION 63 (1989); Cheever, *supra* note 2, at 143.

40. 46 Fed. Reg. 54,748 (1981).

41. *Id.* The 1981 rule remains unaltered. 50 C.F.R. § 17.3.

and that activities that significantly degraded the palila's habitat, and caused actual injury to the palila, remained prohibited.[42] Likewise, the court rejected the notion that "potential" harm to listed species was not "actual harm" as contemplated by the new definition.[43]

Though *Palila II* was by no means the only opinion of its era holding habitat modification to be a prohibited harm of listed species,[44] the scope and clarity of the opinion was such that it could be not be ignored by other circuits.

4.5.2   *Sweet Home:* "Harm" Definition Upheld

In 1994, the U.S. Court of Appeals for the D.C. Circuit handed down a decision in direct conflict with *Palila II*. The plaintiffs in *Sweet Home* were landowners and logging industry representatives who claimed economic injury due to application of the "harm" regulation to protect red-cockaded woodpeckers and the northern spotted owl.[45] In response to the plaintiffs' facial challenge to the FWS's 1981 regulation defining *harm* (the same regulation considered in *Palila II*), the D.C. Circuit held that the ESA prohibition on take prohibited only those activities amounting to "a direct application of force against the animal taken";[46] thus, the "harm" regulation was held invalid. The Supreme Court granted certiorari to resolve the "square conflict"[47] between the D.C. Circuit's *Sweet Home* decision and the Ninth Circuit's *Palila II* decision. Adding to the palila bird's legacy, on April 14, 1995, the Court reversed the D.C. Circuit and reaffirmed the application of the "harm" prohibition to habitat modification.[48]

---

42. Palila v. Haw. Dep't of Land & Nat. Res. (*Palila II*), 649 F. Supp. 1070, 1075 (D. Haw. 1986), *aff'd*, 852 F.2d 1106 (9th Cir. 1988).

43. *Palila II*, 852 F.2d at 1108. As discussed in section 4.6, courts continue to struggle to determine when potential harm to a listed species is sufficiently imminent or causally related to the habitat-modifying behavior as to constitute a take.

44. *See, e.g.,* Sierra Club v. Lyng, 694 F. Supp. 1260 (E.D. Tex. 1988), *aff'd in part, vacated in part sub nom.* Sierra Club v. Yeuter, 926 F.2d 437 (5th Cir. 1991) (holding that U.S. Forest Service logging practices harmed red-cockaded woodpeckers); Defenders of Wildlife v. Adm'r of EPA, 688 F. Supp. 1334 (D. Minn. 1988), *rev'd on other grounds,* 882 F.2d 1294 (8th Cir. 1989).

45. Sweet Home Chapter of Cmtys. for a Great Or. v. Babbitt, 17 F.3d 1463 (D.C. Cir. 1994), *rev'd,* 515 U.S. 687 (1995).

46. *Id.,* 17 F.3d at 1465.

47. *Sweet Home,* 515 U.S. at 695.

48. *Id.* at 707.

The *Sweet Home* plaintiffs framed their case as a facial challenge to the "harm" regulation, as opposed to an as-applied challenge. The Court, therefore, assumed arguendo that the plaintiffs' logging activities would have the effect, though unintended, "of detrimentally changing the natural habitat of both listed species and that, as a consequence, members of those species will be killed or injured."[49] The only question then before the Court was whether the "harm" regulation was a permissible construction of the ESA. The Court ultimately concluded that "the Secretary reasonably construed the intent of Congress when he defined 'harm' to include 'significant habitat modification or degradation that actually kills or injures wildlife.'"[50]

Writing for the majority, Justice Stevens found support for the Secretary's definition of the word *harm* in the dictionary definition of the term. Webster's defines *harm* as "to cause hurt or damage to: injure."[51] Habitat modification that results in actual injury to members of listed species meets the dictionary definition of *harm*. Likewise, the dictionary definition is devoid of any reference to "direct" application of force, as opposed to indirect injury.[52] Moreover, the majority held that if harm were limited to direct injuries, the term would have no meaning that did not duplicate the meaning of the other words included in the statutory definition of *take*.[53] Simply put, the ordinary meaning of the word *harm* was held to support the Secretary's definition.

The majority also concluded that the comprehensive nature of the ESA, combined with Congress's explicit reference in the Act to conservation of "the *ecosystems* upon which endangered and threatened species depend," supported the Secretary's broad definition of *harm*.[54] Referencing its 1978 decision in *Tennessee Valley Authority v. Hill*, where the Court elaborated on the comprehensive nature of the ESA, the *Sweet Home* Court noted that the Secretary's inclusion of habitat modification in the "harm" definition had added weight to the Court's conclusion that the Tellico Dam would "harm" the snail darter.[55]

---

49. *Id.* at 696.
50. *Id.* at 708.
51. *Id.* at 697 (quoting Webster's Third New International Dictionary 1034 (1966)).
52. *Id.*
53. *Id.* at 697–98.
54. *Id.* at 698–99 (emphasis added) (quoting 16 U.S.C. § 1531(b)) (citing Tenn. Valley Auth. v. Hill, 437 U.S. 153 (1978).
55. *Id.* at 697–99 (citing *Hill,* 437 U.S. at 184 n.30).

The Court similarly suggested that the Secretary's "harm" definition comported with the Act's legislative history, particularly the 1982 ESA amendments authorizing limited takings, when such takings are "incidental to, and not the purpose of, the carrying out of an otherwise lawful activity."[56] Recognizing that incidental take permits under section 10 provide an exception to the section 9 takings prohibition, and that such permits are available only when the taking is unintended or indirect (i.e., "incidental to, and not the purpose of" the proposed activity), the Court concluded that Congress must have intended to apply the "harm" prohibition to unintended takings, such as habitat modification, or the section 10 permit provision would be meaningless.[57] In response to the dissent's suggestion that the section 9 take prohibition is limited to the deliberate actions of hunters and trappers, the majority cited instances in the ESA's legislative history where Congress expressed its intent to define take broadly, and where Congress even gave examples of prohibited, indirect harm or harassment of listed species.[58] The majority found nothing in the legislative history of the Act that weighed against the Secretary's application of the "harm" prohibition to habitat modification.

Applying *Chevron*[59] deference, the Court concluded that Congress delegated broad administrative and interpretive power to the Secretary under the ESA, and that, based on the text, structure, and legislative history of the Act, the Secretary reasonably construed the intent of Congress when defining *harm* to include habitat modification or degradation that actually kills or injures wildlife. With respect to whether the current definition of *harm* is facially valid, therefore, the issue is settled. Yet, as discussed next, the Court's majority recognized that much uncertainty remains with respect to actual application of the "harm" prohibition to individual fact patterns.[60]

---

56. *Id.* at 700 (quoting 16 U.S.C. § 1539(a)(1)(B)). Incidental take permits are discussed in chapter 6, section 6.2.

57. *Id.* at 700–01. The Court was also persuaded that the legislative history of the 1982 amendments illustrates that Congress clearly had habitat modification in mind when crafting the section 10 incidental take permit provision. *Id.* at 707 (citing S. Rep. No. 97-418, at 10 (1982); H.R. Conf. Rep. No. 97-835, at 30–32 (1982)).

58. *Id.* at 704–06.

59. Chevron U.S.A. Inc. v. Nat. Res. Def. Council, Inc., 467 U.S. 837, 865–66 (1984).

60. *Sweet Home,* 515 U.S. at 708. In spite of this uncertainty, however, section 9 litigants cannot invoke the "rule of lenity" with respect to the "harm" definition; the *Sweet Home* Court rejected the notion, concluding that the "harm"

4.6   Causation: Reasonable Certainty and the New Era of Section 9 Litigation

Although the *Sweet Home* Court validated the broad regulatory definition of *harm,* the Court also noted that actual application of the "harm" standard could prove difficult. The Court's discussion of causation touched on issues that have permeated section 9 litigation since its inception; until *Sweet Home,* though, they were rarely articulated in terms of causation. Words such as *certain, imminent, proximate, foreseeable, speculative,* and *conjectural* likely will remain part of the ESA section 9 lexicon for years to come.

The *Sweet Home* majority held that the "harm" regulation incorporates "ordinary requirements of proximate causation and foreseeability."[61] In addition, the Court apparently adopted but-for causation as the proper means of establishing whether a particular activity is, or will be, the cause of a prohibited harm to listed species.[62] With the exception of some interesting discussion by Justice O'Connor in her concurring opinion, the Court did not attempt to precisely define proximate cause, foreseeability, or but-for causation, but the majority suggested that under some circumstances, "minimal or unforeseeable harm" may not violate the ESA.[63]

Justice O'Connor captured the state of the law for proximate cause by noting that "proximate causation is not a concept susceptible of precise definition," and the Justice further opined that the concept "normally eliminates the bizarre."[64] Justice O'Connor also observed that proximate cause injects "a foreseeability element into the [ESA]" and the "harm" regulation.[65] But Justice O'Connor parted company with the majority, when she stated that she would have overturned *Palila II,*[66] and that she did not believe

---

regulation provided fair notice and fair warning of its consequence. *Id.* at 704 n.18.

61.   *Id.* at 700 n.13. *See* Lawrence R. Liebesman & Steven G. Davison, *Takings of Wildlife Under the Endangered Species Act after Babbitt v. Sweet Home Chapter of Communities for a Great Oregon,* 5 U. BALT. J. ENVTL. L. 137, 155–58 (1997) (providing a detailed discussion of section 9 causation). For Professor Davison's follow-up article, see Steven G. Davison, *The Aftermath of Sweet Home Chapter: Modification of Wildlife Habitat as a Prohibited Taking in Violation of the Endangered Species Act,* 27 WM. & MARY ENVTL. L. & POL'Y REV. 541 (2003).

62.   515 U.S. at 700 n.13.

63.   *Id.* at 699.

64.   *Id.* at 713 (O'Connor, J., concurring) (quoting Jerome B. Grubart, Inc. v. Great Lakes Dredge & Dock Co., 513 U.S. 527, 536 (1995)).

65.   *Id.*

66.   The majority specifically noted the conflict between *Palila II* and the D.C. Circuit's *Sweet Home* decision, and chose to reverse the D.C. Circuit; *Palila II* survives.

the mouflon sheep consumption of mumane seeds proximately caused "actual death or injury to identifiable [palila] birds."[67] Yet both the majority and Justice O'Connor agreed in acknowledging that application of the harm prohibition to individual fact patterns will have to be resolved on a case-by-case basis.[68]

Lower court opinions predating and following *Sweet Home* provide guidance—albeit limited—on instances when harm might occur, or not. For example, in what one commentator termed "the extreme end of the spectrum,"[69] the Eighth Circuit held that EPA's decision to register strychnine as a pesticide "was critical to the resulting poisonings" of listed species.[70] Courts also have found a causal link to exist between

- state licensing of fishing and lobstering equipment and subsequent whale entanglement in the equipment[71]
- Forest Service timber management practices and woodpecker abandonment of nesting cavities[72]
- town permitting of vehicles on beaches and crushing deaths of plovers[73]
- county permitting of beachfront lighting and disorientation of turtles[74]
- railroad company spillage of corn on railroad tracks and subsequent killing of grizzly bears that were struck while feeding on the spilled corn[75]
- logging and the impairment of breeding by marbled murrelets[76]

---

67. 515 U.S. at 714.

68. *Id.* at 713. The majority had noted that "all persons who must comply with the [ESA] will confront difficult questions of proximity and degree . . . [which must be addressed] through case-by-case resolution and adjudication." *Id.* at 708.

69. James C. Kilbourne, *The Endangered Species Act Under the Microscope: A Closeup Look from a Litigator's Perspective*, 21 Envtl. L. 499, 583 (1991).

70. Defenders of Wildlife v. EPA, 882 F.2d 1294, 1301 (8th Cir. 1989).

71. Strahan v. Coxe, 127 F.3d 155, 159 (1st Cir. 1997), *cert. denied*, 525 U.S. 830 (1998).

72. Sierra Club v. Yeutter, 926 F.2d 437 (5th Cir. 1991).

73. United States v. Town of Plymouth, CV No. 98-10566-PBS at 20–21 (D. Mass. May 15, 1998) (memorandum and order).

74. Loggerhead Turtle v. Cnty. Council of Volusia Cnty., 148 F.3d 1231 (11th Cir. 1998) (for standing purposes, the court determined that a causal link existed between county permitting of beachfront lighting and the resulting disorientation of turtle hatchlings).

75. Nat'l Wildlife Fed'n v. Burlington N. R.R., 23 F.3d 1508 (9th Cir. 1994).

76. Marbled Murrelet v. Babbitt, 83 F.3d 1060, 1067–68 (9th Cir. 1996) (court also determined that the proposed logging would increase the likelihood of attack by predators).

Conversely, several courts have dismissed section 9 claims when causation was found lacking or too attenuated. For example, the Ninth Circuit (in a post–*Palila II* opinion) held that one year's diversion of water to lands leased by the U.S. Navy did not cause harm to the endangered cui-ui fish.[77] Likewise, the First Circuit held that causation was not sufficient to find that the U.S. Coast Guard had violated section 9 by issuing certificates of documentation (analogous to automobile and drivers' licenses) for non–Coast Guard vessels, when those vessels struck endangered whales.[78] In an earlier First Circuit case, the court declined a request to hold that a "one in a million" risk of harm is sufficient to find a section 9 violation.[79] The court refused to enjoin a deer hunt that allegedly created a risk to eagles because the eagles might ingest carrion containing lead slugs; the court considered the low likelihood of lead ingestion by eagles, as well as the fact that the plaintiffs had not introduced any evidence that any eagle had ever ingested lead in such a fashion.[80]

One of the principal issues that surfaces in cases involving section 9 is the standard of proof necessary for a court to enjoin potential take liability, before evidence exists that the defendant's conduct actually has resulted in the loss of an individual member of the species. Although the *Sweet Home* majority may have left room for some argument on the issue of future versus past injury,[81] lower courts confronted with the issue consistently find liability when the defendant's conduct is reasonably certain to cause a take of the species.

The Ninth Circuit explicitly rejects any need for "historic injury," holding that liability can arise when a "reasonably certain" and "imminent" threat of harm to listed species can be established.[82] Likewise, the First Circuit recognized that "actual injury"

---

77. Pyramid Lake Paiute Tribe v. U. S. Dep't of Navy, 898 F.2d 1410, 1420 (9th Cir. 1990).

78. Strahan v. Coxe, 127 F.3d 155 (1st Cir. 1997), *cert. denied,* 525 U.S. 830 (1998).

79. Am. Bald Eagle v. Bhatti, 9 F.3d 163, 165 (1st Cir. 1993).

80. *Id.* at 166.

81. Babbitt v. Sweet Home Chapter of Cmtys. for a Great Or., 515 U.S. 687, 700 n.13 (1995) ("the Government cannot enforce the section 9 prohibition until an animal has actually been killed or harmed"). Language accompanying the 1981 FWS regulation redefining *harm* arguably lends credence to the notion that historic death or injury is required for harm. *See* 46 Fed. Reg. 54,749, at 54,749–50 (1981).

82. Forest Conservation Council v. Rosboro Lumber Co., 50 F.3d 781, 784–87 (9th Cir. 1995). *See also* Defenders of Wildlife v. Bernal, 204 F.3d 920 (9th Cir. 2005); Envtl. Prot. Info. Ctr. v. Simpson Timber Co., 255 F.3d 1073 (9th Cir. 2001);

may be shown when the activity "actually harmed the species *or* if continued *will* actually, as opposed to potentially, cause harm to the species."[83] The court also limited application of section 9 to future harm by requiring the threat of harm to be greater than "substantial."[84] In a recent high profile district court opinion in Maryland, the court held that the Ninth Circuit standard applied to a wind project that the court determined was reasonably certain to produce take of the protected Indiana bat.[85]

Little doubt exists that injury to a particular animal can result in a section 9 violation. It remains unclear, however, to what extent injury to a species or population as a whole can be said to be a prohibited act. The *Sweet Home* majority apparently would have limited the application of the "harm" prohibition to injury to "particular animals."[86] Likewise, Justice O'Connor stated in her concurring opinion that "the [harm] regulation is limited by its terms to actions that actually kill or injure individual animals."[87] But the Court's discussion of this issue is inconclusive, and most of the cases appear to avoid the issue because they involve plaintiffs' efforts to address reasonably certain harms to individual members of species.

This raises the apparent tension between the *Sweet Home* majority opinion and *Palila II*—the very case it relied upon (and implicitly upheld) as one-half of the circuit split justifying certiorari. The *Palila II* court held that death or injury to individual members of a species is not required to show harm.[88] *Sierra Club v. Lyng* illustrates that, like the Ninth Circuit, the Fifth Circuit (at least prior to *Sweet Home*) would not have required proof "of the death of specific or individual members of the species."[89] Given that the Supreme Court's discussion of this issue may be dictum,

---

Marbled Murrelet, 83 F.3d at 1064–65 (holding that language in *Sweet Home,* which apparently precludes application of section 9 to future harm, is "dictum"); Greenpeace v. NMFS, 106 F. Supp. 2d 1066 (W.D. Wash. 2000). *Cf.* Protect Our Waters v. Flowers, 377 F. Supp. 2d 844, 879–81 (E.D. Cal. 2004) (re take of kit fox and red-legged frogs).

83. *Am. Bald Eagle,* 9 F.3d at 166 (emphasis added). *See also* Strahan v. Coxe, 127 F.3d at 164 (discussing activity in terms of whether it "is likely to result" in a violation of section 9).

84. *Am. Bald Eagle,* 9 F.3d at 166 n.5.

85. Animal Welfare Inst. v. Beech Ridge Energy, LLC, 675 F. Supp. 2d 540 (D. Md. 2009).

86. *Sweet Home,* 515 U.S. at 700 n.13.

87. *Id.* at 709 (O'Connor, J., concurring).

88. Palila v. Haw. Dep't of Land & Nat. Res. (*Palila II*), 649 F. Supp. 1070, 1075 (D. Haw. 1986) (noting that an act that "prevents the recovery of the species" is prohibited).

89. Sierra Club v. Lyng, 694 F. Supp. 1260, 1270 (E.D. Tex. 1988).

and that the Court did not single out *Palila II* or *Lyng*[90] for reversal on the issue, and that the Court in fact implicitly affirmed *Palila II* with respect to its application of the "harm" regulation, the issue legitimately remains unresolved.

4.7   Section 11 Penalties: Overview

Section 11 of the ESA[91] establishes the penalties that may be levied against one who violates section 9. These penalties collectively present a comprehensive and severe suite of preventative and punitive measures, including civil penalties, criminal fines, injunctions,[92] forfeiture, attorneys' fees, and license/permit revocation.

4.7.1   Monetary Penalties, Imprisonment, Forfeiture

Any person who "knowingly"[93] violates any section 9 prohibition or implementing regulation (with the exception of limited record-keeping requirements), with respect to any *endangered* animal or plant, is subject to a civil penalty[94] of up to $25,000 (as otherwise adjusted)[95] and a criminal penalty of up to $100,000 (as otherwise adjusted) and up to one year of imprisonment.[96] Any person who knowingly violates any regulation with respect to *threatened* animals or plants is subject to as much as a $12,000 (as otherwise adjusted)[97] civil penalty and a criminal penalty of up to $25,000

90. *See* Liebesman & Davison, *supra* note 61, at 168–69 (suggesting that *Sweet Home* modifies *Lyng*'s determination that death or injury to individual animals is not required to find a prohibited harm).
91. 16 U.S.C. § 1540.
92. *Id.* § 1540(e)(6) (providing that the U.S. attorney general may seek to enjoin any person who is alleged to be in violation of any provision of the ESA or its implementing regulations). See chapter 11 for a discussion of section 11's "citizen suit" provision.
93. *See infra* notes 101–109 and accompanying text.
94. Civil penalties may be assessed only after proper notice and opportunity for hearing. 16 U.S.C. § 1540(a)(1). See 5 U.S.C. § 554 and 50 C.F.R. pt. 11 for hearing procedures.
95. 16 U.S.C. §§ 1540(a)(1).
96. *Id.* § 1540(b)(1). Because a criminal violation of the ESA relating to endangered species is a class A misdemeanor as defined by 18 U.S.C. § 3559(a)(6), ESA section 11's fine is supplanted by 18 U.S.C. § 3571(b)(5).
97. 16 U.S.C. § 1540(a)(1). Interestingly, persons "engaged in business" as importers of fish, wildlife, or plants may be subject to the same civil penalty levied by this subsection, for knowing *or unknowing* violations.

(as otherwise adjusted) and up to six months of imprisonment.[98] Any person who "otherwise violates any provision" of the ESA is subject to a civil penalty of up to $500 (as otherwise adjusted).[99] Finally, any equipment or vehicles used to aid any violation of the Act may be seized and are subject to permanent forfeiture.[100]

4.7.2   Scienter

Criminal or civil violations of the ESA may be proven only upon a showing that the defendant "knowingly" violated the Act.[101] In 1978, Congress changed the ESA's intent requirement to "reduce" the standard for violations of the ESA "from 'willfully' to 'knowingly,'" and to clarify that "criminal violations of the Act [are] a general rather than a specific intent crime."[102] In spite of this seemingly clear statement of the degree of intent required for an ESA civil or criminal violation,[103] enough ambiguity remains that defendants continue to plead that their state of mind precludes conviction on ESA criminal counts.[104]

In 1990, the U.S. Circuit Court of Appeals for the Fifth Circuit upheld the conviction of defendant Nguyen on charges that he violated the ESA by possessing a threatened loggerhead sea turtle.[105] Although some facts in evidence indicated that the defendant knew it was illegal to keep the turtle, the court held these facts irrelevant,[106] concluding that "it is sufficient that Nguyen

---

98.   *Id.* § 1540(b)(1).

99.   *Id.*

100.   16 U.S.C. § 1540(e)(4)(B). Likewise, all fish, wildlife, and plants "taken, possessed, sold, purchased, offered for sale or purchase, transported, delivered, received, carried, shipped, exported or imported" in violation of the Act are subject to forfeiture.

101.   16 U.S.C. § 1540(a)(1).

102.   H.R. Rep. No. 95-1625, at 26 (1978), *reprinted in* 1978 U.S.C.C.A.N. 9453, 9476.

103.   Neither civil nor criminal penalties require a showing of specific intent. *See* H.R. Conf. Rep. No. 95-1804, at 26, *reprinted in* 1978 U.S.C.C.A.N. 9484, 9493 (noting that "the Conferees do not intend to make knowledge of the law an element of *either civil penalty or criminal violations* of the [Endangered Species] Act") (emphasis added).

104.   *See, e.g.,* Babbitt v. Sweet Home Chapter of Cmtys. for a Great Or., 515 U.S. 687, 696 n.9 (1995) (speculating that the Court might impute a scienter requirement to the section 11(a)(1) civil penalty applicable when one "otherwise violates" the Act, but stating that the instant case was not a challenge to enforcement of that provision).

105.   United States v. Nguyen, 916 F.2d 1016 (5th Cir. 1990).

106.   *Id.* at 1018.

knew that he was in possession of a turtle," and that "the govern-ment was not required to prove that Nguyen knew that this turtle is a threatened species or that it is illegal to transport or import it."[107] In another Fifth Circuit opinion rendered only one year after *Nguyen,* the court opined that requiring a showing of spe-cific intent would render the ESA "ineffective because it would be nearly impossible to show that an accused intended to violate the Act."[108]

Likewise, in 1998 the Court of Appeals for the Ninth Circuit was unmoved by defendant Chad McKittrick's argument that he thought he was shooting a wild dog, when in fact the animal turned out to be an endangered gray wolf.[109] The important fact, in the court's view, was that McKittrick knew he "was shooting an animal."[110] As in situations involving less direct means of "take" than shooting, the lack of a specific intent to take a member of a listed species is generally no defense.

4.8   Bodily Harm Defense

Among the several exceptions to liability found in the ESA, section 11 provides explicitly that no civil or criminal liability will attach for any ESA offense when the otherwise illegal act was committed "based on a good faith belief that [the actor] was acting to protect himself or herself, a member of his or her family, or any other individual, from bodily harm from any endangered or threatened species."[111] This defense does not extend to actions taken to pro-tect property of any kind, including livestock and pets.[112]

---

107. *Id.* (emphasis added).
108. United States v. Ivey, 949 F.2d 759, 766 (5th Cir. 1991).
109. United States v. McKittrick, 142 F.3d 1170, 1177 (9th Cir. 1998).
110. *Id.* The same rationale was applied in two other cases involving shooting of listed wildlife. *See* United States v. Billie, 667 F. Supp. 1485, 1492–93 (S.D. Fla. 1987) (rejecting argument that government must prove that defendant knew the animal he shot was an endangered Florida panther); United States v. St. Onge, 676 F. Supp. 1044, 1045 (D. Mont. 1988) (holding that government only had to prove that the defendant knew he was shooting an animal, which consequently turned out to be a threatened grizzly bear; defendant's claim that he thought he was shooting an elk was irrelevant).
111. 16 U.S.C. § 1540(a)(3), (b)(3).
112. *See* Christy v. Hodel, 857 F.2d 1324 (9th Cir. 1988), *cert. denied,* 490 U.S. 1114 (1989) (upholding fine imposed against rancher who shot a listed griz-zly bear that was killing the rancher's sheep).

5 Consultation: Section 7(a)(2)

5.1 Overview

Federal action agencies must comply with section 7 by, when appropriate, consulting with the National Marine Fisheries Service (NMFS) or Fish and Wildlife Service (FWS) and by avoiding activities that are likely to jeopardize listed species or adversely modify those species' critical habitat. Courts and legal commentators alike often quote the Supreme Court's admonition in *Tennessee Valley Authority v. Hill* that "one would be hard pressed to find a statutory provision whose terms were any plainer" than section 7 of the Endangered Species Act (ESA).[1] The volume of legal commentary, regulation, and litigation arising from section 7[2] attests to its fairly unambiguous and far-reaching language.

Section 7(a)(2) of the ESA applies exclusively to federal agencies (and indirectly to private applicants for federal permits, approvals, or funding), and it imposes both a procedural and substantive obligation on federal agencies when they authorize, fund, or carry out any action.[3] It requires that each federal agency

> shall, *in consultation with* and with the assistance of [NMFS or FWS], insure that any action authorized, funded, or carried out by such agency . . . is *not likely to jeopardize* the continued existence of any endangered species or threatened species or result in the *destruction or adverse modification* of [critical habitat].[4]

---

1. Tenn. Valley Auth. v. Hill, 437 U.S. 153, 173 (1978).
2. *See* James C. Kilbourne, *The Endangered Species Act under the Microscope: A Closeup Look from a Litigator's Perspective,* 21 Envtl. L. 499, 525 (1991) (noting that ESA section 7(a)(2) is "undoubtedly the most well known, and certainly the most frequently litigated, obligation pertaining to federal agencies").
3. 16 U.S.C. § 1536(a)(2).
4. *Id.* (emphasis added); 50 C.F.R. § 402.01. *See* 16 U.S.C. § 1532(7) (defining "federal agency" as "any department, agency, or instrumentality of the United States").

The procedural and substantive mandates are designed to ensure that agencies (1) engage in appropriate consultation with FWS or NMFS when a proposed action may affect listed species or designated critical habitat, and (2) avoid jeopardizing listed species or destroying or adversely modifying designated critical habitat.

The section 7 consultation process is guided generally by what are called the 402 Joint Section 7 Consultation Regulations, which are at 50 C.F.R. 402, and the Services' *Section 7 Consultation Handbook*.[5] The 402 regulations further contemplate that the federal agencies can develop "counterpart" regulations to supplement the 402 regulations,[6] and agencies also can enter into memorandum of agreements or other similar documents to assist in the consultation process.[7] Overall, the consultation process is divided into an informal consultation and a formal consultation process, with the former occasionally obviating the need for the latter. The charts at the end of this chapter from the *Consultation Handbook* illustrate the process for each of these consultations.

5.2   Agency Action

Because section 7(a)(2) of the ESA applies only to federal agency actions, the first inquiry is whether any "federal agency" is engaging in any "action." Although *action* is not defined in the ESA, the Services have defined the term in their Joint Section 7 Consultation Regulations, as follows:

---

5.   U.S. Fish & Wildlife Serv. & Nat'l Marine Fisheries Serv., Endangered Species Consultation Handbook (Mar. 1998) [hereinafter Consultation Handbook]. *See* 64 Fed. Reg. 31,285 (1999) (announcing availability of handbook).

6.   The history of counterpart regulations has not necessarily been promising. Counterpart regulations, for instance, were developed for the national fire plan, 68 Fed. Reg. 68,254 (Dec. 8, 2003) (50 C.F.R. § 402.30), but in December 2011, BLM indicated that the alternative consultation process had not proved effective. Assistant Director, Renewable Resources, Bureau of Land Management, Instruction Memorandum No. 2012-049 (Dec. 11, 2011). *See* Defenders of Wildlife v. Salazar, 2012 WL 366901 (D.D.C. 2012) (reviewing national fire plan consultation regulations). *See also* Joint Counterpart Regulations re Actions Under the Federal Insecticide, Fungicide, and Rodenticide Act, 69 Fed. Reg. 47,732 (Aug. 5, 2004). *But cf.* Wash. Toxics Coal. v. U.S. Fish & Wildlife Serv., 457 F. Supp. 2d 1158 (W.D. Wash. 2006) (reviewing counterpart regulations).

7.   *E.g.*, Memorandum of Agreement Between the Environmental Protection Agency, Fish and Wildlife Service, and National Marine Fisheries Service Regarding Enhanced Coordination Under the Clean Water Act and Endangered Species Act, 66 Fed. Reg. 11,201 (2001).

Action means all activities or programs of any kind authorized, funded, or carried out, in whole or in part, by federal agencies in the United States or upon the high seas. Examples include, but are not limited to:

> (a) actions intended to conserve listed species or their habitat;
> (b) the promulgation of regulations;
> (c) the granting of licenses, contracts, leases, or grants-in-aid; or
> (d) actions directly or indirectly causing modifications to the land, water, or air.[8]

As the succeeding discussion notes, clearly identifying a "federal agency . . . action" is critical: It informs the entire consultation process. And courts generally construe the term *action* very broadly.[9]

Examples of federal agency activities that courts have determined satisfy the ESA definition of *agency action* include federal program activities as well as federal permitting and licensing activities. Federal program activities triggering section 7 are quite varied, and they include agency development of management plans for public lands,[10] timber sales,[11] operation of federal dams,[12] and providing funding for programs that are not federally operated.[13] A similarly broad approach toward *agency action* applies to private activities requiring some form of federal agency approval, whether in issuing a license or permit, granting a right-of-way, or entering into a contract. Section 7, therefore, has applied to the U.S. Army Corps of Engineers' issuance of Clean Water Act section 404 dredge and fill material (wetlands) permits,[14] licenses and permits issued by the Federal Energy Regulatory Commission,[15] and the Bureau of Reclamation's renewal

---

8.   50 C.F.R. § 402.02.

9.   *See, e.g.,* Tenn. Valley Auth. v. Hill, 437 U.S. 153 (1978) (rejecting notion that section 7 applies only to projects in planning stage); Conner v. Burford, 848 F.2d 1441, 1453 (9th Cir. 1982), *cert. denied,* 489 U.S. 1012 (1989).

10.   *E.g.,* Ctr. for Biological Diversity v. BLM, 422 F. Supp. 2d 1115 (N.D. Cal. 2006).

11.   Lane Cnty. Audubon Soc'y v. Jamison, 958 F.2d 290, 294–95 (9th Cir. 1992) (BLM timber sales enjoined pending consultation on interim strategy).

12.   Bennett v. Spear, 520 U.S. 154 (1997).

13.   *E.g.,* Fla. Key Deer v. Paulison, 522 F.3d 1133 (11th Cir. 2008) (FEMA's implementation of the National Flood Insurance Program); Nat'l Wildlife Fed'n v. FEMA, 345 F. Supp. 2d 1151 (W.D. Wash. 2004) (same); Fla. Key Deer v. Stickney, 864 F. Supp. 1222 (S.D. Fla. 1994) (same).

14.   Nat'l Wildlife Fed'n v. Norton, 332 F. Supp. 2d 170 (D.D.C. 2004).

15.   *See* Cal. Sportfishing Prot. Alliance v. FERC, 472 F.3d 593, 599 (9th Cir. 2006) (issuance of hydroelectric license triggers section 7(a)(2)).

of existing water service contracts[16] and annual delivery of water under existing water service contracts.[17] But, conversely, merely giving advice to a private entity does not necessarily rise to the level of an agency action,[18] nor would generic funding of state programs "federalize" state agency actions, requiring the state agency to engage in a section 7(a)(2) consultation.[19]

The identification of an agency action can become controversial or difficult when one of three interrelated circumstances exists: when an agency fails to act, when an agency previously acted but the action is ongoing, or when the agency lacks sufficient discretion when undertaking an action. When, for instance, an agency fails to act in light of alleged ongoing threats to a species, it is essential to distinguish the agency's failure to act from the agency's ongoing actions. The Ninth Circuit has indicated that the failure to act does not itself trigger section 7(a)(2).[20] But when the agency retains sufficient discretion to alter its ongoing actions, that same court has held that section 7(a)(2) applies.[21] In *Hill*, for

---

16.   Nat. Res. Def. Council v. Houston, 146 F.3d 1118, 1125 (9th Cir. 1998).

17.   O'Neil v. United States, 50 F.3d 677, 680–81 (9th Cir. 1995) (consultation requirement triggered because Bureau of Reclamation must act annually to deliver water pursuant to existing contracts). *But cf.* Natural Resources Defense Council v. Salazar, 686 F.3d 1092 (9th Cir. 2012) (settlement contracts not subject to section 7(a)(2)).

18.   Marbled Murrelet v. Babbitt, 83 F.3d 1068, 1073–75 (9th Cir. 1996) (FWS advice to lumber company, as to how to avoid take of listed species during logging operation, did not represent discretionary involvement or control for purposes of ESA section 7). When the agency's action has little or no effect on the activity, and does not operate as any form of an approval for the activity, section 7(a)(2) might not apply. *E.g.*, Ark Initiative v. U.S. Forest Serv., 2010 WL 3323661 (D. Colo. 2010) (agency acceptance of a vision document), *aff'd on other grounds,* 660 F.3d 1256 (10th Cir. 2011); Tex. Indep. Producers & Royalty Owners Ass'n v. EPA, 410 F.3d 964, 979 (7th Cir. 2005) (section 7 not triggered by ministerial acceptance of a notice); Ctr. for Biological Diversity v. Chertoff, 2009 WL 839042 (N.D. Cal. 2009) (unpublished) (Coast Guard's issuance of advisory notices did not trigger section 7(a)(2)). *Cf.* Turtle Island Restoration Network v. NMFS, 340 F.3d 969 (9th Cir. 2003) (agency action existed when NMFS exercised discretion and conditioning authority).

19.   *See* Or. Nat. Res. Council v. Hallock, 2006 WL 3463432 (D. Or. 2006) (unpublished). Federal funding often creates a difficult question under section 7. *See* Ctr. for Biological Diversity v. HUD, 541 F. Supp. 2d 1091 (D. Ariz. 2008) (consultation not required), *aff'd unpublished opinion,* 359 F. App'x 781 (9th Cir. 2009).

20.   *See* W. Watershed Project v. Matejko, 468 F.3d 1099, 1108 (9th Cir. 2006).

21.   *See* Karuk Tribe of Cal. v. U.S. Forest Serv., 681 F.3d 1006 (9th Cir. 2012) (en banc) (ESA applied to notice of intent to conduct mining activities on national forest lands); Turtle Island Restoration Network v. NMFS, 340 F.3d 969, 976–77 (9th Cir. 2003) (section 7 applied to ongoing actions); Klamath Water Users Protective Ass'n v. Patterson, 191 F.3d 1115 (9th Cir. 1999) (Bureau of Reclamation ownership and retention of management discretion at a dam were held to trigger consultation on operation of the dam); Pac. Rivers Council v. Thomas, 30 F.3d 1050, 1053–56 (9th Cir. 1994) (Forest Service is required to consult on its existing

instance, the Court emphasized that section 7 still applied even though the project was almost completed, because the agency still had left to carry out an activity. But when an agency lacks discretion over an action, including an ongoing agency action, section 7(a)(2) does not apply. The 402 regulations expressly note that section 7(a)(2) applies only to discretionary agency actions.[22] And in *National Ass'n of Homebuilders v. Defenders of Wildlife,*[23] the Supreme Court upheld this interpretation of the Act, concluding that the Environmental Protection Agency's delegation of Clean Water Act permitting authority under section 402 of that act did not trigger section 7(a)(2) because the agency lacked sufficient discretion under the Clean Water Act to apply ESA criteria to its decision. The issue for ongoing agency actions, therefore, generally becomes whether the agency has retained sufficient discretion to alter or control the activity presenting a threat to listed species or their designated critical habitat.[24]

5.3 Effects of the Action

Once an agency determines that a particular activity is an "action," the agency must then determine the effects of the action on listed species or critical habitat. The "effects of an action" include (1) *direct and indirect effects* of an action, and (2) the effects of other

---

land and resource management plans whenever a species is listed that may be affected by ongoing and future forest management projects).

22. 50 C.F.R. § 402.03 ("Section 7 and the requirements of this Part apply to all actions in which there is discretionary federal involvement and control.").

23. 551 U.S. 644 (2007).

24. *See, e.g.,* Grand Canyon Trust v. U.S. Bureau of Reclamation, 2012 WL 326499 (9th Cir. Aug. 13, 2012) (annual operating plans not trigger section 7); Natural Resources Defense Council v. Salazar, 686 F.3d 1092 (9th Cir. 2012) (renewal of settlement contracts not trigger section 7); Cal. Sportfishing Prot. Alliance v. FERC, 472 F.3d 593 (9th Cir. 2006) (ongoing hydroelectric operation is not an agency action when agency lacks authority to control); W. Watershed Project v. Matejko, 468 F.3d 1099, 1108, 1110 (9th Cir. 2006) (agency did not retain discretion); Wash. Toxics Coal. v. EPA, 413 F.3d 1024 (9th Cir. 2005) (pesticide program requires ESA compliance); Ground Zero Ctr. for Non-Violent Action v. Dep't of Navy, 383 F.3d 1082 (9th Cir. 2004) (consultation not required); Envtl. Prot. Info. Ctr. v. Simpson Timber Co., 255 F.3d 1073, 1083 (9th Cir. 2001) (no retained discretion); Platte River Whooping Crane Trust v. FERC, 962 F.2d 27, 32–33 (D.C. Cir. 1992) (no "action" existed when FERC was required to issue an annual operation license "under the terms and conditions of the existing license"); Sierra Club v. Babbitt, 65 F.3d 1502 (9th Cir. 1995) (no action exists when reciprocal right-of-way agreement did not give Bureau of Land Management authority to affect road construction by private parties).

activities that are *interrelated or interdependent* with that action, each of which will be added to the *environmental baseline*.[25]

A determination of the effects of a proposed action will dictate whether,[26] and to what extent, consultation is required for a particular action, and will ultimately determine whether the proposed action may proceed. In many respects, then, section 7 compliance begins and ends with a critical focus on the effects of a proposed action.

5.3.1   The Environmental Baseline

The logical first question for an analysis of a project's likely effects is, "Effects on what?" Determining the likely effects of an action on a species or its critical habitat requires an evaluation of the "status of the species or critical habitat at issue," including the status of the "present environment in which the species or critical habitat exist."[27] This snapshot in time,[28] referred to as the "environmental baseline," directs agencies to identify and understand existing conditions before considering the effects of a proposed action on those conditions.

The *environmental baseline* for section 7 consultation purposes is defined as follows:

> The environmental baseline includes the past and present impacts of all federal, state, or private actions and other human activities in the action area, the anticipated impacts of all proposed federal projects in the action area that have already undergone formal or early section 7 consultation, and the impact of state or private actions which are contemporaneous with the consultation in process.[29]

---

25. 50 C.F.R. § 402.02.

26. Consultation is not required for federal actions that are "environmentally neutral" and thus have no effect on a listed species. Marin Audubon Soc'y v. Seidman, Civ. No. 91-2029 (N.D. Cal. Nov. 21, 1991), *aff'd,* No. 92-15003, 1993 U.S. App. LEXIS 18198 (9th Cir. July 13, 1993) (FDIC sale of note, secured by property that was habitat for listed species, was not an action affecting the species).

27. Proposed Joint Consultation Regulations, Supplementary Information, 48 Fed. Reg. 29,990, 29,994 (1983).

28. THE CONSULTATION HANDBOOK, *supra* note 5, at 4-22, describes the environmental baseline as "a snapshot of a species' health at a specific point in time."

29. 50 C.F.R. § 402.02 (definition of "environmental baseline" is included within definition of "effects of the action"). This purportedly structured approach toward identifying the likely effects of an action is not necessarily completely congruent with modern ecological principles. *See* Fred Bosselman, *What Lawmak-*

Of particular note is the inclusion in the baseline of the impacts of federal actions that already have undergone consultation. Agencies are well advised to meet their consultation obligations sooner rather than later, before the baseline becomes further degraded as other federal actions complete consultation. This approach arguably creates a veritable "race to the baseline," with the last-in-time agency action running a higher risk that the environmental baseline can handle no further degradation without jeopardizing a listed species or resulting in adverse modification of critical habitat. The Ninth Circuit, after all, suggests that "the proper baseline analysis is not the proportional share of responsibility the federal agency bears for the decline in the species, but what jeopardy might result from the agency's proposed actions in the present and future human and natural contexts."[30]

But often identifying an environmental baseline is difficult, particularly when the proposed action involves the continuation of prior activities or an extension or modification of those ongoing prior activities. This has become particularly evident in the struggle over defining the environmental baseline for the operation of the federal hydroelectric dams that constitute the Federal Columbia River Power System.[31] It also has surfaced elsewhere, when parties engage in debates over natural conditions or the period for those conditions that are said to preexist the prior activity.[32] In

---

ers Can Learn From Large-Scale Ecology, 17 J. LAND USE & ENVTL. L. 207 (2002); J.B. Ruhl & James Salzman, Gaming the Past: The Theory and Practice of Historic Baselines in the Administrative State, 64 VAND. L. REV. 1 (2011).

30. Nat'l Wildlife Fed'n v. NMFS, 524 F.3d 917, 930 (9th Cir. 2008). Nor may an agency exclude from its baseline past effects from nondiscretionary actions that continue to the present and possibly the future. See Nat'l Wildlife Fed'n v. NMFS, 524 F.3d at 926, 928; see also Ctr. for Biological Diversity v. BLM, 746 F. Supp. 2d 1055, 1106 (N.D. Cal. 2009), vacated in part on other grounds, 2011 WL 33764 (N.D. Cal. Jan. 29, 2011); Pac. Coast Fed'n of Fishermen's Ass'n v. Gutierrez, 606 F. Supp. 2d 1122, 1176 (E.D. Cal. 2008) (emphasis in original) (citations and internal quotation marks omitted):

> The approach enunciated by the court in NWF v. NMFS does not require NMFS to include the entire environmental baseline in the agency action subject to review. It simply requires that NMFS appropriately consider the effects of its actions within the context of other existing human activities that impact the listed species. [T]he proper baseline analysis is not the proportional share of responsibility the federal agency bears for the decline in the species, but what jeopardy might result from the agency's proposed actions in the present and future human and natural contexts.

31. See Michael C. Blumm et al., Practiced in the Art of Deception: The Failure of Columbia Basin Salmon Recovery Under the Endangered Species Act, 36 ENVTL. L. 709, 736 (2006).

32. E.g., In re Operation of the Mo. River Sys. Litig., 421 F.3d 618, 632–33 (8th Cir. 2005), cert. denied, 547 U.S. 1097 (2006); Klamath Water Users Protective

addition, rising greenhouse gas emissions and the resulting effect on climate, makes the process even more difficult because of the influence on any baseline analysis.

5.3.2   Direct and Indirect Effects

For ESA section 7 consultation purposes, the "effects" of a proposed action include both the "direct" and "indirect" effects.[33] The term *direct effects* is somewhat self-explanatory.[34] *Indirect effects* is defined to include any effects caused or induced by the action that are "reasonably certain to occur";[35] put another way, indirect effects are "caused by or result from the proposed agency action, are later in time, and are reasonably certain to occur."[36] In an important example of an indirect effect, the Fifth Circuit held that the Department of Transportation had failed to consider the effects on sandhill cranes of future private development that would result from highway construction.[37] The Supplementary Information accompanying the 402 regulations explains that the definition of *effects of the action*,[38] with its requirement to consider private actions reasonably certain to occur, is intended to be consistent with *National Wildlife Federation v. Coleman*.[39]

In another case, the Tenth Circuit held that the Corps, in considering whether to grant the Clean Water Act permit necessary for construction of a dam, must consider the future effects of the increased consumptive use of water that will result from the dam and affect whooping cranes 150 miles away.[40] The court explained that ignoring these indirect effects would allow

---

Ass'n v. Patterson, 191 F.3d 1115 (9th Cir. 1999). *See* A. Dan Tarlock, *Ecosystem Services in the Klamath Basin: Battlefield Casualties or the Future,* 22 J. LAND USE & ENVTL. L. 207, 240 (2007). *See also* San Luis & Delta-Mendota Water Auth. v. Salazar, 760 F. Supp. 2d 855 (E.D. Cal. 2010).

33.   50 C.F.R. § 402.02.

34.   "Direct effects" is not defined in the ESA or the Joint Consultation Regulations.

35.   50 C.F.R. § 402.02.

36.   CONSULTATION HANDBOOK, *supra* note 5, at 4-27.

37.   Nat'l Wildlife Fed'n v. Coleman, 529 F.2d 359, 373 (5th Cir. 1976) (holding that residential and commercial development "that can be expected to result from the construction of the highway" must be considered as an indirect effect of highway construction).

38.   50 C.F.R. § 402.02.

39.   51 Fed. Reg. 19,926, 19,932 (1986).

40.   Riverside Irrigation Dist. v. Andrews, 758 F.2d 508, 512 (10th Cir. 1985), *cited with approval in* CONSULTATION HANDBOOK, *supra* note 5, at 4-28.

the agency to "wear blinders that Congress has not chosen to impose."[41]

The *Consultation Handbook* discusses indirect effects in some detail,[42] and includes the following example of a federal action with indirect effects:

> A very complex example of indirect effects arose in determining effects of renewing water service contracts from a large reclamation project (Friant Unit of the Central Valley Project) in the San Joaquin Basin of California. Upon checking with other Federal and State agencies, the FWS determined that the distribution of water for agricultural use on the higher east side of the Valley provided a hydrologic head maintaining the groundwater table on the west side of the Valley at a level making it economical to pump. As a result, occupied habitats for several species on the west side of the Valley were being destroyed because the pumped water could be used to convert this land to agriculture. . . .[43]

Future groundwater development, for instance, was considered an indirect effect of water service contract renewal. Although purely speculative actions do not meet the definition of a "reasonably certain to occur" action, the phrase does not require a guarantee that the action will occur.[44]

5.3.3   Cumulative Effects

When a particular agency action leads to formal consultation,[45] FWS or NMFS must evaluate both the effects of the action and the cumulative effects on the listed species or critical habitat.[46] Unlike direct, indirect, interdependent, or interrelated effects, which are all part of an agency's initial determination of the "effects of the action," cumulative effects are not initially considered by an action agency to determine the extent of its consultation obligations.[47] Rather, once an agency has determined that the effects of a proposed action warrant formal consultation, cumulative

---

41. *Id.*
42. CONSULTATION HANDBOOK, *supra* note 5, at 4-27 through 4-31.
43. *Id.* at 4–28.
44. *Id.* at 4–30.
45. See section 5.4.4 for a discussion of formal consultation.
46. 50 C.F.R. § 402.14(g)(3).
47. *See, e.g.,* Sierra Club v. Marsh, 816 F.2d 1376, 1387 (9th Cir. 1987) (cumulative effects not relevant for determining whether agency must reinitiate consultation).

effects are added to the effects of the action to determine whether the proposed action will result in jeopardy to a listed species or adverse modification or destruction of critical habitat.

Cumulative effects are defined in the 402 regulations as "those effects of future state or private activities, not involving federal activities, that are reasonably certain to occur within the action area of the federal action subject to consultation."[48] Like indirect effects, cumulative effects exist only when they are "reasonably certain to occur."[49] To meet this standard, there must exist more than a "mere possibility that the action may proceed . . . bearing in mind the economic, administrative, or legal hurdles which remain to be cleared."[50]

If a biological assessment (BA) is prepared,[51] the 402 regulations recommend that it contain a "consideration" of cumulative effects.[52] Likewise, if an agency initiates formal consultation, the 402 regulations require the action agency to include, in its request to initiate formal consultation, an "analysis of any cumulative effects."[53]

5.3.4   Interrelated and Interdependent Activities

The effects of the action include "the effects of other activities that are interrelated or interdependent with that action."[54] *Interrelated and interdependent actions* are defined as follows:

> Interrelated actions are those that are part of a larger action and depend on the larger action for their justification. Interdependent actions are those that have no significant independent utility apart from the action that is under consideration.[55]

If a particular private activity would not occur "but for"[56] the occurrence of the proposed federal action, the effects of that

---

48. 50 C.F.R. § 402.02. *See also* CONSULTATION HANDBOOK, *supra* note 5, at 4-30 through 4-31 (discussing cumulative effects).

49. 50 C.F.R. § 402.02.

50. Preamble to Final Joint Consultation Rules, 51 Fed. Reg. 19,926, 19,933 (1986).

51. See section 5.4.3 for a discussion of the BA requirement.

52. 50 C.F.R. § 402.12(f)(4).

53. 50 C.F.R. § 402.14(c)(4).

54. 50 C.F.R. § 402.02 (defined in "effects of the action" definition).

55. *Id.*

56. Joint Consultation Regulations, Preamble to Final Rule, 51 Fed. Reg. 19,932 (1986).

private action are interdependent and interrelated to the federal action, and the effects of that private action are attributable to the federal action for consultation purposes. Conversely, activities that would occur anyway, with or without the occurrence of the federal action at issue, are not interdependent or interrelated to the proposed federal action.[57]

Determining what activities are interdependent and interrelated is often complicated. Agencies must make difficult judgments about whether a particular proposed private activity would or would not occur absent the federal action.

5.3.5 "Incremental Step" Consultation

Many federal agency actions or processes employ multilayered decision-making, often raising the question of when section 7 consultation is appropriate and what the scope of that consultation should cover. Should, for instance, the consultation process apply to the leasing of public lands to a private entity or, instead, only to when the private entity eventually develops and submits for approval an actual plan for the use of those lands? Potentially, however, an agency could segregate a possibly harmful proposed action into a series of small steps, each of which would, when examined separately, appear environmentally benign.

The ESA and its implementing regulations attempt to address these issues by foreclosing consultation on project segments, except in very narrowly prescribed circumstances. The 402 regulations allow "incremental step" consultations only when the action is authorized by a statute that allows the agency to take incremental steps toward completion of the action.[58] In such a case, the Services may issue a biological opinion (BO) on the

---

57. See Consultation Handbook, *supra* note 5, at 4-26 through 4-24 for helpful examples of interdependent and interrelated activities. *See also* Sierra Club v. Marsh, 816 F.2d 1376, 1387 (9th Cir. 1987) (holding that private developments that are "not part of the federal project, and are not related to or dependent on it" are not interdependent or interrelated activities). The Fifth Circuit afforded the *Consultation Handbook* deference, and held that the entire tract development was not interrelated. Medina Cnty. Envtl. Action Ass'n v. Surface Transp. Bd., 602 F.3d 687, 700 (5th Cir. 2010).

58. 50 C.F.R. § 402.14(k). *See* Preamble to Joint Consultation Regulations, 51 Fed. Reg. 19,926, 19,954 (1986) (noting the intended consistency of the regulations with N. Slope Borough v. Andrus, 642 F.2d 589 (D.C. Cir. 1980)).

incremental step being considered.[59] The action agency may then proceed with the incremental step if

- the BO does not conclude that the incremental step would violate section 7(a)(2);
- the action agency continues consulting with respect to the entire action;
- the action agency fulfills its obligation to obtain data upon which to base a final decision on the entire action;
- the incremental step does not violate section 7(d) of the ESA;[60] and
- there is a reasonable likelihood that the entire action will not violate section 7(a)(2) of the ESA.[61]

These fairly demanding criteria, combined with an agency's obligation to consider the indirect effects ("reasonably certain to occur")[62] of any action, effectively preclude an agency from segmenting the consultation process into phases based on its processes or decisions. One prominent instance where an incremental approach has received a judicial endorsement is in the leasing of oil and gas on the Outer Continental Shelf.[63]

5.4   The Consultation Process

If a federal agency determines that it is proposing to take an "action" that triggers section 7(a)(2), the 402 regulations and *Consultation Handbook* contemplate that the agency then determine whether that action "may affect" a listed species or its critical

---

59.   50 C.F.R. § 402.14(k). In doing so, the Service also will include "its views on the entire action." *Id.*

60.   See section 5.6 for a discussion of ESA section 7(d).

61.   50 C.F.R. §§ 402.14(k)(1)–(5).

62.   See section 5.3.2 for a discussion of indirect effects.

63.   Ctr. for Biological Diversity v. Dep't of the Interior, 563 F.3d 466, 482–83 (D.C. Cir. 2009) (ESA claim not ripe at leasing stage); *see also N. Slope Borough,* 642 F.2d at 608 (holding that segmented consultation was appropriate for offshore leasing activities, in light of "checks and balances" provided by Outer Continental Shelf Land Act (OCSLA)); Vill. of False Pass v. Watt, 565 F. Supp. 1123, 1156 (D. Alaska 1983), *aff'd sub nom.* Vill. of False Pass v. Clark, 733 F.2d 605 (9th Cir. 1984) (following rationale of *N. Slope,* allowed incremental-step consultation under OCSLA). *But see* Conner v. Burford, 848 F.2d 1441, 1453 (9th Cir. 1988) (holding that the Minerals Leasing Act, unlike the OCSLA, did not contemplate incremental-step activities).

habitat, and if so the agency must then "consult" with NMFS or FWS[64] (depending on the particular species affected[65]) to ensure that the action does not jeopardize the listed species or adversely modify its critical habitat.[66] In satisfying the section 7 consultation requirements, agencies must utilize the best scientific and commercial data available,[67] and agencies that fail to consult properly risk that a court might enjoin their activity.[68]

The consultation process unfolds depending upon how the agency and the Secretary answer a sequence of questions regarding the nature of the proposed agency action and its potential effects on listed species or critical habitat. The following discussion generally mirrors the chronological sequence of the ESA section 7 process.

5.4.1   Presence of Listed Species or Critical Habitat in the Action Area

To evaluate the effects of a proposed project on listed species or critical habitat, agencies initially must determine what species or critical habitat is present in the "action area." The *action area* for any proposed project is defined quite broadly to include all areas directly or indirectly affected by the action, not merely those "in the immediate area involved in the action."[69] For "major construction activities,"[70] the ESA and 402 regulations require the action agency to communicate with the Services in writing to identify listed species or designated critical habitat that may be present in

---

64. For purposes of this chapter, NMFS and FWS are alternatively referred to as "the Services," "the Secretary," "the Director," or "the consulting agencies." Other federal agencies are the "action agencies" for purposes of section 7 consultation.

65. *See* 50 C.F.R. §§ 223.102 and 224.101 for lists of endangered and threatened species under NMFS jurisdiction, and 50 C.F.R. §§ 17.11(wildlife) and 17.12 (plants) for lists of endangered and threatened species under FWS jurisdiction.

66. 16 U.S.C. § 1536(a)(2).

67. *Id.*

68. *See, e.g.,* Pac. Rivers Council v. Robertson, 854 F. Supp. 713, 724 (D. Or. 1993) (holding that procedural violations of the ESA, such as not initiating section 7 consultation when required, mandate that the underlying action be enjoined), *aff'd in part, rev'd in part sub nom.* Pac. Rivers Council v. Thomas, 30 F.3d 1050 (9th Cir. 1994).

69. 50 C.F.R § 402.02.

70. See section 5.4.3 for a discussion of major construction activities.

the action area.[71] And for "major construction activities" occurring in the presence of listed species or critical habitat, the action agency must prepare a BA.[72] For other actions, the regulations provide that an action agency may (and often does) solicit assistance from the Secretary when determining what species and critical habitat might be present in the action area.[73] Once a species or its habitat is identified, the agency and the Secretary must then determine if and to what degree that species or habitat will be affected.

5.4.2　"May Affect" Determination

Upon determining that a listed species or designated critical habitat may be present in the action area, the action agency should then determine whether the proposed action "may affect" a listed species.[74] The 402 regulations contemplate that, if a BA is required, this determination may be made in the BA itself. For other activities, the "may affect" determination need not be contained in a formal document, although a detailed written record is advisable.

The term *may affect* is not defined in the ESA or the 402 regulations, but the *Consultation Handbook* defines it as "the appropriate conclusion when a proposed action may pose *any* effects on listed species or designated critical habitat."[75] This definition, combined with the breadth of the previously discussed "effects of the action,"[76] sets the "may effect" threshold quite low.

Agencies may conclude the informal consultation process if they determine that the action will have "no effect" on listed

---

71.　50 C.F.R. § 402.12(c). The Service must respond to the action agency's request for a list of species affected within 30 days. 50 C.F.R. § 402.12(d).

72.　16 U.S.C. § 1536(c)(1); 50 C.F.R. § 402.13. "Major construction activities" are those construction projects, or any undertakings having "similar physical impacts," that are major federal actions significantly affecting the quality of the human environment as referred to in the National Environmental Policy Act (NEPA). 50 C.F.R. § 402.02.

73.　Agencies often seek the expertise of the Services in developing species and critical habitat lists for nonconstruction activities, and the Services will meet the same 30-day response time when possible. CONSULTATION HANDBOOK, *supra* note 5, at 3-2.

74.　50 C.F.R. § 402.14(a) (providing that agencies should review their actions at the "earliest possible time to determine whether any action may affect listed species or critical habitat").

75.　CONSULTATION HANDBOOK, *supra* note 5, at xvi.

76.　*See* section 5.3 (discussing effects of the action).

species or critical habitat.[77] Although not required, an agency may voluntarily request from the Services a written concurrence with the "no effect" determination; this concurrence can be "useful for the Administrative Record"[78] should the agency's determination be challenged.

5.4.3   Biological Assessment Preparation or Informal Consultation

If the action agency determines, in consultation with the appropriate Service and possibly state and tribal resource agencies, that listed species or their critical habitat may be present in the action area and affected, the next question is whether any such species or habitat is "likely to be adversely affected." Section 7(c) of the ESA generally contemplates that the action agency can answer this question through the preparation of a BA, and possibly in combination with the development of an environmental document under NEPA.[79] Whether required or not, in practice many agencies prepare BAs, particularly for proposed actions that arguably might impact species or their habitat. Failure to prepare a necessary BA is a "substantial" violation of the ESA.[80] The Act requires that, in particular, an agency must complete its BA prior to executing any contract for construction, and before any construction is begun.[81]

Determining whether any listed species or critical habitat might be adversely affected occurs during the process often referred to as informal consultation. Informal consultation generally means "all discussions, correspondence, etc. between the Service and the federal agency," designed to assist the action agency in determining whether formal consultation will be necessary.[82] During this process, the Service may suggest modifications to the

---

77. *See* Newton Cnty. Wildlife Ass'n v. Rogers, 141 F.3d 803, 810 (8th Cir. 1998) ("A finding of no effect obviates the need for consultation.").

78. Consultation Handbook, *supra* note 5, at 3-12.

79. 16 U.S.C. § 1736(c). 50 C.F.R. § 402.14(b) (formal consultation is not required for actions that are not likely to adversely affect listed species or critical habitat). Also, where appropriate, a state, or local agency, private organization, or individual may voluntarily prepare a biological assessment. *See* Preamble to Final Joint Consultation Rules, 51 Fed. Reg. 19,926, 19,945 (1986).

80. Thomas v. Peterson, 841 F.2d 332 (9th Cir. 1988) (Forest Service road construction enjoined because of failure to prepare BA).

81. 16 U.S.C. § 1536(c); 50 C.F.R. § 402.12(b)(2).

82. *Id.*

action that the federal agencies could implement to avoid the likelihood of adverse effects to listed species or critical habitat.[83]

The contents of the BA are "at the discretion" of the action agency; the 402 regulations advise that the following types of information be considered for inclusion:

- the results of an on-site inspection of the area affected by the action
- the views of recognized experts on the species at issue
- a review of the literature and other information
- an analysis of the effects of the action on the species and habitat, including consideration of cumulative effects
- an analysis of alternate actions considered by the federal agency for the proposed action[84]

At a minimum, the BA by definition should evaluate potential effects of the action on listed species and designated critical habitat.[85] Regardless of the information included in the BA, the agency must use the "best scientific and commercial data available."[86] The BA is supposed to be completed within 180 days of the agency's receipt of a list of species present in the action area, unless the Secretary and action agency agree to a longer time period.[87]

The goal of the BA, as with the informal consultation period itself, is to determine whether the proposed action is, or is not, likely to adversely affect listed species or critical habitat.[88] If the action agency concludes that its proposed action is not likely to

---

83.   50 C.F.R. § 402.14(b).

84.   50 C.F.R. § 402.02(f). *See* Strahan v. Linnon, 967 F. Supp. 581, 594 (D. Mass. 1997) (holding that "the contents of the BA are discretionary").

85.   50 C.F.R. § 402.02 (definition of "biological assessment").

86.   16 U.S.C. § 1536(a)(2). *See* Bennett v. Spear, 520 U.S. 154, 176–77 (1997) (discussing the purposes of the requirement to use the best available scientific and commercial data); Greenpeace Action v. Franklin, 14 F.3d 1324 (9th Cir. 1992) (discussing "uncertainty" with regard to scientific data); DANIEL J. ROHLF, THE ENDANGERED SPECIES ACT: A GUIDE TO ITS PROTECTIONS AND IMPLEMENTATION 125–33 (1989) (discussing earlier cases interpreting the "best scientific and commercial data available" requirement). The purpose of this requirement has been said to ensure that the agency does not ignore available scientific evidence. *See* Am. Wildlands v. Kempthorne, 530 F.3d 991, 998 (D.C. Cir. 2008). *Cf.* Kern Cnty. Farm Bureau v. Allen, 450 F.3d 1072, 1080 (9th Cir. 2006) (agency cannot ignore available evidence that appears better than evidence relied upon); Rock Creek Alliance v. U.S. Fish & Wildlife Serv., 390 F. Supp. 2d 993 (D. Mont. 2005) (agency cannot rely upon disputed report that expressly indicated not applicable to situation).

87.   50 C.F.R. § 402.12(i). If an applicant is involved, the 180-day period may not be extended without first notifying the applicant of the estimated length of the proposed extension and the reasons why the extension is necessary. *Id.*

88.   50 C.F.R. § 402.12(k).

cause either of these results, and the Service concurs in writing,[89] no further consultation is required. It is imperative, however, that to avoid engaging in formal consultation the Service issue a *written concurrence* before the action agency can proceed with its proposed action; otherwise, formal consultation is required.[90] The determination that a species may be affected but is not likely to be adversely affected is subject to judicial scrutiny.[91] And, conversely, if the action agency or the BA indicates that the action is likely to adversely affect a listed species or critical habitat, formal consultation must occur.

When the consultation process involves a private applicant seeking some form of federal authorization, that private applicant has the ability to suggest that the federal action agency designate the applicant as a "designated nonfederal representative."[92] Often this option is attractive for the private applicant, because it allows the applicant to engage with the Service early in the process.

5.4.4   Formal Consultation and the Biological Opinion

If the action agency determines (through its own analysis, informal consultation, or preparation of a BA) that its proposed action is likely to adversely affect[93] listed species or critical habitat, formal consultation is required.[94] The formal consultation process begins with a written request from the action agency to the

---

89. 50 C.F.R. § 402.12(j). The Service must respond to the action agency within 30 days of receipt of the BA, stating whether it concurs with the action agency's conclusions. *Id.*

90. *E.g.,* Pac. Rivers Council v. Thomas, 30 F.3d 1050 (9th Cir. 1994). In *Western Watersheds Project v. Kraayenbrink,* 630 F.3d 1187, 1208–12 (9th Cir. 2010), the court held that the Bureau of Land Management acted arbitrarily and capriciously in concluding that 18 amendments to grazing regulations did not adversely affect listed species, and therefore failed to consult.

91. *E.g.,* Sierra Club v. Van Antwerp, 661 F.3d 1147 (D.C. Cir. 2011) (remanded for more reasoned explanation for why not likely to adversely affect eastern Indigo Snake); Pres. Our Island v. U.S. Army Corps of Eng'rs, 2009 WL 2511953 (W.D. Wash. 2009) (unpublished).

92. *See* 50 C.F.R. § 402.2. A federal agency may, usually upon request of the private applicant, designate the applicant as its nonfederal representative by giving the Secretary notice in writing of the designation. *Id.* at 402.08. *See also* section 5.9 (role of the applicant).

93. *See* CONSULTATION HANDBOOK, *supra* note 5, at 3-13 (defining "is likely to adversely affect" as the appropriate conclusion when "any" adverse affect may occur that is not insignificant, discountable, or beneficial).

94. 50 C.F.R. §§ 402.14(a), (b).

Service, and ends with issuance by the Service of a BO.[95] The 402 regulations require that any written request to initiate formal consultation include

- a description of the action to be considered;
- a description of the specific area that may be affected by the action;
- a description of any listed species or any critical habitat that may be affected by the action;
- a description of the manner in which the action may affect any listed species or critical habitat and an analysis of any cumulative effects;
- relevant reports, including any environmental impact statement (EIS), environmental assessment (EA), or BA; and
- any other relevant available information on the action, the affected listed species, or critical habitat.[96]

Agencies should strongly consider these criteria during preparation of any BA, as formal consultation is often initiated by transmitting the BA to the Service.

5.4.5   Biological Opinion

The term *biological opinion* is a regulatory creation not specifically identified in the ESA. Rather, section 7(b) of the Act requires that, promptly after conclusion of consultation,[97] the Secretary provide to the action agency (and any applicant) a "written statement setting forth the Secretary's opinion, and a summary of the information on which the opinion is based, detailing how the agency action affects the species or its critical habitat."[98] Through regulation, these "written statements" have gained credibility as "biological opinions."[99]

The contents of a BO are prescribed by the 402 regulations. Every BO must include a summary of the information on which the opinion is based, a detailed discussion of the effects of the action on listed species or critical habitat, and the Service's

---

95.   50 C.F.R. § 402.02 (definition of "formal consultation").

96.   *Id.* § 402.14(c).

97.   Consultation must conclude within 90 days of its initiation, or within such other time mutually agreed to by the Service and the agency. 16 U.S.C. § 1536(b).

98.   16 U.S.C. § 1536(b)(3)(A).

99.   50 C.F.R. § 402.02 (defining "biological opinion").

opinion as to whether the action is likely to jeopardize the continued existence of a listed species or result in destruction or adverse modification of critical habitat.[100] Any BO finding jeopardy or adverse modification of critical habitat must also include "reasonable and prudent alternatives" (RPAs) to the proposed action, if any.[101] Consequently, there are three types of biological opinions: a "no jeopardy" opinion, a jeopardy opinion with RPAs, and a jeopardy opinion with no RPAs.

After receipt of a BO, it is the action agency's responsibility—not the Service's—to decide how to proceed.[102] Although technically BOs serve only an "advisory function,"[103] in practice they carry considerable weight and action agencies are hesitant to act contrary to a BO's conclusions. Action agencies generally recognize that a court is not likely to afford the agency's scientific expertise greater deference than the expertise of the Services, with whom Congress has entrusted the administration of the Act; as such, an action agency must "articulate its reasons for disagreement" with the BO, and the agency "runs a substantial risk if its (inexpert) reasons turn out to be wrong."[104] By the same token, however, even when a BO concludes that the proposed action will not jeopardize a listed species or adversely modify or destroy critical habitat, an action agency may not simply rubber-stamp the Service's analysis.[105] Nonetheless, an action agency need not undertake a separate, independent analysis in the absence of new information not already considered by the Service.[106]

5.4.5.1   Jeopardy

The substantive purposes of the section 7 consultation process are to ensure that agencies do not jeopardize listed species or adversely modify or destroy those species' critical habitat.[107] The

---

100. 50 C.F.R. § 402.14(h).

101. *Id. See* section 5.4.5.3 (discussing RPAs in more detail).

102. 50 C.F.R. § 402.15(a); Aluminum Co. of Am. v. Adm'r of EPA, 175 F.3d 1156, 1160–61 (9th Cir. 1999). *See* Tribal Vill. of Akutan v. Hodel, 869 F.2d 1185, 1193 (9th Cir. 1988) (action agency's deviations from BO do not constitute violation of the ESA if agency implements adequate alternative measures).

103. Preamble to Final Joint Consultation Regulations, 51 Fed. Reg. 19,926, 19,928 (1986).

104. Bennett v. Spear, 520 U.S. 154, 169 (1997).

105. *Aluminum Co. of Am.,* 175 F.3d at 1161 (citing Res. Ltd, Inc. v. Robertson, 35 F.3d 1300, 1304 (9th Cir. 1994)).

106. *Id.* (citing Stop H-3 Ass'n v. Dole, 740 F.2d 1441, 1460 (9th Cir. 1984)).

107. 16 U.S.C. § 1536(a)(2).

Supreme Court has deemed this an affirmative "command," and concluded in 1978 that the then-existing language of section 7 "admits of no exception."[108] Though Congress responded to *Tennessee Valley Authority v. Hill* by creating certain limited exceptions to section 7's substantive mandates,[109] the mandatory nature of section 7 remains intact. Agencies must avoid "jeopardy" and "adverse modification" and "destruction of" critical habitat.

The BO must contain a determination of whether the effects of the action, taken together with cumulative effects,[110] are likely to jeopardize the species as a whole or adversely modify critical habitat.[111] The 402 regulations contemplate that to *jeopardize the continued existence* of a listed species means "to engage in an action that reasonably would be expected, directly or indirectly, to reduce appreciably the likelihood of both the survival and recovery of a listed species in the wild by reducing the reproduction, numbers, or distribution of that species."[112] The Ninth Circuit, in *National Wildlife Federation v. NMFS*,[113] held that the jeopardy analysis requires considering both the likely effect on survival of the species as well as the likely effect on recovery.

5.4.5.2   Adverse Modification or Destruction

Section 7(a)(2) not only prohibits actions that are likely to jeopardize listed species, but also independently prohibits any *adverse modification* or *destruction* of *critical habitat*—regardless of the action's likely affect on the species itself. The phrase *destruction or adverse modification* of critical habitat is defined in the 402 regulations as

> a direct or indirect alteration that appreciably diminishes the value of critical habitat for both the survival and recovery of a listed species. Such alterations include, but are not limited to, alterations adversely modifying any of those physical or biological features that were the basis for determining the habitat to be critical.[114]

---

108. Tenn. Valley Auth. v. Hill, 437 U.S. 153, 173 (1978).
109. *See* section 5.4.5.4 (discussing incidental take associated with federal actions) and chapter 7 (discussing the section 7 exemption process).
110. 50 C.F.R. § 402.14(g)(4).
111. *See* CONSULTATION HANDBOOK, *supra* note 5, at 4-34; *see also* Butte Envtl. Council v. U.S. Army Corps of Eng'rs, 620 F.3d 936, 948 (9th Cir. 2010) (citing same).
112. 50 C.F.R. § 402.02.
113. 481 F.3d 1224 (9th Cir. 2007), *amended and superseded by* 524 F.3d 917 (9th Cir. 2008).
114. 50 C.F.R. § 402.02

The interpretation of the statutory standard for adverse modification has become problematic, triggering the question of whether appreciably reducing the recovery of the species is sufficient to establish adverse modification or destruction, or whether, as the 402 regulations suggest, there must be an impact on both survival and recovery. A standard that can look only at recovery would be a broader inquiry.[115] In *Gifford Pinchot Task Force v. U.S. Fish & Wildlife Service*,[116] the Ninth Circuit reviewed the regulation in light of the statutory mandate and held that the Services erred in concluding that the proposed action had to impact both the survival *and* the recovery of the species. Instead, adverse modification or destruction can occur when the proposed action appreciably reduces the likelihood of species recovery. And section 7(a)(2) does not per se bar the mere loss of some critical habitat, unless the amount of lost habitat satisfies the threshold.[117]

5.4.5.3   Reasonable and Prudent Alternatives

When a BO concludes that the prohibited jeopardy or adverse modification is likely, the opinion must also contain RPAs to the proposed action, if any exist.[118] By definition, a *reasonable and prudent alternative* is one that

- can be implemented in a manner consistent with the purposes of the action;
- can be implemented consistent with the scope of the action agency's legal authority and jurisdiction;
- is economically and technologically feasible; and
- would avoid jeopardy or adverse modification of critical habitat.[119]

115. *See* Ctr. for Biological Diversity v. BLM, 746 F. Supp. 2d 1055, 1100–1104 (N.D. Cal. 2009), *vacated in part by* 2011 WL 337364 (N.D. Cal. Jan. 29, 2011).
116.   378 F.3d 1059 (9th Cir. 2004), *amended by* 387 F.3d 968 (9th Cir. 2004). *See also* Miccosukee Tribe of Indians v. United States, 566 F.3d 1257 (11th Cir. 2009); N.M. Cattle Growers Ass'n v. U.S. Fish & Wildlife Serv., 248 F.3d 1277 (10th Cir. 2001); Sierra Club v. U.S. Fish & Wildlife Serv., 245 F.3d 434, 441–42 (5th Cir. 2001).
117. *See* Butte Envtl. Council v. U.S. Army Corps of Eng'rs, 620 F.3d 936 (9th Cir. 2010). *See also* 77 Fed. Reg. 51,503, 51,507 (Aug. 24, 2012) (discussing adverse modification or destruction standard). For an analysis of the adverse modification and destruction language, see Dave Owen, *Critical Habitat and the Challenge of Regulating Small Harms*, 64 FLA. L. REV. 141 (2012) (providing an empirical analysis).
118.   50 C.F.R. § 402.14(h)(3).
119.   *Id.* § 402.02.

When developing RPAs, the Services may propose alternatives that "permeate the full range of discretionary authority held by [the action] agency" and may specify an RPA that "involves the maximum exercise of federal agency authority" when necessary to avoid jeopardy.[120] Often, recovery plans for species can inform the development of RPAs.

The final determination of whether a proposed alternative is in fact reasonable and prudent lies with the action agency. The action agency is not required to select the first RPA developed, nor must the action agency select an RPA that might be the "best" alternative.[121] Rather, the agency may select an RPA that otherwise meets the section 7 mandate to avoid jeopardy to listed species, or destruction or adverse modification of critical habitat. Often the action agency and the Service engage in discussions about the reasonableness, appropriateness, or ability to implement a possible RPA. If a private applicant is involved, it is often prudent for that applicant to engage in the dialogue about whether a particular RPA is technologically or economically feasible, as well as whether the legal authority exists to implement the RPA.[122] However, once an RPA is selected, the agency must ensure implementation of the RPA provisions prior to engaging in activities that adversely affect the species or critical habitat.[123]

In addition to RPAs, the Service can include in its BO "conservation recommendations." *Conservation recommendations* are purely discretionary recommendations made by the Service to the action agency, and are intended to serve as nonbinding measures that will help minimize or avoid adverse effects on listed species or their habitat.[124] These conservation recommendations also can serve as part of an agency's conservation program under section 7(a)(1) of the Act.[125]

---

120.   Preamble to Joint Consultation Regulations, 51 Fed. Reg. 19,926, 19,937 (1986).

121.   Sw. Ctr. for Biological Diversity v. Bureau of Reclamation, 143 F.3d 515, 522–23 (9th Cir. 1998).

122.   *See* 50 C.F.R. § 402.02.

123.   Sierra Club v. Marsh, 816 F.2d 1376, 1389 (9th Cir. 1987) (Corps of Engineers failed to ensure implementation of mitigation plans prior to constructing highway and flood control devices).

124.   50 C.F.R. § 402.02.

125.   See chapter 3, section 3.2 for a discussion of section 7(a)(1).

5.4.5.4 Incidental Take Statements

Federal agencies often confront scenarios where their particular action may result in some "take" of individual members of a listed species, without causing prohibited jeopardy or adverse modification of critical habitat. Without some permit allowing such take, the agency or the private party acting pursuant to a federal permit would be violating section 9 of the Act.[126] Congress remedied this "dilemma"[127] in 1982, when it amended the ESA to allow for the "incidental" taking of listed species in connection with otherwise lawful federal actions.[128]

As long as an action may proceed (whether as originally proposed or in accordance with an RPA) without violating section 7(a)(2)'s substantive prohibitions, any BO issued with respect to that action must include an incidental take statement (ITS), which permits take of listed species incidental to the agency actions.[129] *Incidental take* refers to "takings that result from, but are not the purpose of, carrying out an otherwise lawful activity conducted by the federal agency or applicant."[130] Any taking that is in compliance with an ITS is exempt from the Act's prohibitions and penalties.[131] The Supreme Court summarized the import of the ITS as follows: "[T]he biological opinion's incidental take statement constitutes a permit authorizing the action agency to 'take' the endangered or threatened species as long as it respects the Service's 'terms and conditions.'"[132]

The contents of an ITS are prescribed by statute. Each ITS must

- specify the impact of the take on the species;
- specify those "reasonable and prudent measures" (RPMs) that the Secretary considers necessary or appropriate to minimize such impact; and

---

126. See chapter 4 for a discussion of section 9's take prohibition.

127. *See* H.R. Rep. No. 567, at 26 (1982), *reprinted in* 1982 U.S.C.C.A.N. 2807, 2826 (describing the purpose behind Congress's 1982 amendment of ESA section 7).

128. *Id.*

129. 16 U.S.C. § 1536(b)(4); 50 C.F.R. § 402.14(i). "The FWS must issue an Incidental Take Statement if the BiOp concludes no jeopardy to listed species or adverse modification of critical habitat will result from the proposed action, but the action is likely to result in incidental taking." Or. Nat. Res. Council v. Allen, 476 F.3d 1031, 1036 (9th Cir. 2007). *See also* Ctr. for Biological Diversity v. Salazar, 2012 WL 3570667 (9th Cir. Aug. 21, 2012) (ITS required even if no section 9 take liability).

130. 50 C.F.R. § 402.02 (defining "incidental take").

131. 16 U.S.C. § 1536(o). *See, e.g.,* Ramsey v. Kantor, 96 F.3d 434 (9th Cir. 1996) (holding that anyone, not just agencies or applicants, may take listed species in a manner contemplated by an ITS).

132. Bennett v. Spear, 520 U.S. 154, 170 (1997).

- set forth terms and conditions to implement those reasonable and prudent measures.[133]

Defining the level or degree of allowable take often is problematic.[134] And yet "Congress has clearly declared a preference for expressing take in numerical form, and an [ITS] that utilizes a surrogate instead of a numerical cap on take must explain why it was impracticable to express a numerical measure of take."[135] A specified take level serves as a trigger that removes the safe harbor of the ITS and requires that the parties reinitiate consultation.[136] The RPMs may not serve a general mitigation purpose, but instead must be designed to actually minimize the amount or extent of the anticipated take.[137] RPMs, and the terms and conditions implementing them, cannot alter the basic design, location, scope, duration, or timing of the action and may involve only "minor changes."[138] Ultimately, the real import of RPMs and terms and conditions is that they must be implemented, or any incidental take occurring pursuant to the action is unlawful.[139]

5.4.5.5   Challenges to Biological Opinions

Once issued, BOs now can be challenged in federal court, for consistency with the Act as well as whether the judgments rendered in the BO are arbitrary or capricious.[140] In *Bennett v.*

133. 16 U.S.C. § 1536(b)(4)(C) (emphasis added). *See also* 50 C.F.R. § 402.14(i) (setting forth additional detail for ITSs).

134. The Ninth Circuit warns that the permissible level of take ought to be expressed in the form of a specific number. *See* Ariz. Cattle Growers Ass'n v. U.S. Fish & Wildlife Serv., 273 F.3d 1229, 1249 (9th Cir. 2001). Yet the court further notes that it has "never held that a numerical limit is required. Indeed, we have upheld Incidental Take Statements that used a combination of numbers and estimates." *Id.* But when a numerical limit is not specified, the Service must "establish that no such numerical value could be practically obtained." *Id.* at 1250. *See also* Ctr. for Biological Diversity v. Salazar, 2012 WL 3570667 (9th Cir. Aug. 21, 2012) (discussing numerical or surrogate take in an ITS).

135. Or. Nat. Res. Council v. Allen, 476 F.3d 1031, 1037 (9th Cir. 2007) (invalidating ITS, concluding no rational connection between take authorization and scope of the underlying proposed action).

136. Ariz. Cattle Growers Ass'n v. U.S. Fish & Wildlife Serv., 273 F.3d 1229, 1249 (9th Cir. 2001).

137. Consultation Handbook, *supra* note 5, at 4-50.

138. 50 C.F.R. § 402.14(i)(2).

139. 16 U.S.C. § 1536(o) (exempting from the ESA's takings prohibitions only takings that are "in compliance" with the ITS).

140. *E.g.,* Miccosukee Tribe of Indians of Fla. v. United States, 566 F.3d 1257 (11th Cir. 2009); Ctr. for Biological Diversity v. U.S. Fish & Wildlife Serv., 450 F.3d 930 (9th Cir. 2006). In *Dow AgroSciences v. NMFS,* 637 F.3d 259 (4th Cir.

Spear,[141] the Supreme Court held that a BO containing an ITS could be challenged under the Administrative Procedure Act (APA) in a district court. Although the ESA contains a citizen suit provision, the Court held that the provision, and its accompanying 60-day-notice requirement, applies to federal agencies only when they are engaging in nondiscretionary agency actions, and that the issues in a challenge to a BO are not nondiscretionary. While in practice many citizen plaintiffs continue to file 60-day-notice letters pursuant to the citizen suit provision, such notice is not required, and parties may initiate a lawsuit challenging a BO in federal district court, invoking the court's jurisdiction under 28 U.S.C. § 1331 and the sovereign immunity waiver and cause of action under the APA. In some circumstances, challenges to a BO must be brought in conjunction with a challenge to the underlying agency action and in the court in which that challenge occurs.[142]

5.5   Reinitiation of Consultation

When a federal agency has retained any discretionary involvement in or control over a particular action, the agency remains under a continuing obligation to reinitiate consultation if conditions so warrant. Pursuant to the 402 regulations, consultation must be reinitiated if any of the following four circumstances arises:

1. The amount or extent of taking specified in the ITS is exceeded.
2. New information reveals effects of the action that may affect listed species or critical habitat in a manner or to an extent not previously considered.
3. The identified action is subsequently modified in a manner that causes an effect to the listed species or critical habitat that was not considered in the biological opinion.
4. A new species is listed or critical habitat designated that may be affected by the identified action.[143]

2011), for instance, the court held that the BO was reviewable under APA section 704, because the underlying EPA program for registration of insecticides did not provide an adequate forum for challenging the BO.
141. 520 U.S. 154 (1997).
142. *Cf.* City of Tacoma v. FERC, 460 F.2d 53, 75 (D.C. Cir. 2006).
143. 50 C.F.R. § 402.16.

Certain agency actions, such as ongoing programmatic land use planning, may require regular reinitiation, particularly when the action area is broad and could encompass many new species' listings.[144]

5.6   Irreversible/Irretrievable Commitments of Resources

Once initiated,[145] until formal consultation is properly concluded no action may proceed if that action may affect listed species or critical habitat. Section 7(d) of the ESA prohibits any agency or applicant, after initiation of consultation, from making any irreversible or irretrievable commitments of resources that would foreclose the formulation or implementation of any RPA.[146] "Section 7(d) was enacted to ensure that the status quo would be maintained during the consultation process to prevent agencies from sinking resources into a project in order to ensure its completion regardless of its impacts on endangered or threatened species."[147] The section 7(d) bar, therefore, joins with the separate section 7(a)(2) procedural requirements to ensure that the consultation process is completed prior to proceeding with any action that may affect a listed species or critical habitat.[148] By regulation, the Services have extended the scope of section 7(d) to "re-initiation" of consultation and have determined that the prohibition is in effect "until the requirements of section 7(a)(2) are satisfied."[149]

---

144.   See Pac. Rivers Council v. Thomas, 30 F.3d 1050 (9th Cir. 1994) (enjoining Forest Service activities because consultation had not been initiated on the Forest Service's land and resource management plans after subsequent listing of chinook salmon).

145.   Initiation of formal consultation occurs upon acceptance of a written request (50 C.F.R. § 402.14(c)).

146.   16 U.S.C. § 1536(d).

147.   Wash. Toxics Coal. v. EPA, 413 F.3d 1024, 1034–35 (9th Cir. 2005), cert. denied sub nom. CropLife Am. v. Wash. Toxics Coal., 546 U.S. 1090 (2006).

148.   Pac. Rivers Council v. Thomas, 30 F.3d 1050, 1056–67 (9th Cir. 1994) (enjoining Forest Service timber sales, range management activities, grazing permits, and road-building projects because the Forest Service had not properly completed consultation).

149.   50 C.F.R. § 402.09. The preamble to the joint Consultation Regulations explains that the "requirements of section 7(a)(2) are satisfied" when the agency either receives a no-jeopardy opinion or chooses a valid reasonable and prudent alternative. 51 Fed. Reg. 19,926, 19,940 (1986). A section 7(d) violation can occur if the agency reinitiates consultation and is likely to exceed any allowable take permitted in an existing BO's ITS. See Ctr. for Biological Diversity v. U.S. Forest Serv.,

Neither the ESA nor its implementing regulations define what constitutes an "irreversible or irretrievable commitment" subject to the section 7(d) prohibition. FWS guidance provides that an "irreversible or irretrievable commitment" is "[a]ny action that has the effect of preventing the formulation or implementation of any reasonable and prudent alternatives needed to avoid jeopardizing the species or adversely modifying critical habitat."[150] The *Consultation Handbook* provides limited guidance regarding the application of section 7(d) during the consultation process other than to state that the section 7(d) restriction is triggered by the determination of "may affect."[151] The *Consultation Handbook* also states that "[n]ot all irreversible and irretrievable commitments of resources are prohibited. The formulation or implementation of any reasonable and prudent alternatives must be foreclosed by the resource commitment to violate section 7(d). Thus, resource commitments may occur as long as the action agency retains sufficient discretion and flexibility to modify its action to allow formulation and implementation of an appropriate reasonable and prudent alternative. Destroying potential alternative habitat within the project area, for example, could violate section 7(d)."[152]

Courts applying section 7(d) have struggled somewhat to provide a measure of consistency. On the one hand, the Ninth Circuit has observed that the purpose of the provision is to "maintain the status quo,"[153] and at least one district court noted that the legislative history of the provision indicates a congressional desire to prevent agencies from "steam-rolling" a project by investing resources during the early stages of the project.[154] A number of courts have held that actions taken during the consultation process constituted a violation of section 7(d). In *Natural Resources Defense Council v. Houston*,[155] environmental groups sought to enjoin the Bureau of Reclamation from entering into renewal

2011 WL 5008514 (D. Ariz. Oct. 11, 2011). *But cf.* Defenders of Wildlife v. Bureau of Ocean Management, 684 F.3d 1242 (11th Cir. 2012) (section 7(d) not necessarily apply when an existing BO still applicable during a reinitiation of consultation).

150. U.S. Fish & Wildlife Serv., Endangered Species Program, Consultations: Frequently Asked Questions, http://www.fws.gov/endangered/what-we-do/faq.html.

151. Consultation Handbook, *supra* note 5, at 2-7.

152. *Id.*

153. Lane Cnty. Audubon Soc'y v. Jamison, 958 F.2d 290, 294 (9th Cir. 1992). *See also* Wash. Toxics Coal. v. EPA, 413 F.3d 1024, 1034–35 (9th Cir. 2005), *cert denied sub nom.* CropLife of Am. v. Wash. Toxics Coal., 546 U.S. 1090 (2006).

154. N. Slope Borough v. Andrus, 486 F. Supp. 332, 356 (D.D.C.), *aff'd in part, rev'd in part,* 642 F.2d 589 (D.C. Cir. 1980).

155. 146 F.3d 1118, 1124 (9th Cir. 1998).

contracts to supply water from a dam unit based on the Bureau's alleged violation of various statutes, including the ESA. The court found that the 40-year water contracts were a prohibited irreversible and irretrievable commitment of resources.[156] The court reasoned that, because the contracts did not allow for a reduction in the amount of water delivered under the contract, the reasonable and prudent alternative of reallocating contracted water from irrigation to conservation was foreclosed.[157] Therefore, the contracts that were entered into before the completion of the consultation process were subject to rescission.[158] In analyzing a timber company's commitment of resources in *Environmental Protection Information Center v. Pacific Lumber Co.*, the court looked to the fact that the logging operations at issue in the case could cause the erosion and mass wasting of steeply sloped hillsides that contribute to the severe degradation of streams and coho salmon habitat.[159] The court found that those effects would foreclose the formulation and implementation of alternative measures.[160] Therefore, the plaintiffs were entitled to a preliminary injunction to stop the logging operations.[161]

Yet other decisions suggest that that sunk costs alone might not violate section 7(d). For example, in *Bays' Legal Fund v. Brown*,[162] the district court determined that an investment of more than $100 million prior to the completion of consultation did not violate section 7(d) because the project proponents retained sufficient flexibility to alter the project's design if necessary to protect endangered whales.[163] Even when courts have enjoined activities found to be in violation of section 7(d), they have implicitly recognized that not all activities are precluded during consultation.[164] In the seminal *Pacific Rivers* case, the Ninth Circuit concluded

---

156. *Id.* at 1128.
157. *Id.*
158. *Id.; see also* Lane Cnty. Audubon Soc'y v. Jamison, 958 F.2d 290 (9th Cir. 1992) (enjoining all timber sales until the timber sale selection criteria and guidelines relied on by the BLM completed the consultation process under section 7(a)(2)).
159. 67 F. Supp. 2d 1113, 1122 (N.D. Cal.), *vacated by* 257 F.3d 1071 (9th Cir. 1999) (after case became moot).
160. 67 F. Supp. 2d at 1126.
161. *Id.*
162. 828 F. Supp. 102 (D. Mass. 1993).
163. *Id.* at 112.
164. *See* Pac. Rivers Council v. Thomas, 30 F.3d 1050, 1057 (9th Cir. 1994) (stating that because consultation had not been initiated at the time of hearing, "we need not address . . . whether the various commitments of resources irreversible and irretrievable"); Nat. Res. Def. Council v. Houston, 146 F.3d 1118, 1128 (9th Cir. 1998) (Bureau of Reclamation contracts, executed prior to conclu-

that timber sales, for instance, are per se violations of ESA section 7(d), when the action agency has not completed the consultation process.[165]

Action agencies, therefore, should be cautioned that, along with any potential standard for awarding preliminary injunctions, section 7(d) is of limited use in many circumstances where an activity may affect a listed species or potentially jeopardize the species or adversely modify or destroy its critical habitat. Section 7(d) does not sanction activities that might take a listed species pending the completion of consultation. On balance, the cases suggest that an underlying consideration in determining whether particular activities constitute an irreversible and irretrievable commitment of resources is whether the actions taken foreclose the possibility to implement reasonable and prudent alternatives. If the resources committed to the project can be used in a manner that does not affect the existence of listed species, and the actions taken do not effectively tie the agencies' hands in identifying any reasonable and prudent alternatives that might be required to avoid jeopardy from the project as proposed, the section 7(d) prohibition should not apply.

5.7   Conferencing

Section 7(a)(4) of the ESA is one of the few provisions protecting species that are not yet listed as endangered or threatened.[166] Section 7(a)(4) requires each federal agency to "confer" with the Secretary with respect to any agency action that is "likely to jeopardize the continued existence" of any species proposed to be listed, or that is likely to result in destruction or adverse modification of proposed critical habitat.[167] A finding of likely jeopardy or adverse modification triggers conferencing. But conferencing does not impose the same substantive obligations on agencies as a consultation (the recommendations are nonbinding), and the

---

sion of consultation, were not adequately conditioned to allow for future needs of endangered species).

165. *Pac. Rivers Council,* 30 F.3d at 1057 (citing *Lane Cnty.,* 958 F.2d at 295).

166. 16 U.S.C. § 1536(a)(4).

167. *Id. See* James C. Kilbourne, *The Endangered Species Act Under the Microscope: A Closeup Look from a Litigator's Perspective,* 21 ENVTL. L. 499, 556–58 (1991) (detailed discussion of the ESA conferencing requirement).

section 7(d) limitation on commitment of resources is not applicable for conferencing.

Like consultation, conferencing may be informal or formal, and the process requires significant interaction between the action agency and the Service. The procedural value of conferencing is that the opinion issued at the conclusion of the conference may ultimately be adopted as the BO if and when the species is listed or critical habitat is designated.[168]

With respect to continuing or ongoing agency actions, the conferencing procedures are useful. If, for instance, a federal agency does not conference on a proposed species, and the particular ongoing action will cause some incidental take of the species, the ongoing action would have to cease upon listing of the species, until the action agency reinitiates and completes consultation and receives an ITS. In contrast, an agency that has conferenced with respect to its ongoing action and the proposed species may find itself with a BO, with any necessary protection through an incidental take statement, upon the effective date of the listing of the species.[169]

5.8   The Role of Tribes

As explained in more detail in chapter 8, tribal interests can play an important role in the administration of the Act. The Secretaries, when administering natural resource programs, appreciate that American Indian lands in the lower 48 states comprise many millions of acres of land, and the same is true for traditional Native lands in Alaska. And when administering programs in the lower 48, the Secretaries exercise a federal trust responsibility and must respect tribal rights and the obligations of the United States toward the tribes. As part of the unique status of tribes, therefore, the Secretaries attempt to ensure a meaningful government-to-government relationship with the tribes when a consultation process might affect tribal interests.[170]

---

168.   50 C.F.R. § 402.10(d).

169.   During the 30-day period between publication of a final rule listing a species and the effective date of the rule, the Service may convert the conference opinion into a biological opinion, pursuant to 50 C.F.R. § 402.10(d).

170.   *E.g.*, Exec. Order No. 13,175, Consultation and Coordination with Indian Tribal Governments (Nov. 6, 2000); Secretarial Order No. 3206, Working with

5.9   The Role of Private Applicants

Section 7 of the ESA affords certain procedural rights to persons who qualify as "applicants." The ESA itself defines the term *applicant* somewhat narrowly:

> The term "permit or license applicant" means, when used with respect to an action of a federal agency for which exemption is sought under section 1536 of this title, any person whose application to such agency for a permit or a license has been denied primarily because of the application of section 1536(a) of this title to such agency action.[171]

The consulting agencies have determined that the statutory definition of *applicant* is "of limited use in the consultation context because it focuses on the exemption process."[172] The 402 regulations define *applicant* more broadly to include "any person, as defined in section 3(13) of the Act, who requires formal approval or authorization from a Federal agency as a prerequisite to conducting the action."[173] For section 7 consultation purposes, applicants include a wide array of individuals seeking permits, licenses, leases, letters of authorization, or "any other form of authorization or approval"[174] from a federal agency as a prerequisite for carrying out an action. But conversely, the consulting agencies have indicated that those merely seeking funding from a federal agency are not applicants, unless the request for funding is coupled with a requirement for separate federal agency authorization or approval prior to carrying out the action for which the funding is sought.[175] Likewise, a "prospective permit applicant" is not an applicant.[176]

Examples of instances where federal agencies have approved a request for applicant status include a mine operator seeking plan of operations and permit approvals on national forest land; floatboat outfitters seeking renewal of a Forest Service special-use permit; a regional water authority seeking a Bureau of Land

Tribes, American Indian Tribal Rights, Federal Trust Responsibilities, and the Endangered Species Act (June 5, 1997). *See* chapter 8, section 8.5.

171.   16 U.S.C. § 1532(12).

172.   Supplementary Information Accompanying Final Section 7 Consultation Rules, 51 Fed. Reg. 19,926, 19,930 (1986).

173.   50 C.F.R. § 402.02.

174.   *See* Supplementary Information Accompanying Final Section 7 Consultation Rules, 51 Fed. Reg. at 19,930.

175.   *Id.*

176.   *Id.*

Management right-of-way; and a permit applicant for a railroad right-of-way across federal land.

The *Section 7 Consultation Handbook* provides further guidance for determining whether one is an applicant. Specifically, the handbook notes that the type, or scope, of a particular section 7 consultation affects the determination of whether applicants exist; the more discrete and narrowly focused the action being consulted on, the more likely it is that persons exist who qualify as applicants.[177] The specific example given in the handbook is worthy of examination:

> Users of public resources (e.g. timber companies harvesting on national forests) are not parties to programmatic Section 7 consultations dealing with an agency's overall management operations, including land management planning and other program level consultations. However, users who are party to a discrete action (i.e., where they are already the successful bidder on a timber sale that becomes the subject of later consultation or re-initiation when a new species is listed or new critical habitat is designated) may participate as applicants in the Section 7 process.[178]

This example apparently recognizes a consultation continuum; on one end of the continuum are broad, programmatic consultations unlikely to confer applicant status on anyone, and on the other end of the continuum are the very narrow, "discrete" consultations involving specific actions.

Any person determined by an action agency to qualify as an applicant is entitled to[179]

- submit information for consideration during consultation;[180]
- be informed by the action agency, in writing, of the estimated length of any delay in preparing a BA, and the reasons for the delay;[181]
- refuse to grant more than a 60-day extension to NMFS or FWS of the 90-day time limit for preparation of a BO;[182]
- review the draft BO and provide comments on the draft through the action agency;[183]

---

177. Consultation Handbook, *supra* note 5, at 2-12.
178. *Id.*
179. *Id.* at 2-13.
180. 50 C.F.R. § 402.14(d).
181. 16 U.S.C. § 1536(c)(1); 50 C.F.R. § 402.12(i).
182. 16 U.S.C. § 1536(b)(1)(B); 50 C.F.R. § 402.14(e).
183. 50 C.F.R. § 402.14(g)(5). The applicant obtains a copy of the draft BO by requesting one from the action agency; all comments "must be submitted to the

- discuss with NMFS or FWS the basis of the biological determinations in the draft BO, and assist in the development of reasonable and prudent alternatives (in the case of a draft "jeopardy opinion");[184]
- receive a copy of the final BO;[185]
- initiate the exemption process if the BO concludes that the proposed action is likely to jeopardize the continued existence of a listed species, and that there are no reasonable and prudent alternatives to the proposed action;[186] and
- request "early consultation" prior to actually applying for a federal license or permit.[187]

In addition, applicants may serve as the designated nonfederal representative of the federal action agency for the purposes of conducting informal consultation and preparing a BA.[188] In fact, the action agency may not designate any other nonfederal representative for these purposes without the agreement of the applicant.[189] From a project applicant's perspective, it can be advantageous to seek applicant status in the consultation and make use of these opportunities for input and review in the consultation process. In that way, the applicant can contribute its expertise, information, and input while its project's future and potential management constraints based on ESA factors are being addressed in the interagency consultation process. The ultimate responsibility for compliance with section 7, however, always remains with the federal action agency.[190]

Service through the Federal agency, although the applicant may send a copy of its comments directly to the Service." *Id.*

184. *Id.*

185. 16 U.S.C. § 1536(b)(3)(A) (providing that the Service must "promptly," after the conclusion of consultation, provide the action agency and the applicant a copy of the BO); 50 C.F.R. § 402.14(e) (providing that the action agency and the applicant will receive a copy of the BO within 45 days of the conclusion of formal consultation).

186. 16 U.S.C. § 1536(g)(1); 50 C.F.R. § 451.02(c).

187. 50 C.F.R. § 402.1 1.

188. 50 C.F.R § 402.08.

189. *Id.*

190. *Id.*

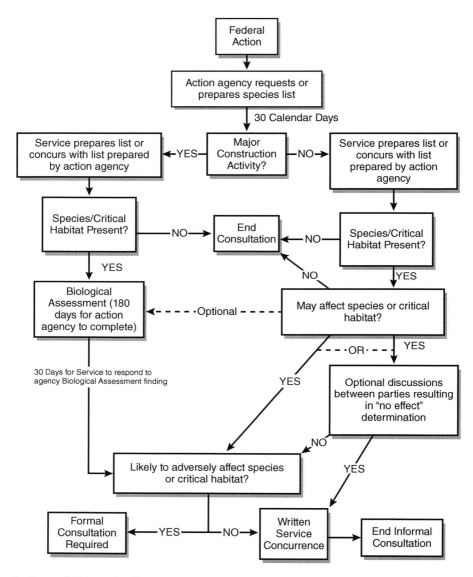

Informal Consultation Process

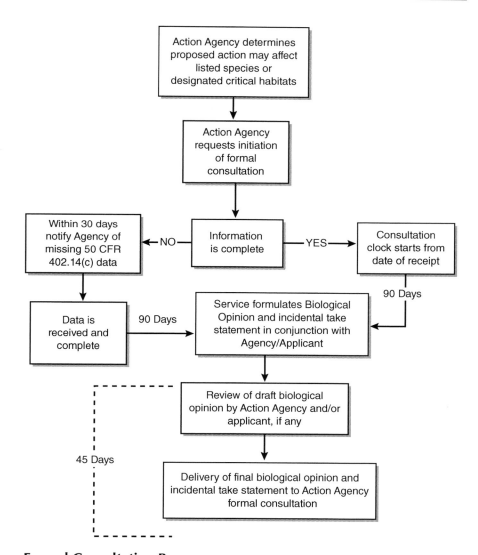

Formal Consultation Process

6 Incidental Take Permits and Other Allowable Take

6.1   Overview

The Endangered Species Act (ESA) includes various mechanisms for allowing parties to engage in otherwise prohibited activities. In some circumstances, even an otherwise illegal "knowing take"[1] of a listed species may be allowed. This chapter provides an overview of the exceptions contained in section 10 of the ESA.[2] Other authorized takings, such as those consistent with and contemplated by an incidental take statement associated with actions authorized, funded, or carried out by federal agencies;[3] those that are consistent with any rule promulgated under section 4(d) for threatened species;[4] or those activities that may affect members of "experimental populations"[5] are discussed elsewhere in this book. Since the 1990s, the section 10 program for permitting the take of species has become a robust aspect of the ESA, particularly as the Services crafted new and creative mechanisms (such as the "no surprises" and "safe harbor" policies discussed later in this chapter) to facilitate making section 10 permits a more attractive option for addressing conflicts between private activities and the needs of endangered and threatened species.[6]

---

1. See chapter 4 for a detailed discussion of section 9 prohibited take of listed species.
2. 16 U.S.C. § 1539.
3. Incidental take of listed species in connection with federal actions is discussed in section 5.4; taking of species pursuant to the Act's exemption process (the so-called God Squad proceeding) is discussed in chapter 7.
4. See section 4.3 for a detailed discussion of 4(d) rules.
5. See chapter 10 for a detailed discussion of experimental populations.
6. *See generally* J.B. Ruhl, *How to Kill Endangered Species, Legally: The Nuts and Bolts of Endangered Species Act "HCP" Permits for Real Estate Development,*

6.2   **Incidental Take Permits**

In 1982, Congress amended the ESA to resolve the "concerns of private landowners who are faced with having otherwise lawful activities . . . prevented by [ESA] Section 9 prohibitions against takings."[7] Through the creation of ESA section 10(a)(1)(B),[8] Congress authorized an otherwise prohibited taking of listed species "if such taking is incidental to, and not the purpose of, the carrying out of an otherwise lawful activity."[9] Congress specifically intended for these section 10 incidental take permits (hereinafter section 10 permits or ITPs) to encourage "unique partnerships" between the public and private sectors and serve the dual purposes of conserving species while providing desirable long-term assurances to participating landowners.[10] During the last decade and a half, section 10 permits have become a popular device for resolving conflicts between the needs of listed species and proposed land-use activities. This has occurred, in part, because the Services during the 1990s developed creative policies, promulgated fairly extensive section 10 permit regulations,[11] and published a comprehensive handbook containing "detailed but flexible guidelines" to guide section 10 permit applicants through the process.[12] Indeed, during the first decade of the program, only 14 ITPs had been issued, while by September 1998 the Services had issued 243 such permits, with hundreds then in development.[13] Today, the Fish and Wildlife Service (FWS) maintains a

---

5 ENVTL. L. 345 (1999); Barton H. Thompson, Jr., *The Endangered Species Act: A Case Study in Takings and Incentives,* 49 STAN. L. REV. 305 (1997).

7.   H.R. CONF. REP. NO. 97-835, at 29 (1982), *reprinted in* 1982 U.S.C.C.A.N. 2860, 2870.

8.   16 U.S.C. § 1539(a)(1)(B).

9.   *Id.*

10.   H.R. REP. NO. 97-567, at 30–31 (1982), *reprinted in* 1982 U.S.C.C.A.N. 2830–31.

11.   FWS regulations governing all Service permits are published at 50 C.F.R. § 13. In addition, FWS has published specific rules governing section 10 permits. 50 C.F.R. § 17.22(b), 17.32(b). Permitting rules for species under NMFS jurisdiction are published at 50 C.F.R. part 222.

12.   *See* U.S. FISH & WILDLIFE SERV. & NAT'L MARINE FISHERIES SERV., JOINT ENDANGERED SPECIES HABITAT CONSERVATION PLANNING HANDBOOK (November 1996) [hereinafter HCP HANDBOOK]; the Services released an addendum to the *Handbook* in 2000, incorporating a five-point policy. 65 Fed. Reg. 35,242 (June 1, 2000). *See also* Response to Public Comments on Amending General Permitting Regulations Relating to Habitat Conservation Plans, Safe Harbor Agreements and Candidate Conservation Agreements with Assurances, 66 Fed. Reg. 6483 (Jan. 22, 2001) (declining to repropose any amendments to parts 13 or 17 of the regulations).

13.   Spirit of the Sage Council v. Norton, 411 F.3d 225, 227 (D.C. Cir. 2005).

database of issued permits, with the number of permits as of May 2012 exceeding 780.[14]

6.3　Habitat Conservation Plans

The essential element of any section 10 permit is the applicant's proposed "conservation plan."[15] This conservation plan, commonly referred to as a "habitat conservation plan"[16] (HCP), must specify

- the impact that will likely result from the taking;
- the steps the applicant will take to "minimize and mitigate" such impacts, and the funding that will be available to implement such steps;
- alternative actions to the taking that the applicant has considered, and the reasons why the alternatives are not being used; and
- such other measures as the Secretary may require as being necessary or appropriate for purposes of the plan.[17]

14.　*See* U.S. Fish & Wildlife Serv., Conservation Plans and Agreements Database, http://ecos.fws.gov/conserv_plans/public.jsp.

15.　16 U.S.C. § 1539(a)(2)(A). Congress modeled the section 10 permit program on a plan developed by private parties to address the impacts of development on endangered butterflies near the San Bruno Mountains in California. The San Bruno Plan was viewed by Congress as the "model for the incidental take permit" and the standard against which the "adequacy of other plans should be measured." H.R. CONF. REP. NO. 97-835, at 31 (1982), *reprinted in* 1982 U.S.C.C.A.N. 2807, 2872. *See* Friends of Endangered Species v. Jantzen, 760 F.2d 976, 982–83 (9th Cir. 1985) (upholding the San Bruno plan largely due to Congress's reliance on that plan). A potential applicant should appreciate that take associated with research or development of the habitat conservation plan itself is not allowed unless carried out pursuant to a valid permit. *See* Hamilton v. City of Austin, 8 F. Supp. 2d 886 (W.D. Tex. 1998) (pre-HCP activities designed to determine the parameters of the incidental take permit required issuance of a section 10(a)(1)(B) scientific research permit).

16.　For two significant early overviews of habitat conservation planning, see MICHAEL J. BEAN ET AL., RECONCILING CONFLICTS UNDER THE ENDANGERED SPECIES ACT: THE HABITAT CONSERVATION PLANNING EXPERIENCE (World Wildlife Fund 1991), and Robert D. Thornton, *Searching for Consensus and Predictability: Habitat Conservation Planning Under the Endangered Species Act of 1973,* 21 ENVTL. L. 605 (1991). *See also* TIMOTHY BEATLEY, HABITAT CONSERVATION PLANNING: ENDANGERED SPECIES AND URBAN GROWTH (1994); Patrick Duggan, *Incidental Extinction: How the Endangered Species Act's Incidental Take Permits Fail to Account for Population Loss,* 41 ENVTL. L. REP. 10,628 (2011).

17.　16 U.S.C. § 1539(a)(2)(A)(i)–(iv).

After receipt of a permit application and an HCP that satisfies these criteria, and then after opportunity for public comment,[18] the Act instructs the Secretary to issue a section 10 permit if the Secretary finds that (1) the proposed taking will be incidental; (2) the applicant will, to the maximum extent practicable, minimize and mitigate the impacts of the taking; (3) the applicant will ensure adequate funding for the HCP; (4) the taking will not "appreciably reduce the likelihood of the survival and recovery of the species in the wild"; and (5) the applicant has agreed to implement such other measures, terms, and conditions as the Secretary deems necessary or appropriate.[19]

Generally, unless the HCP is considered a low-effect HCP, parties to the HCP enter into what is called an implementing agreement (IA). The IA serves as the contractual mechanism ostensibly binding the parties to the terms of the IA and accompanying HCP.

6.3.1   Scope of an HCP

A single HCP may address one or many different species, including both listed and unlisted species.[20] Alternatively, an HCP may focus on particular habitat types and address all species within certain habitat types present in the plan area.[21] At a minimum, a permit applicant is well advised to include all listed species of plants[22] and wildlife that incidentally might be taken during

---

18.   Section 10(c) of the Act requires that the Service ensure that the public has an opportunity to review the delineated area being addressed by the HCP. In *Gerber v. Norton,* 294 F.3d 173, 179, 184 (D.C. Cir. 2002), the court invalidated an HCP, in part, because the Service failed to make publicly available a map of the off-site mitigation. The Services' five-point policy addendum to the *HCP Handbook* included expanded use of public participation as an important policy. 65 Fed. Reg. 35,246–47 (June 1, 2000).

19.   16 U.S.C. § 1539(a)(2)(B)(i)–(v). At least one court has rejected that this language operates as a nondiscretionary duty to issue the ITP. Sw. Ctr. for Biological Diversity v. Bartel, 470 F. Supp. 2d 1118, 1135 (S.D. Cal. 2006), *appeal dismissed and remanded,* 409 F. App'x 143 (9th Cir. 2011).

20.   HCP HANDBOOK, *supra* note 12, at 3-7 through 3-8 (addressing HCP species selection generally), and 4-1 through 4-4 (addressing unlisted species in an HCP). Candidate conservation agreements are addressed in section 6.5.

21.   *Id.* at 3-37 through 3-38.

22.   Although plants generally are not the object of a section 10 permit (because the section 9 prohibitions against takings do not apply to plants), the Services cannot approve a section 10 permit for an action that would result in jeopardy to any listed species, including plants. HCP HANDBOOK, *supra* note 12, at 3-8 (citing 16 U.S.C. § 1536(a)(2)).

the life of the proposed project. Simply stated, the covered species should be identified clearly in the HCP and subsequent section 10 permit (or some other permit); failure to include all covered species that might subsequently be taken could result in enforcement, project delays, or a even a permanent enjoining of the project.[23]

An HCP may be limited to a specifically identifiable action, such as the construction of residential properties,[24] or it may apply to broad categories of activities, such as county building permit programs or statewide logging activities affecting a listed species.[25] A section 10 permit for a "programmatic HCP," for example, might be issued to a county or state government, allowing entities subsequently permitted by the county or state government to conduct activities covered by the programmatic HCP and then avail themselves of incidental take protection under certain circumstances.[26] With respect to a programmatic section 10 permit issued by the National Marine Fisheries Service (NMFS), a person seeking coverage under the permit must apply for and receive a "certificate of inclusion."[27] In the case of an FWS-issued programmatic section 10 permit, the permit itself may identify persons under the jurisdiction of the permittee who are allowed to conduct activities pursuant to the permit, or the permittee may issue subsequent permits, through any "written instrument" consistent with implementation of the HCP.[28]

---

23. *Id.* at 3-7. See chapter 4 for a discussion of actions prohibited by section 9 of the ESA. Regardless of the scope of an HCP, all proposed activities must be consistent with and contemplated by the HCP and resulting section 10 permit for the shield against section 9 liability to apply. *See* Loggerhead Turtle v. Cnty. Council of Volusia Cnty., 148 F.3d 1231, 1242 (11th Cir. 1998).

24. *See, e.g.,* 74 Fed. Reg. 58,653 (Nov. 13, 2009) (noticing availability of HCPs for residential development regarding the Alabama beach mouse).

25. HCP HANDBOOK, *supra* note 12, at 3-39. See 64 Fed. Reg. 40,616 (July 27, 1999) for an example of a statewide section 10 permit application. *See generally* J.B. Ruhl, *Regional Habitat Conservation Planning Under the Endangered Species Act: Pushing the Legal and Practical Limits of Species Protection,* 44 Sw. L.J. 1393 (1991).

26. *See* HCP HANDBOOK, *supra* note 12, at 3-39. Such a regional-scale HCP was the subject of the litigation in *Southwest Center for Biological Diversity v. Bartel,* 470 F. Supp. 2d 1118 (S.D. Cal. 2006), *appeal dismissed and remanded,* 409 F. App'x 143 (9th Cir. 2011).

27. 50 C.F.R. § 222.307(f) (NMFS criteria for issuance of "certificates of inclusion").

28. 50 C.F.R. §§ 13.25(d), (e).

6.3.2   HCP Mitigation Requirements

The critical features of any HCP are the measures required to "minimize and mitigate" the impacts of the proposed taking to the "maximum extent practicable." The precise scope of this requirement is somewhat vague, because neither the ESA nor the section 10 permit regulations define "maximum extent practicable."[29] The Services require that mitigation be based on "sound biological rationale" and that it be "commensurate with the impacts" addressed.[30] The *HCP Handbook* identifies two threshold factors relevant when determining the adequacy of proposed mitigation: (1) the extent to which the proposed measures provide substantial benefits to the species, and (2) whether the amount of mitigation proposed is the maximum practicable in light of such factors as the relative costs and benefits of additional mitigation, the abilities of the applicant, and the amount of mitigation provided by other applicants in similar situations.[31] And it is incumbent upon the Service to make a determination that no practicable alternative to the development plan exists that would minimize the taking of the species.[32]

The Services suggest that HCP mitigation programs are "as varied as the projects they address," and that unyielding rules for mitigation would limit the "creative potential inherent in any good HCP effort."[33] Nonetheless, mitigation should be as con-

---

29.   *See* Nat'l Wildlife Fed'n v. Norton, 306 F. Supp. 2d 920, 927 (E.D. Cal. 2004).
30.   HCP HANDBOOK, *supra* note 12, at 3-19. Mitigation actions usually take one of the following forms:

1. Avoiding the impact (such as through relocation of facilities within the project area);
2. Minimizing the impact (such as through timing restrictions and buffer zones);
3. Rectifying the impact (such as through restoration and revegetation of disturbed project areas);
4. Reducing or eliminating the impact over time (such as through proper management, monitoring, and adaptive management); or
5. Compensating for the impact (such as through restoring or protecting habitat at an onsite or offsite location).

Id. at 3-19 through 3-20.
31.   *Id.* at 7-3. A 2000 addendum to the *Handbook* emphasized focusing on adaptive management, as well. 65 Fed. Reg. 35,242 (June 1, 2000).
32.   *See* Gerber v. Norton, 294 F.3d 173, 185 (D.C. Cir. 2002). The "FWS must make an independent determination of practicability and make a finding that the impacts of the taking will be minimized and mitigated 'to the maximum extent practicable.'" Sw. Ctr. for Biological Diversity v. Bartel, 470 F. Supp. 2d 1118, 1158 (S.D. Cal. 2006), *appeal dismissed and remanded,* 409 F. App'x 143 (9th Cir. 2011).
33.   HCP HANDBOOK, *supra* note 12, at 3-19.

sistent as possible for the same species,[34] and the administrative record should support both the amount and level of mitigation ultimately required by the HCP. Federal courts most likely will examine the administrative record for some "rational basis" to support any decision approving an HCP and issuing the associated section 10 permit.[35] This suggests that the record should contain at least some analysis of whether the amount or level of mitigation provided in the HCP is the maximum practicable.[36] The Services, moreover, may not justify their approval of an HCP on a mere speculative possibility of future actions (such as an unknown amount of funding from an unknown third party).[37]

6.3.3   No Surprises Policy and Adaptive Management

A section 10 HCP permit seeks to achieve two arguably competing goals. On the one hand, it should be flexible enough to

---

34. *Id.* at 3-23. *See also* Sierra Club v. Babbitt, 15 F. Supp. 2d 1274, 1281 (S.D. Ala. 1998) (overturning the issuance of a section 10 incidental take permit because, among other reasons, of the uncertainty surrounding proposed mitigation plan); Sierra Club v. Norton, 207 F. Supp. 2d 1310 (S.D. Ala. 2002) (enjoining incidental take authorized by two Alabama beach mouse ITPs based on plaintiffs' likelihood of success on alleged NEPA challenge); Sierra Club v. Kempthorne, 2009 WL 323072 (S.D. Ala. Feb. 9, 2009) (recognizing subsequent ESA injunction against reissued ITPs following remand in *Sierra Club v. Norton,* and dissolving injunction based on revisions to real estate development plans requiring submittal of new HCPs and ITP applications).

35. Sierra Club v. Babbitt, 15 F. Supp. 2d at 1282 (court overturned FWS issuance of two section 10 permits to incidentally take the Alabama beach mouse, finding that the Service had not demonstrated that the effects of the development were minimized and mitigated to the maximum extent practicable). For a helpful discussion of the Alabama beach mouse HCPs and the holding in *Sierra Club v. Babbitt,* see Jennifer Jester, Note, *Habitat Conservation Plans Under Section 10 of the Endangered Species Act: The Alabama Beach Mouse and the Unfulfilled Mandate of Species Recovery,* 26 B.C. Envtl. Aff. L. Rev. 131 (1998). For further developments in the HCP effort for Fort Morgan, see 77 Fed. Reg. 18,857 (Mar. 28, 2012) (announcing issuance of record of decision and accompanying NEPA document). *See also* Friends of Endangered Species v. Jantzen, 760 F.2d 976, 982–84 (9th Cir. 1985) (upholding FWS determination that permanent protection of 86 percent of the Mission Blue butterfly's habitat, coupled with funding for halting incursion of brush into the butterfly's habitat, constituted the appropriate mitigation required for an HCP).

36. Sierra Club v. Babbitt, 15 F. Supp. 2d at 1282 (citing Sierra Club v. Marsh, 816 F.2d 1376 (9th Cir. 1987)) (action agency cannot be sure that project will not jeopardize species based upon promise of future mitigation measures); Nat'l Wildlife Fed'n v. Coleman, 529 F.2d 359 (5th Cir. 1976) (proposed actions by others do not ensure that a project will not jeopardize listed species). In WildEarth Guardians v. U.S Fish & Wildlife Serv., 622 F. Supp. 2d 1155 (D. Utah 2009), the court rejected the argument that the ITP needed to identify a precise number of species covered by the take permit.

37. Sierra Club v. Babbitt, 15 F. Supp. 2d at 1282.

adapt to changes in circumstances and new information regarding the needs of listed species. The Services during the 1990s generally emphasized the need to incorporate into decisions adequate mechanisms for adaptive management.[38] And they added an addendum to the *HCP Handbook* to that effect in 2000.[39] Conversely, applicants desire as much regulatory and economic certainty as they can secure, and for as long a period as possible. Yet Congress provided little guidance to the Secretary on how to balance these competing demands, at one point in the legislative history suggesting only that the Secretary is vested with broad discretion and should address the situation by including in every long-term HCP "a procedure by which the parties will deal with unforeseen circumstances."[40] Courts appear to accept adaptive management provisions in an HCP, provided that the Service is not merely employing adaptive management as a surrogate for avoiding making difficult choices.[41]

In February 1998, FWS and NMFS promulgated the Habitat Conservation Plan Assurances ("No Surprises") Rule.[42] This final rule formally implemented the FWS's no surprises policy, a policy described by one key Interior Department official as "the single most important catalyst in stimulating renewed interest in Habitat

---

38. For one review of the program and its effectiveness, see Alejandro E. Camacho, *Can Regulation Evolve? Lessons from a Study in Maladaptive Management,* 55 UCLA L. Rev. 293 (2007). The FWS has a technical guide for strategic habitat conservation that emphasizes the iterative process for habitat conservation strategies. U.S Fish & Wildlife Serv., Strategic Habitat Conservation Handbook: A Guide to Implementing the Technical Elements of Strategic Habitat Conservation (Version 1.0, 2008), http://www.fws.gov/science/doc/SHCTechnicalHandbook.pdf.

39. 65 Fed. Reg. 35,242 (June 1, 2000).

40. H.R. Rep. No. 97-835, at 30 (1982), *reprinted in* 1982 U.S.C.C.A.N. 2860, 2872.

41. In *National Wildlife Federation v. Babbitt,* 128 F. Supp. 2d 1274 (E.D. Cal. 2000), the court approved the adaptive management strategy, although otherwise concluding that the ITP was too broad. *See also* Nat. Res. Def. Council v. Kempthorne, 506 F. Supp. 2d 322 (E.D. Cal. 2007); Sw. Ctr. for Biological Diversity v. Bartel, 470 F. Supp. 2d 1118 (S.D. Cal. 2006); Ctr. for Biological Diversity v. U.S. Fish & Wildlife Serv., 202 F. Supp. 2d 594 (W.D. Tex. 2002). Indeed, the absence of adaptive management could be problematic, because one court suggested the need for adaptive management in lieu of what the court described as a "lock-in ineffective, unstudied, and inadequate mitigation" plan for the particular species for 50 years. Sw. Ctr. for Biological Diversity v. Bartel, 470 F. Supp. 2d 1118, 1146 (S.D. Cal. 2006), *appeal dismissed and remanded,* 409 F. App'x 143 (9th Cir. 2011).

42. 63 Fed. Reg. 8,859 (1998) (codified at 50 C.F.R. pt. 17) [hereinafter No Surprises Rule]. For the litigation surrounding the rule and a discussion of the rule, see Spirit of the Sage Council v. Norton, 294 F. Supp. 2d 67 (D.D.C. 2003), *appeal dismissed and orders vacated as moot,* 411 F.3d 225 (D.C. Cir. 2005).

Conservation Planning."[43] The Services described the policy as follows:

> The No Surprises policy announced in 1994 provides regulatory assurances to the holder of a Habitat Conservation Plan (HCP) incidental take permit issued under section 10(a) of the ESA that no additional land use restrictions or financial compensation will be required of the permit holder with respect to species covered by the permit, even if unforeseen circumstances arise after the permit is issued indicating that additional mitigation is needed for a given species covered by a permit.[44]

The ITP theoretically operates as a firm arrangement between the permit holder and the government for species covered in the HCP; landowners properly implementing the terms of their HCP essentially are shielding from being responsible for significant additional measures that may become necessary to respond to "unforeseen circumstances." This arrangement became further solidified once the FWS issued a procedurally proper permit revocation rule, effectively providing that a permit would not be revoked unless the permittee was not complying with its terms or if continuation of the permit might threaten to jeopardize the species.[45]

A few significant aspects of the no surprises policy are worth noting. First, the policy is applicable only to nonfederal parties seeking an ESA section 10(a)(1)(B) ITP;[46] second, the assurances provided to the permit holder are valid for the life of the permit and only with respect to species "adequately covered"[47] by the permit; third, the assurances provided to the permit holder are valid only when the HCP is being "properly implemented."[48]

---

43. Donald J. Barry, Opportunity in the Face of Danger: The Pragmatic Development of Habitat Conservation Plans, Keynote Address Before the West-Northwest Symposium (Mar. 1, 1997), in 4 HASTINGS W.-NW. J. ENVTL. L. & POL'Y 129, 130 (Summer 1998).

44. No Surprises Rule, *supra* note 42, 63 Fed. Reg. 8859 (1998).

45. 69 Fed. Reg. 71,723 (Dec. 10, 2004); 69 Fed. Reg. 29,681 (May 25, 2004) (proposing permit revocation regulations); 69 Fed. Reg. 29,669 (May 25, 2004) (withdrawing certain permit revocation regulations); 64 Fed. Reg. 32,706 (June 17, 1999). The permit revocation survived a challenge based upon the argument that ITPs must promote the recovery of listed species. Spirit of the Sage Council v. Kempthorne, 511 F. Supp. 2d 31 (D.D.C. 2007). The court disagreed with other courts that suggested that HCPs must promote recovery, not just survival. *Id.* at 43 n.4.

46. No Surprises Rule, *supra* note 42, 63 Fed. Reg. at 8,868.

47. 50 C.F.R. § 17.22(b)(5); 50 C.F.R. § 17.32(b)(5); 50 C.F.R. § 222.307(g). The term *adequately covered* is defined in 50 C.F.R. §§ 17.3 and 222.102.

48. *A properly implemented conservation plan* is defined as "any conservation plan, implementing agreement and permit whose commitments and

The larger issue, of course, is the scope and extent of the actual assurances provided to permit holders. The nature of the available assurances depends on whether a particular change in circumstances, affecting species covered by an HCP, is foreseeable or unforeseeable. Neither NMFS nor FWS define the term *foreseeable;* instead, the Services employ their respective definitions of the term *changed circumstances* for applying the No Surprises Rule. *Changed circumstances* means

> changes in circumstances affecting a species or geographic area covered by a conservation plan or agreement that can reasonably be anticipated by plan or agreement developers and the Service and that can be planned for (e.g., the listing of new species, or a fire or other natural catastrophic event in areas prone to such events).[49]

And the term *unforeseen circumstances* is defined as

> changes in circumstances affecting a species or geographic area covered by a conservation plan or agreement that could not reasonably have been anticipated by plan or agreement developers and the Service at the time of the conservation plan's or agreement's negotiation and development, and that result in a substantial and adverse change in the status of the covered species.[50]

When developing an HCP, the parties should attempt to address all reasonably foreseeable changes in circumstances.[51] By definition, these changed circumstances are foreseeable, and when (or if) they occur during the life of the HCP, the permittee must address them as called for in the plan.[52] Rarely should a foreseeable change in circumstances not have been addressed in an HCP, but should such an event occur, the permittee will not be required to implement additional conservation and mitigation measures without its "consent."[53]

---

provisions have been or are being fully implemented by the permittee." 50 C.F.R. § 17.3.

49. 50 C.F.R. § 17.3 (FWS); 50 C.F.R. § 222.102 (NMFS).

50. *Id.*

51. No Surprises Rule, *supra* note 42, 63 Fed. Reg. at 8863. The final No Surprises Rule is silent with respect to the extent of a party's obligation to address changes in circumstances. The supplementary information accompanying the final rule provides that reasonably foreseeable changes in circumstances "need to be addressed in an HCP," and that all reasonably foreseeable circumstances, including natural catastrophes that normally occur in the area, "should be addressed in the HCP." *Id.*

52. 50 C.F.R. § 17.22(b)(5)(i)–(ii) (FWS Regulations for Endangered Wildlife); 50 C.F.R. § 17.32(b)(5)(i)–(ii) (FWS Regulations for Threatened Wildlife); 50 C.F.R. § 222.307(g)(1), (2) (NMFS regulations).

53. 50 C.F.R. §§ 17.22(b)(5)(ii), 17.32(b)(5)(ii), 222.307(g)(ii).

The import of unforeseen circumstances is that when and if they occur, the government may only require minimal additional measures of the permittee. The original terms of the HCP must be maintained to the maximum extent possible and, importantly, the Services may not require "commitments of additional land, water or financial compensation or additional restrictions on the use of land, water, or other natural resources" without the permittee's consent.[54] The Services recognize that the needs of a species in such an instance may mandate that some action be taken on behalf of the species. As such, the Services noted in the No Surprises Rule that nothing in the rule should be read to limit or constrain any governmental entity (including the Services) from taking additional action at its own expense to protect or conserve a species included in an HCP.

6.4   Enhancement of Survival and Safe Harbor Permits

Section 10(a)(1)(A)[55] of the ESA allows the Services to authorize otherwise prohibited acts when carried out to enhance the propagation or survival of a listed species. Examples of enhancement activities include capture, study, tagging, banding, and other scientific activities.

In addition, the FWS promulgated regulations[56] in mid-1999 formalizing the use of a device called a safe harbor agreement (SHA).[57] While an HCP is developed in concert with an application for an incidental take permit, an SHA is developed in conjunction with an application for an "enhancement of survival" permit. An SHA is a voluntary agreement, not necessarily provoked by immediate concerns over potential take liability associated with

---

54. 50 C.F.R. § 17.22(b)(5)(iii) (FWS); 50 C.F.R. § 222.307(g)(3) (NMFS).
55. 16 U.S.C. § 1539(a)(1)(A).
56. 50 C.F.R. pts. 13 and 17. *See* FWS Final Safe Harbor Rule, 64 Fed. Reg. 32,706 (1999).
57. Announcement of Final Safe Harbor Policy [hereinafter Joint Safe Harbor Policy], 64 Fed. Reg. 32,717 (1999). The Services described the rules as "creating a new category of enhancement of survival permit." *Id.* at 32,722. Because of the prior informal safe harbor policy, there were in fact more than 40 SHAs in effect as of August 1999. U.S. Fish & Wildlife Serv., Safe Harbor Agreements for Private Property Owners, Questions & Answers (Sept. 1999). The Service revised its regulations in 2004. 69 Fed. Reg. 24,084 (May 3, 2004). And as of May 2012, the Service reports that it has approved 80 SHAs.

specific activities on particular private lands. Rather, the SHA-based enhancement of survival permit is appropriate when a landowner proposes engaging in activities that may restore, enhance, or maintain habitat for listed species, possibly increasing numbers of the particular species present on his or her private land. In exchange for the landowner's commitment to implement these species-friendly measures, the landowner receives certain assurances limiting future land-use restrictions and is assured of some future incidental take of covered species, back down to an agreed-upon baseline level. The FWS reports that it has enrolled approximately 3 million acres into the SHA program.[58]

Any person requesting an SHA-based permit must submit a permit application (FWS Form 3-200.54).[59] In addition to the general information required for any wildlife taking permit application,[60] an applicant for a SHA must include in the application (1) the common and scientific names of species for which a permit is sought, (2) a description of the land use or water management activity proposed, and (3) a safe harbor agreement that complies with the FWS's safe harbor policy.[61] With this third criterion, the "development of an 'enhancement of survival' Section 10(a)(1)(A) permit application *and* an adequate Safe Harbor Agreement are intricately linked."[62]

The Service will work with prospective applicants to develop an appropriate SHA.[63] Initially, the parties must determine the "baseline condition" of the property to be covered by the agreement.[64] This baseline condition reflects the "known biological

---

58. *See* U.S. Fish & Wildlife Serv., Endangered Species Permits: Safe Harbor Agreements, http://www.fws.gov/midwest/endangered/permits/enhancement/sha/index.html.

59. 50 C.F.R. §§ 17.22(c)(1) (for endangered wildlife), 17.32(c)(1) (for threatened wildlife). Similar to other permits, the FWS will allow parties to enter into "umbrella" or programmatic SHAs. *See* 69 Fed. Reg. at 24,085. The FWS amended its regulations in 2004 to clarify nonfederal property owners entitled to request a SHA (as well as a CCAA). 69 Fed. Reg. at 24,086; 50 C.F.R. § 17.3.

60. *See, e.g.,* 50 C.F.R. § 13.12 (information required of all permit applicants includes personal information about the applicant, location information regarding the proposed permitted activity, the desired effective date of the permit, etc.).

61. 50 C.F.R. §§ 17.22(c)(1)(i)–(iii).

62. Joint Safe Harbor Policy, *supra* note 57, 64 Fed. Reg. at 32,722 (emphasis added).

63. *Id.*

64. *Baseline condition* is defined in the Joint Safe Harbor Policy as

[P]opulation estimates and distribution and/or habitat characteristics and determined area of the enrolled property that sustain seasonal or permanent use by the covered species at the time the Safe Harbor Agreement is executed between the Services and the property owner.

Id.

and habitat characteristics that support existing levels of use of the property by species covered in the agreement."[65] The baseline determination serves as a precursor to the next step in developing the SHA: the identification of species-friendly measures or activities to be undertaken that are reasonably expected to accomplish a "net conservation benefit"[66] relative to the baseline conditions. This net conservation benefit need not be permanent, as landowners ultimately may degrade the habitat back down to the baseline.[67] Upon a finding that implementation of the SHA would provide a net conservation benefit, among other things,[68] the Service may issue a section 10(a)(1)(A) enhancement permit allowing the permittee to "incidentally"[69] take species covered by the agreement. The permit holder is then authorized to "use the property in any manner that does not result in moving the enrolled property to below baseline conditions."[70] The permit holder also is assured, consistent with the no surprises policy,[71] that no additional commitments of land, water, or financial resources will be required.[72]

---

65. *Id.* at 32,723.

66. *Id.* at 32,722. *Net conservation benefits* are defined as

The cumulative benefits of the management activities identified in a Safe Harbor Agreement that provide for an increase in a species' population and/or the enhancement, restoration, or maintenance of covered species' suitable habitat within the enrolled property, taking into account the length of the agreement and any off-setting adverse effects attributable to the incidental taking allowed by the enhancement of survival permit. Net conservation benefits must be sufficient to contribute, either directly or indirectly, to the recovery of the covered species.

Id.

67. The Services justify this aspect of SHAs by noting that although the agreement may not permanently conserve or recover species, they nevertheless offer conservation benefits, such as reduced fragmentation of habitats, increased connectivity of habitats, maintenance or increase in populations to insure against catastrophic events, and creation of areas for testing and implementation of new conservation strategies. *Id.* at 32,721–22.

68. The Secretary may issue an enhancement of survival permit only upon finding that (1) the taking will be incidental to an otherwise lawful activity, (2) the taking and its direct and indirect effects will not appreciably reduce the likelihood of survival and recovery of species covered by the permit, (3) implementation of the agreement is consistent with federal/state/tribal laws and regulations, (4) implementation is consistent with any ongoing recovery program, and (5) the applicant has shown both the capability for and the commitment to implementing the safe harbor agreement. 50 C.F.R. §§ 17.22(c)(2)(i)–(iv), 17.32(c)(2)(i)–(iv). *See* 64 Fed. Reg. at 32,712.

69. A landowner cannot create a storehouse of specimens for later intentional "harvest" or take. Rather, the taking must be "incidental to otherwise lawful activities." 50 C.F.R. §§ 17.22(c)(2)(i), 17.32(c)(2)(i). *See* 64 Fed. Reg. at 32,712.

70. Joint Safe Harbor Policy, *supra* note 57, 64 Fed. Reg. at 32,724.

71. *See* section 6.3.3.

72. *See* FWS Safe Harbor Rule, 64 Fed. Reg. at 32,712.

In order to provide a measure of "certainty relative to future property use restrictions," the duration of a safe harbor–based permit may extend for quite some time[73] and may be revoked only under very narrowly prescribed circumstances. Similar to other permits, of course, an enhancement of survival permit may be revoked for such acts as violating laws involving the conditions of the permit, failing to correct deficiencies in implementation of the permit, or becoming disqualified to hold any wildlife permit.[74] An SHA-based permit also may be revoked if a change in the statute or regulations authorizing the permit prohibits its continuation.[75] Beyond these limited revocation criteria, however, an enhancement of survival permit may be revoked only "[a]s a 'last resort' in the narrow and unlikely situation in which unforeseen circumstances result in likely jeopardy to a species covered by the permit and the Service has not been successful in remedying the situation through other means."[76]

6.5   Candidate Conservation Agreements

Corresponding to the FWS's agreements with private landowners to conserve candidate species on their property, the NMFS created the candidate conservation agreement with assurances (CCAA).[77] For candidate species, or any "species that will likely become candidates in the near future,"[78] any nonfederal property owner[79] that enters into a CCAA and implements conservation

---

73. The duration of a safe harbor agreement and accompanying permit must be sufficient to provide a net conservation benefit to species covered by the permit. However, there appears to be no maximum duration for these permits; as long as the participating landowner is implementing the terms of the agreement and the permit, the permit "runs with the land." *Id.* at 32,713; Joint Safe Harbor Policy, *supra* note 57, 64 Fed. Reg. at 37,721.

74. 50 C.F.R. § 13.28(a)(1)–(3).

75. *Id.* at § 13.28(a)(4).

76. Preamble to FWS Safe Harbor Rule, 64 Fed. Reg. at 32,709.

77. 64 Fed. Reg. 32,706 (1999). NMFS concurrently adopted the FWS policy with regard to candidate conservation agreements, without promulgating formal rules. 64 Fed. Reg. 32,726 (1999). The FWS subsequently released a *Draft Handbook for Candidate Conservation Agreements with Assurances and Enhancement of Survival Permit Processing.* 68 Fed. Reg. 37,170 (June 23, 2003).

78. The Services explicitly chose not to adopt a strict regulatory definition of the phrase "species that will likely become candidates in the near future," instead indicating that species to be covered by a candidate conservation agreement will be reviewed on a case-by-case basis. 64 Fed. Reg. at 32,732.

79. *A nonfederal property owner* includes any individual, small business, large corporation, state and local agency, or private organization. 64 Fed. Reg.

measures on nonfederal property designed to benefit such species will receive assurances from the Services that additional conservation measures will not be required of the landowner should the species subsequently become listed.[80] These are "voluntary agreements between the [Service] and non-Federal property owners to benefit proposed species, candidate species, and species likely to become candidates in the near future."[81] The goal of such agreements is to incent voluntary conservation activities that might make a listing unnecessary. Before approving a CCAA, therefore, the "Services must determine that the benefits of the conservation measures implemented by the property owner under a [CCAA], when combined with those benefits that would be achieved if it is assumed that conservation measures were also to be implemented on other necessary properties, would preclude or remove any need to list the covered species."[82]

The mechanism for implementing these assurances, in the event a candidate species is ultimately listed, is a section 10(a)(1)(A) enhancement of survival permit,[83] issued at the time of entering into the CCAA, but with a delayed effective date tied to the date of any future listing of the covered species.[84] Upon receipt of an enhancement of survival permit application for a candidate species, the FWS, for instance, may issue the permit only upon finding all of the following:

- The take will be incidental to an otherwise lawful activity and in accordance with the terms of the CCAA.
- The CCAA complies with the requirements of FWS/NMFS policy.[85]

---

at 32,710. The Service clarified the types of property owners entitled to apply for CCAAs, as well as SHAs, in 2004, noting that the important issue is the ability to carry out the management activities. 69 Fed. Reg. at 24,085. The FWS excludes federal agencies from participating in CCAAs, because the Service considers the assurances under a CCAA to conflict with obligations on agencies to promote conservation of species pursuant to § 7(a)(1). 64 Fed. Reg. 32,726 (June 17, 1999).

80. 64 Fed. Reg. at 37,727.

81. 69 Fed. Reg. at 24,084. The FWS, similar to with HCPs, will permit "umbrella" or programmatic CCAAs. *Id.* at 24,085.

82. 64 Fed. Reg. at 32,727. "'Other necessary properties' are other properties on which conservation measures would have to be implemented in order to preclude or remove any need to list the covered species." *Id.*

83. 16 U.S.C. § 1539(a)(1)(A).

84. 50 C.F.R. §§ 17.22(d)(4) (endangered species), 17.32(d)(4) (threatened species). *See* 64 Fed. Reg. at 32,735.

85. The relevant policy provides that the CCAA must identify or include the following: "a) the population levels of the covered species at the time of the agreement, b) the conservation measures the participating property owner is willing to

- The probable direct and indirect effects of the authorized take will not appreciably reduce the likelihood of survival and recovery of any species in the wild.
- Implementation of the terms of the CCAA is consistent with all applicable law and regulations.
- Implementation of the CCAA will not be in conflict with any ongoing conservation programs for species covered by the permit.
- The applicant has shown the capability for and the commitment to implementing the terms of the CCAA.[86]

CCAAs follow a similar approach as the no surprises policy. If the permittee properly implements the terms of the CCAA, then for those species adequately covered by the agreement,[87] changed circumstances will not require any conservation or mitigation measures in addition to those provided for in the agreement, and unforeseen circumstances will not result in any "commitment of additional land, water, or financial compensation or additional restriction on the use of land, water, or other natural resources beyond the level otherwise agreed upon for the species covered in the agreement."[88] The regulations contemplate that in the event of changed or unforeseen circumstances, the Service, or any state, local, or tribal government, would at its "own expense" take additional actions to conserve a species covered by a CCAA.[89] And the Service can revoke a CCAA only under limited circumstances; in addition to being revocable under the same conditions as any permit issued by the FWS, a CCAA is revocable upon a finding that continuation of the permitted activity would "appreciably reduce the likelihood of survival and recovery in the wild of any species."[90]

---

undertake to conserve the species, c) the benefits expected from the conservation agreement measures, d) the assurances provided by the Service that no additional measures will be required, e) monitoring, and f) notification requirements to give the Services an opportunity to rescue individuals of the species before any authorized incidental take occurs." 64 Fed. Reg. at 32,734–35.

86. 50 C.F.R. §§ 17.22(d)(2), 17.32(d)(2). See 64 Fed. Reg. at 32,713.

87. 50 C.F.R. §§ 17.22(d)(5), 17.32(d)(5). See 64 Fed. Reg. at 32,713 and 32,715.

88. Id.

89. 50 C.F.R. §§ 17.22(d)(6), 17.32(d)(6)).

90. 50 C.F.R. §§ 17.22(d)(7), 17.32(d)(7). See also 50 C.F.R. § 13.28(a)(1)–(4) (containing general conditions upon which any permit, including a CCAA, may be revoked).

A related tool is the candidate conservation agreement (CCA), designed to avoid the need for an ESA listing by having parties to the agreement engage in proconservation efforts. A CCA, unlike a CCAA, does not result in the issuance of an enhancement of survival permit. The Services' 2003 Policy for Evaluation of Conservation Efforts When Making Listing Determinations (PECE) promotes the development of CCAs, by taking into account CCAs when making listing decisions.[91] While it mostly serves as a mechanism for the Services to negotiate with federal or state land managers how lands might be managed to promote species conservation, and possibly avert a listing, a CCA can apply to activities on both federal and nonfederal lands.[92] One example of such an agreement is the effort to protect the Louisiana pine snake's habitat and avoid having the snake listed. The snake was found only in limited habitat areas in Louisiana and Texas, and in March 2004 state and federal agencies signed an agreement to protect habitat and the physical and biological features necessary to benefit the species.[93] And more recently, the Service entered into CCAs and CCAAs covering approximately 95 percent of the habitat for the dunes sagebrush lizard, potentially threatened by oil and gas activities in Texas and New Mexico.

6.6 Transferability

Many of these permits are transferable; for permits issued by the FWS, for instance, transferability and other matters are generally governed by the general permit procedures in 50 C.F.R. part 13.

---

91. 68 Fed. Reg. 15,100 (Mar. 28, 2003). The PECE policy requires reasonable certainty that the conservation measures will be implemented and effective. *See generally* Hadassah M. Reimer & Murray D. Feldman, *Give PECE a Chance: Evaluating Conservation Programs to Avoid Endangered Species Act Listings*, 56 ROCKY MTN. MIN. L. INST. 21 (2010). CCAAs are promoted as a tool that too can be used to avoid a listing decision, although their ability to do so is considered more difficult. *See* Michael J. Bean, *Landowner Incentives and the Endangered Species Act*, *in* ENDANGERED SPECIES ACT: LAW, POLICY, AND PERSPECTIVES 207, 212–13 (Donald C. Baur & Wm. Robert Irvin eds., 2010).

92. *See* U.S. Fish & Wildlife Serv., Using Existing Tools to Expand Cooperative Conservation for Candidate Species Across Federal and Non-Federal Lands (undated), http://www.fws.gov/endangered/esa-library/pdf/CCA-CCAA%20%20 final%20guidance%20signed%208Sept08.PDF.

93. *See* Angie Thorne, *Sneaky Snake Makes Support Challenging for Conservation Branch*, FT. POLK GUARDIAN, July 8, 2009, http://www.army.mil/article/24022/ sneaky-snake-makes-support-challenging-for-conservation-branch/.

Any transferees or successors to an individual holding a permit may avail themselves of the permit protections so long as they are otherwise qualified to hold such a permit[94] and provide adequate written assurances that they will fund and implement the terms of the permit.[95] For SHAs, the Services declined to require that a transferee renegotiate the baseline.[96]

6.7   Conservation Banks

Building on the idea of mitigation banking in the wetlands area, the FWS has begun to explore employing conservation banks as a mechanism for promoting species conservation. In 2003, the FWS issued a policy guidance intended to "provide a collaborative incentive-based approach to endangered species conservation."[97] Then, in 2008, the FWS issued recovery credit guidance.[98] The Service now has approved more than 120 such banks nationwide, although mostly in California, conserving roughly 100,000 acres. An essential element of this program is that lands will be managed for their ecological value and protected through a conservation easement or other property instrument, and in return the bank owner will receive credits for the identified species, which credits can then be used as mitigation for those species elsewhere.[99]

---

94.   50 C.F.R. § 13.25(b). See also 50 C.F.R. § 13.21(c) for a list of factors that may disqualify one from receiving any FWS permit.

95.   50 C.F.R. §§ 13.24 (successors), 13.25 (transferees).

96.   69 Fed. Reg. at 24,085.

97.   *See* Guidance for the Establishment, Use, and Operation of Conservation Banks (May 8, 2003), 68 Fed. Reg. 24,753, *available at* http://www.fws.gov/ endangered/esa-library/pdf/Conservation_Banking_Guidance.pdf.

98.   *See* Notice of Availability of Recovery Crediting Guidance, 73 Fed. Reg. 44,761 (July 31, 2008); Notice of Availability for Draft Recovery Crediting Guidance, 72 Fed. Reg. 62,258 (Nov. 2, 2007). *See also* U.S Fish & Wildlife Serv., Recovery Credits and Tax Deductions for Landowners, http://www.fws.gov/ endangered/landowners/recovery-credits.html.

99.   As of the writing of this book, the FWS is attempting to develop regulations that would create further incentives for landowners to implement voluntary conservation measures. Advance Notice of Proposed Rulemaking, Endangered and Threatened Wildlife and Plants: Expanding Incentives for Voluntary Conservation Actions Under the Endangered Species Act, 77 Fed. Reg. 15,352 (Mar. 15, 2012).

6.8   Intra-agency Section 7 Consultation Requirement and NEPA

The decision to grant a section 10 incidental take permit must be made, in part, "using the same standard as found in section 7(a)(2) of the Act."[100] Thus, the Act provides that prior to issuance of any section 10 permit, the Secretary must determine that the contemplated taking "will not appreciably reduce the likelihood of the survival and recovery of [any] species in the wild."[101] Because the issuance of a section 10 permit is a federal action, the issuing agency will engage in an internal section 7 consultation to ensure that no species of animal or plant is jeopardized by issuance of the permit.[102] If the level of take authorized in the section 10 permit and embedded in the intraservice consultation biological opinion subsequently exceeds that which is allowed, the parties must reinitiate consultation, possibly necessitating the issuance of a new biological opinion.[103] The Service also must comply with the requirements of the National Environmental Policy Act (NEPA).[104] This may require the preparation of either an environmental assessment (EA) or an environmental impact statement (EIS), depending upon the nature of the proposed activities. An HCP that qualifies as a low-effect HCP may be categorically excluded, however, from the requirement to prepare either an EA or an EIS.

6.9   Other Specific Section 10 Exceptions

In addition to the more common incidental take and enhancement of survival permits, the ESA provides for a variety of exceptions

---

100. H.R. Conf. Rep. No. 97-835, at 29 (1982), *reprinted in* 1982 U.S.C.C.A.N. 2860, 2870.

101. 16 U.S.C. § 1539(a)(2)(B)(iv). *See generally* Oliver A. Houck, *The Endangered Species Act and Its Implementation by the U.S. Departments of Interior and Commerce*, 64 U. Colo. L. Rev. 277, 353–54 (1993) (discussing the overlap of sections 7 and 9 of the ESA).

102. HCP Handbook, *supra* note 12, at 7-4. The section 7 conference process applies to proposed species. 16 U.S.C. § 1536(a)(4); 50 C.F.R. § 401.10.

103. *E.g.*, WildEarth Guardians v. U.S. Fish & Wildlife Serv., 622 F. Supp. 2d 1155, 1161 (D. Utah 2009) (noting that a new biological opinion had been issued).

104. Also, the Services may be required to comply with the National Historic Preservation Act, if applicable, as well as section 401 of the Clean Water Act, again if applicable. *See also* cases cited *supra* note 34 (application of NEPA).

applicable to specific situations, involving particular species, and in some cases applying only to particular persons.

For example, the ESA's hardship exemption provides that, under certain circumstances, the Secretary may, to minimize economic hardship, issue a permit exempting a person from application of the ESA's prohibitions for up to a year. The hardship exemption applies to situations in which a person has entered into a "contract with respect to a species" prior to publication in the *Federal Register* of notice of consideration of the species for listing, and prior to the final listing of the species, but only if application of the ESA's prohibitions would cause "undue economic hardship."[105]

In addition, section 10 of the ESA also authorizes trade in certain "pre-Act endangered species parts" (sperm whale oil and scrimshaw products);[106] certain takings and trade of listed species by Alaska natives;[107] and importation or possession of certain antique articles (at least 100 years old) composed of listed species.[108] Section 9 of the Act authorizes take in defense of human safety,[109] as well as activities associated with wildlife that was held in captivity or in a controlled environment, for noncommercial purposes, on December 28, 1973, or on the date the particular species was listed under the Act.[110] Finally, the ESA's takings prohibitions do not apply to raptors legally held in captivity or in a controlled environment on November 10, 1978, nor to the progeny of any such raptor.[111]

---

105. Section 10(b)(2) of the ESA defines *undue economic hardship* to include economic loss: "(A) resulting from inability to perform contracts with respect to species of fish and wildlife entered into prior to the date of publication in the *Federal Register* of a notice of consideration of such species as an endangered species; (B) to persons who for the year prior to the notice of consideration of such species . . . derived a substantial portion of their income from the lawful taking of the species; or (C) due to curtailment of certain subsistence takings of listed species." 16 U.S.C. § 1539(b)(2)(A)–(C).

106. 16 U.S.C. § 1539(f). For more about these exceptions, see Sam Kalen & Adam Pan, *Exceptions to the Take Prohibition, in* ENDANGERED SPECIES ACT: LAW, POLICY, AND PERSPECTIVES 193 (Donald C. Baur & Wm. Robert Irvin eds., 2010).

107. 16 U.S.C. § 1539(e) (defining *Alaska natives* to mean "any Indian, Aleut, or Eskimo who is an Alaskan Native who resides in Alaska; or any nonnative permanent resident of an Alaskan native village").

108. *Id.* § 1539(h).

109. *See* chapter 4, section 4.8.

110. 16 U.S.C. § 1538(b)(1).

111. *Id.* § 1538(b)(2)(A).

7 Section 7 Exemption Process

7.1   Overview

The exceptions to the Endangered Species Act's (ESA's) various prohibitions are limited and narrowly defined. Nonetheless, two circumstances exist when the ESA could conceivably allow the knowing elimination of an entire species. First, albeit highly unlikely, a person could lawfully kill even the last living member of a species in order to protect human safety.[1] Second, the Endangered Species Committee (ESC or "God Squad") may grant an exemption under section 7 of the Act, allowing a particular federal project to proceed despite its destructive effect on a listed species, even if it would lead to the extinction of that species.[2]

In 1978, the Supreme Court warned that federal actions that are likely to jeopardize the continued existence of listed species, or that adversely modify or destroy critical habitat, may not proceed.[3] Congress responded to the Court's decision by creating the ESA section 7 exemption process to resolve conflicts between proposed federal actions and ESA section 7 mandates.[4] The exemption process is available only in the rare instance when a section 7 consultation has yielded a determination both that a proposed federal action will jeopardize a listed species or will

---

1. *See* chapter 4, section 4.8.
2. *See generally* Jared des Rosiers, Note, *The Exemption Process Under the Endangered Species Act: How the "God Squad" Works and Why,* 66 Notre Dame L. Rev. 825 (1991).
3. Tenn. Valley Auth. v. Hill, 437 U.S. 153 (1978).
4. H.R. Rep. No. 95-1627, at 13 (1978), *reprinted in* 1978 U.S.C.C.A.N. 9461, 9463. Congress streamlined the exemption process in 1982. 1982 Endangered Species Act Amendments, Pub. L. No. 97-304, *reprinted in* 1982 U.S.C.C.A.N. 1411.

adversely modify critical habitat, and that no reasonable and prudent alternatives to the proposed federal action exist.[5] Although few exemptions have been granted by the Endangered Species Committee,[6] and most observers today believe that the process is not a viable option anymore, the exemption process nevertheless remains available (however remote) as a potential avenue for addressing otherwise irreconcilable conflicts between the needs of listed species and proposed federal activities.

7.2   Applying for an Exemption

Given the potential magnitude of an exemption decision, Congress narrowly defined who may apply for an exemption, and how and when an exemption application will be considered. The Fish and Wildlife Service (FWS) and the National Marine Fisheries Service (NMFS) likewise have promulgated extensive regulations governing nearly every aspect of the exemption process.[7]

7.2.1   Who May Apply for an Exemption

Three categories of persons may apply for an ESA section 7 exemption: (1) a federal agency, (2) the governor of a state in which an agency action will occur, and (3) a permit or license applicant.[8] The phrase "permit or license applicant" is defined more narrowly in the exemption context than in the ESA section 7 consultation context;[9] only those individuals whose applications for federal permits or licenses have been denied on ESA section

---

5. *See* chapter 5, section 5.4 (discussing jeopardy BOs and RPAs).
6. The most recent vote exempted 13 Bureau of Land Management timber sales, allowing impacts to northern spotted owls. Endangered Species Committee Notice of Decision, 57 Fed. Reg. 23,405 (1992). Prior to the spotted owl decision, the ESC voted to exempt the Grayrocks Reservoir project in Wyoming, allowing impacts to whooping cranes, but denied an exemption request to allow the Tellico Dam to proceed in spite of its impacts to the snail darter. *See generally* M. Lynn Corn & Pamela Baldwin, Cong. Research Serv., Endangered Species Act: The Listing and Exemption Processes 7–29 (May 8, 1990).
7. *See* 50 C.F.R. §§ 450–453.
8. 16 U.S.C. § 1536(g)(1); 50 C.F.R. § 451.02(c).
9. See chapter 5, section 5.9 for discussion of applicants in the section 7 consultation context.

7 grounds may apply for an exemption.[10] A private party whose proposed activities have no nexus to a federal project is not eligible to seek a section 7 exemption.

7.2.2   When to Apply for an Exemption

Section 7 consultation is a mandatory precursor to an application for an exemption.[11] The application must be submitted within 90 days "after the completion of the consultation process." A permit or license applicant, however, may wait up to 90 days after the federal agency has formally denied the license or permit at issue before filing.[12] If an applicant chooses to seek administrative review of an agency's denial of a permit or license, the period for seeking an exemption is tolled, pending final disposition of the administrative appeal.[13] And an applicant may not simultaneously seek administrative review of a permit or license denial while applying for an exemption.[14]

7.2.3   Contents of the Exemption Application

An exemption application is mailed to the appropriate Secretary at the address provided for by regulation,[15] and must contain

- basic information identifying the exemption applicant[16]
- a "comprehensive" description of the proposed action (and of the permit or license sought, when applicable)[17]
- a description of any remaining permit, license, or legal requirements that remain to be satisfied[18]
- a description of the consultation process that preceded the exemption application[19]

---

10.   16 U.S.C. § 1536(g)(1); 50 C.F.R. §§ 450.01, 451.02(c).
11.   16 U.S.C. § 1536(g)(2)(A).
12.   16 U.S.C. § 1536(g)(2)(A); 50 C.F.R. § 451(d).
13.   16 U.S.C. § 1536(g)(2)(A); 50 C.F.R. § 451(d).
14.   50 C.F.R. § 451.02(d)(2).
15.   50 C.F.R. § 451.02(b).
16.   50 C.F.R. § 451.02(e)(1) (requiring the exemption applicant to provide his or her name, mailing address, telephone number, and point of contact).
17.   *Id.* § 451.02(e)(2)(i)–(ii), (3)(i)–(ii), (4)(i)–(ii).
18.   *Id.* § 451.02(e)(2)(iii), (3)(iii), (4)(iii).
19.   *Id.* § 451.02(e)(2)(iv), (3)(vii), (4)(vi).

- copies of any biological assessment or biological opinion prepared[20]
- a statement describing why the proposed action cannot be modified to avoid violating section 7(a)(2) of the ESA[21]
- a description of the resources committed by the federal agency (or any permit or license applicant) to the proposed action subsequent to the initiation of consultation[22]

An exemption application also must include

- a complete statement of the nature and extent of the benefits of the proposed action
- a complete discussion of why the benefits of the project clearly outweigh the benefits of each considered alternative to the action
- a complete discussion of why none of the considered alternatives is reasonable and prudent
- a complete statement explaining why the proposed action is in the public interest
- a complete explanation of why the action is of regional or national significance
- a complete discussion of mitigation and enhancement measures proposed to be undertaken if an exemption is granted[23]

When the exemption applicant is a governor or a permit or license applicant, a copy of the application also must be provided (concurrent with filing the application) to the federal agency that denied the relevant license or permit.[24]

7.2.4   Initial Secretarial Action on the Application

Within 10 days of receiving an exemption application, the Secretary must determine whether it contains all the required

20. *Id.* § 451.02(e)(2)(v)–(vi), (3)(v)–(vi), (4)(iv), (4)(vi).
21. *Id.* § 451.02(e)(2)(viii), (3)(ix), (4)(viii).
22. *Id.* § 451.02(e)(2)(viii), 3(x); (4)(ix).
23. *Id.* § 451.02(e)(5)(i)–(vi).
24. *Id.* § 451.02(e)(6).

information.[25] If the Secretary rejects the application for lack of required information, the applicant may resubmit the application, but only within the original 90-day period provided for by regulation.[26] An exemption applicant, therefore, should consider submitting an application as soon as possible to allow time to cure any potential deficiencies. Upon receipt of the application, the Secretary will transmit a copy to the Secretary of State,[27] publish notice of the application in the *Federal Register*,[28] and promptly notify the members of the ESC[29] and the governor of each affected state.[30]

7.3   The Exemption Process, Phase I: Consideration by the Secretary

Having determined that an exemption application contains all the required information, the Secretary must quickly turn to a more demanding, substantive examination of the consultation process that preceded the application. During this early phase of the process, the Secretary alone determines whether the application will be summarily denied or submitted to the ESC.

7.3.1   Threshold Determinations

Within 20 days after receiving an exemption application (or longer if the exemption applicant agrees), the Secretary must make the following three findings:

1.   Whether any required biological assessment was conducted;
2.   To the extent determinable within the time period provided, whether the federal agency or permit or license

---

25.   *Id.* § 450.02(f).
26.   *Id.* § 450.02(f)(2).
27.   *Id.* § 450.02(g). This allows the Secretary of State to determine whether granting the exemption would violate treaties or other United States international obligations.
28.   *Id.* § 402.02(h). The *Federal Register* notice will summarize the information contained in the application, and will designate a place where anyone may obtain a copy of the application. *Id.*
29.   *Id.*
30.   50 C.F.R. § 451.03(b). After notification by the Secretary, the governor has 10 days to submit recommendations of individuals that the state wishes to represent the state on the ESC. *Id.*

applicant has refrained from making irreversible or irretrievable commitments of resources; and

3. Whether the federal agency and any permit or license applicant have carried out consultation in "good faith" and have made reasonable and responsible efforts to develop and fairly consider modifications or reasonable and prudent alternatives to the proposed action.[31]

If the Secretary makes a negative finding on any of these three threshold issues, the Secretary must deny the application and terminate the exemption process.[32] The Secretary also must notify the applicant in writing of such a finding, and the Secretary's denial constitutes final agency action for purposes of judicial review.[33] Conversely, if the Secretary makes a positive finding with respect to each threshold criterion, the Secretary notifies the exemption applicant in writing that the application will be submitted to the ESC.[34]

7.3.2   Hearings

Having determined that the application meets the threshold criteria, the Secretary must designate an administrative law judge (ALJ) to preside over at least one public hearing on the application.[35] The ALJ must be someone uninvolved in the underlying ESA consultation and issue, and ex parte communications with the ALJ are prohibited.[36] Although the Secretary sets the time period for conducting the hearing and closing the record,[37] the ALJ presides over the hearing, and is responsible for conducting any prehearing conference, ruling on motions, and determining whether the evidence offered is "relevant, material, and reliable."[38] The ALJ possesses broad latitude in conducting the hearing, and may subpoena the production of evidence and compel the attendance and testimony of witnesses.[39]

---

31.   16 U.S.C. § 1536(g)(3); 50 C.F.R. § 452.03(a)(1)–(3).
32.   16 U.S.C. § 1536(g)(3)(B); 50 C.F.R. § 452.03(c).
33.   16 U.S.C. § 1536(g)(3)(B); 50 C.F.R. § 452.03(c).
34.   16 U.S.C. § 1536(g)(3)(B); 50 C.F.R. § 452.03(c).
35.   16 U.S.C. § 1536(g)(4); 50 C.F.R. § 452.05(a).
36.   50 C.F.R. § 452.07.
37.   *Id.* § 452.05(a)(3).
38.   *Id.* § 452.05(b), (d).
39.   *Id.* § 452.05(g).

The hearing itself, to the extent practicable, must be conducted in accordance with the Administrative Procedure Act (APA),[40] and must be open to the public.[41] The parties to the hearing consist of the exemption applicant, the federal action agency proposing the underlying action, the Service (i.e., NMFS or FWS), and interveners whose motions to intervene have been granted.[42] At all times, the exemption applicant bears the burden of going forward with evidence to show that the criteria for exemption are met.[43] The hearing does not culminate in an ALJ's decision. Rather, the ALJ's responsibilities are fulfilled by certifying the record and transmitting it to the Secretary.[44] The Secretary bases a report on the record produced at the hearing, but may direct the ALJ to reopen the record and obtain additional information.[45]

7.3.3   The Secretary's Report

After receiving the ALJ's hearing record and transcript, and within 140 days from the date the Secretary initially determined that the threshold criteria for an eligible exemption had been met, the Secretary must submit a report to the ESC.[46] The report must discuss and summarize the following:

- the availability of reasonable and prudent alternatives to the proposed action
- the nature and extent of the benefits of the proposed action
- the nature and extent of the benefits of alternative courses of action consistent with conserving the species or its critical habitat

---

40. 16 U.S.C. § 1536(g)(4), (6). The Ninth Circuit overturned a 5–2 grant of an exemption to the Bureau of Land Management for certain timber sales, 57 Fed. Reg. 23,405 (June 3, 1992), because of impermissible ex parte contacts. Portland Audubon Soc'y v. Endangered Species Comm., 984 F.2d 1534 (9th Cir. 1993).
41. *Id.* § 1536(g)(8).
42. 50 C.F.R. § 452.06. The ALJ must approve a party's motion to intervene upon a finding that the intervener would contribute to a fair determination of the issues. *Id.*
43. 50 C.F.R. § 452.05(e).
44. *Id.* § 452.08.
45. *Id.*
46. 16 U.S.C. § 1536(g)(5); 50 C.F.R. § 452.08(b). The 140-day time limit may be modified by mutual agreement of the Secretary and the exemption applicant. *Id.*

- whether the proposed action is of national or regional significance
- whether the proposed action is in the public interest
- appropriate and reasonable mitigation and enhancement measures
- whether the federal agency and permit or license applicant, if any, have refrained from making any irreversible or irretrievable commitment of resources[47]

The next stage of the exemption process may now proceed, and the ESC must make a decision.

7.4   The Exemption Process, Phase II: The Endangered Species Committee

Congress created the ESC as "an administrative court of last resort."[48] Having been kept informed of the Secretary's progress in preparing his or her report,[49] the ESC must vote, and the members of this cabinet-level body must be personally accountable for their votes; no member may delegate his or her vote to anyone.[50]

7.4.1   The Committee

The ESC is composed of the following members:

- The Secretary of Agriculture
- The Secretary of the Army
- The Chairman of the Council of Economic Advisors
- The Administrator of the Environmental Protection Agency
- The Secretary of the Interior

---

47.   16 U.S.C. § 1536(g)(5)(A)–(D); 50 C.F.R. § 452.04(1)–(7).

48.   Portland Audubon Soc'y v. Endangered Species Comm., 984 F.2d 1534, 1541 (9th Cir. 1992) (quoting S. Rep. No. 97-418, at 17 (1982)).

49.   See, e.g., 16 U.S.C. § 1536(g)(4) (requiring that the hearing set by the Secretary be held "in consultation with" the members of the ESC); H.R. Rep. No. 97-567, at 29 (1982), reprinted in 1982 U.S.C.C.A.N. 2807, 2828–29 (noting that Congress intended the ESC to be fully informed and "thoroughly familiar" with the background evidence by the time it receives the Secretary's report).

50.   16 U.S.C. § 1536(e)(10); 50 C.F.R. § 453.05(c).

- The Administrator of the National Oceanic and Atmospheric Administration (NOAA)
- One individual from each affected state[51]

The Secretary of the Interior serves as the chair of the ESC,[52] and five members of the committee constitute the required quorum.[53] With respect to members from affected states, when more than one state is involved, the state members collectively have one vote on the committee and must determine among themselves how it will be cast.[54]

7.4.2   The Exemption Decision

Upon receipt of the Secretary's report, the ESC must, within 30 days, determine whether to grant the exemption.[55] Within this 30-day window, the ESC considers the report and may gather additional information on its own initiative;[56] the ESC may solicit written submissions from interested persons[57] and may even hold its own informal hearing.[58] The committee's hearing must be open to the public, and is governed by the provisions of the APA applicable to formal adjudications, including the prohibition on ex parte communications.[59] The committee shall grant an exemption if at least five members agree that

- there are no reasonable and prudent alternatives to the agency action;
- the benefits of such action clearly outweigh the benefits of alternative courses of action consistent with conserving the species or its critical habitat, and such action is in the public interest;
- the action is of regional or national significance; and

---

51.   16 U.S.C. § 1536(e)(3).
52.   *Id.* § 1536(e)(5)(B).
53.   *Id.* § 1536(e)(5)(A).
54.   50 C.F.R. § 453.05(d).
55.   16 U.S.C. § 1536(h)(1).
56.   *Id.* § 1536(h)(1)(A) (ESC may base its decision on the report of the Secretary and such other testimony or evidence" as it may receive).
57.   50 C.F.R. § 453.04(a).
58.   50 C.F.R. § 453.04(b).
59.   Portland Audubon Soc'y v. Endangered Species Comm., 984 F.2d 1534, 1549 (9th Cir. 1993).

- neither the federal agency concerned nor the exemption applicant made any irreversible or irretrievable commitment of resources.[60]

Once granted, an exemption is generally permanent in nature and covers all listed species that might be affected by the action, whether or not those species were covered in the biological assessment.[61]

7.4.3   Mitigation and Enhancement

When granting an exemption, the ESC must specify reasonable mitigation and enhancement measures to be implemented by the exemption applicant.[62] For example, when the ESC exempted 13 Bureau of Land Management (BLM) timber sales in 1992, the ESC required the BLM to mitigate the impacts of these sales on northern spotted owls by implementing the final recovery plan for the owl.[63] The exemption applicant is responsible for the cost of implementing mitigation and enhancement measures, and must report annually on its compliance efforts until all mitigation and enhancement measures have been completed.[64]

7.5   Special Cases

The ESA recognizes three circumstances when the normal exemption rules do not apply. First, in any area declared by the president to be a major disaster area, the president may exempt from

---

60. 16 U.S.C. § 1536(h)(1)(A); 50 C.F.R. § 453.03(a)(1). *See* Endangered Species Committee Notice of Decision, 57 Fed. Reg. 23,405 (1992) (applying the exemption criteria to deny exemption to 31 of 44 BLM timber sales).

61. 16 U.S.C. § 1536(h)(2); 50 C.F.R. § 453.03(c). Such blanket, permanent exemptions are available only if a BA was actually prepared. Likewise, an exemption may be declared temporary in nature if it would result in the extinction of species not considered during consultation. 16 U.S.C. § 1536(h)(2); 50 C.F.R. § 453.03(c).

62. 16 U.S.C. § 1536(h)(1)(B) and 50 C.F.R. § 450.01 (providing examples of appropriate mitigation and enhancement measures).

63. 57 Fed. Reg. at 23,408.

64. 16 U.S.C. § 1536(*l*). *E.g.,* Annual Report on Endangered Species Act Exemption, 64 Fed. Reg. 9153 (1999) (summarizing implementation of mitigation and enhancement measures for Grayrocks Reservoir exemption).

from the ESA any project to repair or replace public facilities, if (1) necessary to prevent recurrence of such a natural disaster and to reduce the potential loss of human lives, and (2) the situation is an emergency that does not allow the ordinary procedures to be followed.[65] Second, the ESC must grant an exemption whenever the Secretary of Defense finds that such exemption is necessary for reasons of national security.[66] Finally, the ESC is prohibited from even considering an exemption application if the Secretary of State determines that granting the exemption would result in a violation of international treaty or other international obligations of the United States.[67]

65. 16 U.S.C. § 1536(p).
66. 16 U.S.C. § 1536(j); 50 C.F.R. § 453.03(d).
67. 16 U.S.C. § 1536(i); 50 C.F.R. § 452.03(e).

8 Federal Interaction with States and Tribes

8.1   Overview

States historically protected wildlife in the United States.[1] Yet, since the passage of the first major national wildlife statute (the Lacey Act) in 1900,[2] Congress repeatedly has demonstrated its willingness to protect wildlife through federal legislation. And federal wildlife agencies now work closely with state wildlife agencies and play a major role in American wildlife conservation.

The Endangered Species Act (ESA), therefore, contemplates that states would play a role in helping conserve species. Nearly every major section of the ESA contains a provision recognizing the states' role in species conservation.[3] Indeed, the Act's legislative history demonstrates Congress's expectation that successful

---

1. See generally MICHAEL J. BEAN & MELANIE J. ROWLAND, THE EVOLUTION OF NATIONAL WILDLIFE LAW (1997); ERIC T. FRYFOGLE & DALE D. GOBLE, WILDLIFE LAW: A PRIMER (2009); see also John R. Ernst, Federalism and the Act, in BALANCING ON THE BRINK OF EXTINCTION: THE ENDANGERED SPECIES ACT AND LESSONS FOR THE FUTURE (Kathryn A. Kohm ed., 1993).

2. 16 U.S.C. § 701.

3. The ESA defines the term State to include "any of the several states, the District of Columbia, the Commonwealth of Puerto Rico, American Samoa, the Virgin Islands, Guam, and the trust territory of the Pacific Islands." 16 U.S.C. § 1532(17). The ESA also separately defines the term State agency to mean "any State agency, department, board, commission, or other governmental entity which is responsible for the management and conservation of fish, plant, or wildlife resources within a State." Id. § 1532(18). Some of the ESA's state role provisions refer to the States themselves and others to the State agency, see, e.g., id. § 1535(a) (calling for cooperation with the States); § 1533(i) (calling for Secretary's written justification to "the State agency" when the Secretary adopts a regulation under section 4 that "is in conflict with such comments" of a State agency submitted on the proposed regulation); San Luis & Delta-Mendota Water Auth. v. Badgley, 136 F. Supp. 2d 1136, 1151 (E.D. Cal. 2000) (holding that FWS violated ESA in listing decision where FWS did not submit the required section 4(i) written justification to the California Department of Fish and Game).

implementation of the ESA involves a good working arrangement between federal agencies and states.[4] Section 6 of the Act, in particular, encourages states to take an active role in the development and implementation of conservation programs. The table at the end of this chapter illustrates the statutory role of states in ESA activities.

8.2   The ESA as a Valid Exercise of Congressional Commerce Power

In 1997, the D.C. Circuit noted that 521 of 1,082 listed species existed wholly within the boundaries of single states.[5] Some, therefore, might question Congress's authority to regulate activities with respect to these intrastate species. Courts uniformly have held that the ESA is a valid exercise of Congress's power under the Constitution's commerce clause, and any state law that provides less protection to listed species is preempted.

Federal courts have long held that Congress's commerce clause power is a valid basis for federal wildlife legislation,[6] including the ESA.[7] But after the Supreme Court held that the federal Gun-Free School Zones Act of 1990 exceeded the congressional commerce clause authority,[8] some thought that the ESA, at least as applied to purely intrastate species, might be vulnerable to a constitutional challenge. In 1995, the National Association of Home Builders, along with other building industry plaintiffs, filed suit alleging that application of the ESA's section 9 prohibitions against take were unconstitutional as applied to the endangered Delhi Sands flower-loving fly.[9] The plaintiffs argued that because the fly was located entirely within an eight-mile radius

---

4. *See* H.R. Conf. Rep. No. 93-740 (1973), *reprinted in* 1973 U.S.C.C.A.N. 3001.

5. Nat'l Ass'n of Home Builders v. Babbitt, 130 F.3d 1041, 1052 (D.C. Cir. 1997), *cert. denied,* 524 U.S. 937 (1998).

6. *Id.* at 1054 n.15 (discussing cases upholding the Migratory Bird Treaty Act, the Lacey Act, and the Eagle Protection Act as valid exercise of Congress's commerce clause authority).

7. Palila v. Haw. Dep't of Land & Nat. Res., 471 F. Supp. 985, 992–95 (D. Haw. 1979) (holding that ESA protection of the palila, a bird found only in Hawaii, was a valid exercise of the commerce power).

8. United States v. Lopez, 514 U.S. 549 (1995).

9. *Nat'l Ass'n of Homebuilders,* 130 F.3d at 1045.

in two California counties, Congress's protection of the fly did not amount to a valid exercise of its commerce clause power. The D.C. Circuit disagreed with the plaintiffs and, citing the legislative history of the ESA, held that the loss of "biodiversity itself" has a substantial effect on interstate commerce;[10] the de minimis impact on commerce from individual circumstances (such as protection of a particular species of fly) "is of no consequence."[11] As such, protection of listed species in the "aggregate" bears a substantial relationship to interstate commerce and the use of the channels of interstate commerce.[12] Other courts similarly have rejected constitutional challenges.[13]

8.3   Preemption of State Law

Section 6(f) of the ESA[14] explicitly preempts state laws inconsistent with the Act. And on programs related to the importation, exportation, and commerce in listed species, state laws or regulations that prohibit what is allowed by the ESA, or that allow what is prohibited by the ESA, are void.[15] With respect to take of listed species, the Act provides that state laws may be more restrictive than the exemptions or permits allowed by the ESA, but may not be less restrictive.[16]

Section 6(g)(2) of the Act,[17] however, contains a provision apparently modifying section 6(f). Section 6(g)(2) provides that the Act's takings prohibitions do not apply with respect to the taking of listed species within any state that is, at the time of the taking,

10. *Id.* at 1052–54.
11. *Id.* at 1046.
12. *Id.*
13. *See* San Luis & Delta-Mendota Water Auth. v. Salazar, 638 F.3d 1163, 1175–77 (9th Cir. 2011), *cert. denied sub nom.* Stewart & Jasper Orchards v. Salazar, 132 S. Ct. 498 (2011); Alabama-Tombigbee Rivers Coal. v. Kempthorne, 477 F.3d 1250, 1277 (11th Cir. 2007); GDF Realty Invs., LTD v. Norton, 326 F.3d 622 (5th Cir. 2003); Rancho Viejo, L.L. Co. v. Norton, 323 F.3d 1062 (D.C. Cir. 2003); Gibbs v. Babbitt, 214 F.3d 483 (4th Cir. 2000).
14. 16 U.S.C. § 1535(f).
15. *Id.*
16. *Id.* In one interesting case, a court determined that regulations promulgated pursuant to another federal statute, the Animal Welfare Act, which also dealt with endangered species, were regulations that "implemented" the ESA for purposes of preemption. In Def. of Animals v. Cleveland Metroparks Zoo, 785 F. Supp. 100 (N.D. Ohio 1991).
17. 16 U.S.C. § 1535(g)(2)(A).

a party to a section 6(c) cooperative agreement, "except to the extent that the taking . . . is contrary to the law of such state."[18] In the only reported decision directly addressing this contradiction, the federal district court for the district of Montana ruled that section 6(f)'s explicit preemption of "less restrictive" state laws, combined with the Act's overriding goal of species conservation, meant that federal takings prohibitions applied in a "cooperative agreements state" despite a less restrictive state law.[19]

8.4   Section 6 Cooperative Agreements

Section 6 of the ESA provides for federal funding of state conservation programs benefiting endangered fish, wildlife, and plants.[20] The ESA cooperative agreement program was considered by Congress to be "essential" to an adequate endangered species program.[21] Any state with an "adequate and active" program for endangered and threatened species conservation[22] is entitled to enter into a cooperative agreement with the Secretary; states with cooperative agreements are eligible to receive as much as a 90 percent federal contribution toward the cost of implementing conservation measures.[23] In 1994, the Fish and Wildlife Service (FWS) and National Marine Fisheries Service (NMFS) promulgated a policy statement reaffirming the agencies' commitment to meeting the ESA section 6 requirement of cooperating, to the

---

18. *Id.* § 1535(g)(2)(A).

19. Swan View Coal., Inc. v. Turner, 824 F. Supp. 923 (D. Mont. 1992).

20. 16 U.S.C. § 1535(c). See 50 C.F.R. pt. 81 (FWS) and pt. 225 (NMFS) for regulations implementing the Cooperative Agreement Program of ESA section 6(c).

21. H.R. Conf. Rep. No. 93-740 (1973), *reprinted in* 1973 U.S.C.C.A.N. 3001, 3005.

22. The Act provides a detailed list of requirements for an adequate state program. *See* 16 U.S.C. §§ 1535(c)(1) (for fish and wildlife), 1535(c)(2) (for plants). Requirements for state programs pertaining to plants differ from those for fish and wildlife; plant programs need not include land acquisition. 16 U.S.C. § 1535(c)(2)(A)–(D).

23. For programs addressing species of interest to only one state, the federal contribution of funds is limited to 75 percent. 16 U.S.C. § 1535(d)(3)(i). With respect to joint agreements among states having a common interest in one or more listed species, the federal contribution of funds may be increased to 90 percent. 16 U.S.C. § 1535(d)(2)(ii). For information about the section 6 grant program, see U.S. Fish & Wildlife Serv., Section 6 of the Endangered Species Act http://www .fws.gov/midwest/endangered/grants/S6_grants.html; NMFS, NOAA Fisheries Serv., Cooperation with States: ESA Section 6 Program, http://www.nmfs.noaa.gov/pr/ conservation/states/.

maximum extent practicable, with the states in carrying out the ESA program.[24] Both Services have entered into agreements with states, and NMFS has its own guidance document for the criteria governing these agreements.[25] Some states appear to be exploring creative section 6 cooperative agreements that include the sharing of section 10 permitting responsibilities; as of the summer of 2012, Florida, for instance, is in the process of finalizing an agreement that is intended to establish "a more effective linkage" between Landscape Conservation Cooperative efforts and the incidental take permitting process for listed species.[26]

8.5   Role of Tribal Governments

Beginning in the 1990s, the Services began to explore how to involve tribal governments in aspects of the ESA decision-making process. This led to the development of the Joint Secretarial Order on American Indian Tribal Rights, Federal-Tribal Trust Responsibilities, and the Endangered Species Act (Secretarial Order No. 3206).[27] In the June 2007 Order, the Secretaries committed to "carry out their responsibilities under the [ESA] in a manner that harmonizes the Federal trust responsibility to tribes, tribal sovereignty and the statutory missions of the Departments and that

---

24. Notice of Interagency Cooperative Policy Regarding the Role of State Agencies in Endangered Species Act Activities, 59 Fed. Reg. 34,275 (1994).

25. *See* NMFS, NOAA Fisheries Serv., Cooperation with States: ESA Section 6 Program: Agreements, http://www.nmfs.noaa.gov/pr/conservation/states/#agreements.

26. *E.g.,* U.S. Fish & Wildlife Serv., North Florida Ecological Servs. Office, http://www.fws.gov/northflorida/Guidance-Docs/FWC_Section_6/20120514_gd_2012_FWS-FWC_Section%206_Coop_Agreement.htm (North Florida Ecological Service Office re Cooperative Agreement between the FWS and the Florida Fish and Wildlife Conservation Commission). Landscape conservation cooperatives are public-private partnerships that transcend political boundaries and employ holistic, collaborative, and adaptive principles to land, water, wildlife, and cultural resource management. *See* U.S. Fish & Wildlife Serv., Landscape Conservation Cooperatives, http://www.fws.gov/science/shc/lcc.html.

27. *See generally* MARREN SANDERS, IMPLEMENTING THE FEDERAL ENDANGERED SPECIES ACT IN INDIAN COUNTRY: THE PROMISE AND REALITY OF SECRETARIAL ORDER 3206 (Joint Occasional Papers on Native Aff., 2007); Charles F. Wilkinson, *The Role of Bilateralism in Fulfilling the Federal-Tribal Relationship: The Tribal Rights-Endangered Species Secretarial Order,* 72 WASH. L. REV. 1063 (1997). For a discussion of the role of tribes under the ESA, see Mary Gray Holt, *Indian Rights and the Endangered Species Act, in* ENDANGERED SPECIES ACT: LAW, POLICY, AND PERSPECTIVES 127 (Donald C. Baur & Wm. Robert Irvin eds., 2010).

strives to ensure that the Indian tribes do not bear a disproportion-
ate burden for the conservation of listed species so as to avoid
or minimize the potential for conflict and confrontation." That
commitment was underscored when President Clinton issued
Executive Order No. 13,175, in November 2000, confirming that
federal agencies must consult and coordinate with Indian tribes
on policies that impact Indian communities.[28] And on December
1, 2011, Secretary Salazar issued Secretarial Order 3317, updat-
ing, expanding, and clarifying the Department's policy on "consultation with American Indian and Alaska Native tribes," and
acknowledging "that the provisions for conducting consultation
in compliance with Executive Order . . . 13175 . . . are expressed
in the Department of the Interior Policy on Consultation with
Indian Tribes."[29]

Also, the FWS maintains a Tribal Wildlife Grant Program,[30]
and NMFS too provides opportunities for tribal grants, commensurate with the section 6 grant program.[31]

---

28. 65 Fed. Reg. 67,249–52 (Nov. 6, 2000).
29. Secretarial Order 3317 is available at http://www.doi.gov/tribes/upload/
SO-3317-Tribal-Consultation-Policy.pdf.
30. *See* U.S. Fish & Wildlife Serv., Tribal Wildlife Grant Overview, http://
www.fws.gov/nativeamerican/grants.html.
31. *See* NMFS, NOAA Fisheries Serv., Species Recovery Grants to Tribes,
http://www.nmfs.noaa.gov/pr/conservation/tribes.htm.

ESA Activities and the Respective Role of States

ESA Activity	State Role
Section 4— Listing and Critical Habitat Designations	Secretary must take into account efforts of the states to protect species, prior to making a listing determination. (16 U.S.C. § 1533(b)(1)(A))
	Secretary must give actual notice of any proposed listing, de-listing, or critical habitat designation to the relevant state wildlife agency and counties in which a species is believed to occur, and must invite comments from the state agency. (16 U.S.C. § 1533(b)(5)(A)(ii))
	Secretary must give actual notice of any emergency listing to the relevant state wildlife agency. (16 U.S.C. § 1533(b)(7)(D))
	Secretary must provide state with written justification upon Secretary's failure to adopt a state's comments or petition with respect to listing, critical habitat, or Section 4(d) rule designation. (16 U.S.C. § 1533(h))
Section 6— Agreements	States may enter into cooperative agreements with the Secretary, whereby the federal government contributes 75–90 percent of covered conservation program costs. (16 U.S.C. § 1535(c) & (d)(2))
	States may enter into management agreements for the administration and management of areas for the conservation of listed species. (16 U.S.C. § 1535(b))
Section 6— Land or Water Acquisition	Secretary must consult with states before acquiring any land or water for conservation of listed species. (16 U.S.C. § 1535(a))
Section 7— Consultation	Governor of a state that may ultimately wish to apply for a Section 7 exemption, pursuant to ESA Section 7(g), may (in cooperation with the Secretary) prepare a biological assessment with respect to a particular proposed federal action. (16 U.S.C. § 1536(c)(2))
	Interagency consultation is to ensure that agency action is not likely to result in the destruction or adverse modification of habitat of such species [consulted upon] which is determined by the Secretary, after consultation as appropriate with affected States, to be critical. (16 U.S.C. § 1536(a)(2))

(continued)

ESA Activities and the Respective Role of States (*continued*)

Section 7— Exemption Process	Governor of an affected state may apply for an exemption and initiate the Endangered Species Committee process. (16 U.S.C. § 1536(g)(1))
	One individual from each affected state may participate as a member of the Endangered Species Committee. (16 U.S.C. § 1536(e)(3)(G))
Section 8— International Conventions	Provisions relating to the Western Hemisphere Convention do not affect state authority, jurisdiction, or responsibility regarding resident fish and wildlife. (16 U.S.C. § 1537a(e)(4))
Section 9— Prohibited Acts with Respect to Listed Plants	The ESA prohibits damage to endangered plants when done in knowing violation of state laws. (16 U.S.C. § 1538(a)(2)(B))
Section 10— Permits	State may apply for and hold takings permits; in some cases, persons regulated by the state may avail themselves of the takings allowed pursuant to the permit. (See chapter 6)
Section 11— Enforcement	Secretary may, by agreement, utilize state personnel and resources to enforce the ESA. (16 U.S.C. § 1540(e)(1))

9 International Application of the ESA

Overview

"A primary factor bringing about the near extinction of many animals has been the demand created by the international trade in animals and animal products."[1] The Endangered Species Act (ESA) not surprisingly reflects this appreciation and implements aspects of the United States' commitment to protecting species worldwide. Congress, in the opening subsection of the ESA, recognized the United States' "international commitments"[2] with respect to conservation of fish, wildlife, and plants, and it further declared that the United States "has pledged itself as a sovereign state in the international community" to conserve to the extent practicable listed species pursuant to

- migratory bird treaties with Canada and Mexico;
- the Migratory and Endangered Bird Treaty with Japan;
- the Convention on Nature Protection and Wildlife Preservation in the Western Hemisphere (the Western Hemisphere Convention);
- the International Convention for the Northwest Atlantic Fisheries;
- the International Convention for the High Seas Fisheries of the North Pacific Ocean;
- the Convention on International Trade in Endangered Species of Wild Fauna and Flora (CITES); and
- other international agreements.[3]

---

1. LEWIS REGENSTEIN, THE POLITICS OF EXTINCTION: THE SHOCKING STORY OF THE WORLD'S ENDANGERED WILDLIFE 120 (1975).
2. 16 U.S.C. § 1531(a)(5).
3. 16 U.S.C. § 1531(a)(4).

In the Act's second subsection, Congress expressly declared that one of the purposes of the ESA is to take such steps as may be appropriate to achieve the purposes of these listed treaties and conventions.[4] To that end, the ESA contains several provisions specifically addressing international concerns. In addition, some, but not all, of the Act's general provisions apply outside United States boundaries. Finally, the ESA formally implements two of the referenced conventions: CITES and the Western Hemisphere Convention.[5] The ESA, on the whole, represents a clear demonstration of a "congressional commitment to worldwide conservation efforts."[6]

9.2   International Applicability

Generally, federal statutes are presumed to apply only within the territorial jurisdiction of the United States, and courts require a clear expression of congressional intent to apply a statute beyond U.S. boundaries.[7] And, while the ESA contains various references to international agreements and concerns, most of its principal provisions apply only within the United States, its territorial waters, or upon the "high seas."[8] The following sections summarize those aspects of the ESA that have some role in the international arena.

9.3   Listing of Species

The ESA, like its predecessor statute, the Endangered Species Conservation Act of 1969,[9] authorizes the listing of any species of fish, wildlife, or plant, without regard to whether a species' range lies

---

4. 16 U.S.C. § 1531(b).

5. *See* section 9.5 (discussing CITES and the Western Hemisphere Convention).

6. Defenders of Wildlife v. Lujan, 911 F.2d 117, 123 (8th Cir. 1990), *rev'd on other grounds,* 504 U.S. 555 (1992).

7. Morrison v. Nat'l Australia Bank Ltd., 130 S. Ct. 2869, 2878 (2010).

8. The term *high seas* is not defined in the ESA or its implementing regulations.

9. Pub. L. No. 91-135, 83 Stat. 275 (1969).

within the United States. Of the more than 1,900 species on the endangered or threatened list, roughly one-fourth occur outside the United States.[10] The ESA, therefore, provides some guidance for the listing of foreign species. For example, when considering any listing, the Secretary must take into account the efforts being made by any foreign nation or political subdivision of a foreign nation to protect the species within any area under its jurisdiction, or on the high seas.[11] In addition, if the Secretary proposes a regulation to implement a listing decision, the Secretary must, insofar as practicable, give notice of the proposed regulation to each foreign nation where the species is believed to occur, or whose citizens harvest the species on the high seas, and the Secretary must invite the comment of such nations on proposed listing regulations.[12]

9.4   Limits on the ESA's Applicability

For the most part, the ESA's section 7 obligations, its requirements for designating critical habitat, and the need to establish recovery plans do not apply to activities abroad. To begin with, the ESA section 4 provision governing the designation of critical habitat is silent with respect to designations of lands in foreign nations. Yet, with the implicit approval of Congress,[13] the Services expressly addressed this issue, by declaring through regulation that "critical habitat shall not be designated within foreign countries or in other areas outside the United States' jurisdiction."[14] Next, section 4 recovery plans similarly are not prepared for foreign species. This reflects the practical reality that the United States would have no means of implementing management activities abroad.

Finally, the ESA's section 7 consultation provision and substantive mandate[15] do not expressly address whether they apply to

---

10. U.S. Fish and Wildlife Serv., Species Reports, http://ecos.fws.gov/tess_public/pub/Boxscore.do (last visited Jan. 5, 2012).
11. 16 U.S.C. § 1533(b)(1)(A).
12. *Id.* §1533(b)(5).
13. *See* H.R. Rep. No. 97-567, at 20 (1982), *reprinted in* 1982 U.S.C.C.A.N. 2807, 2820 (agreeing with the Department of the Interior's Solicitor's Office that critical habitat designation in foreign countries or on the high seas would be "inappropriate").
14. 50 C.F.R. § 424.13(h).
15. *See* chapter 5 (discussing the section 7 consultation process).

federal agency actions carried out in foreign countries. The joint consultation regulations promulgated by the Services in 1978 extended the scope of section 7 to foreign countries,[16] but the Services reversed themselves in the 1986 (and still current) regulations, concluding that section 7 extends only to federal actions carried out in whole or in part by federal agencies in the United States or upon the high seas.[17] The Services justified this change in approach based upon "the apparent domestic orientation of the consultation and exemption processes," and because of potential "interference with the sovereignty of foreign nations."[18] One federal appeals court held that the 1986 regulations improperly limited the geographic scope of section 7,[19] but the U.S. Supreme Court reversed the decision on procedural grounds, concluding that the plaintiffs lacked standing.[20] The 1986 rule limiting section 7 to the United States and the high seas still applies.

9.5   Implementation of CITES and the Western Hemisphere Convention

A detailed discussion of international wildlife treaties and conventions is well beyond the scope of this book. Indeed, several chapters would be necessary to fully explain the operation of CITES,[21] its complicated import/export requirements, and its permit application processes. This section provides a brief overview

---

16.   43 Fed. Reg. 874 (1978).
17.   50 C.F.R. § 402.02.
18.   Preamble to Final Rule, 51 Fed. Reg. 19,926, 19,929 (1986).
19.   *See* Defenders of Wildlife v. Lujan, 911 F.2d 117, 122–25 (8th Cir. 1990).
20.   Defenders of Wildlife v. Lujan, 504 U.S. 555 (1992). Concurring, Justice Stevens disagreed with the majority's opinion on standing, but on the merits expressed the view that section 7 does not apply to activities in foreign countries. 504 U.S. at 581 (Stevens, J., concurring).
21.   Convention on International Trade in Endangered Species of Wild Fauna and Flora, Mar. 3, 1973, 27 U.S.T. 1087, T.I.A.S. No. 8249 [hereinafter CITES]. For an overview of CITES, see Pervaze A. Sheikh & M. Lynne Corn, Cong. Res. Serv., The Convention on International Trade in Endangered Species of Wild Fauna and Flora (CITES): Background and Issues (Feb. 5, 2008). *See also* W. Michael Young & Holly Wheeler, *The Convention on International Trade in Endangered Species of Wild Fauna and Flora, in* Endangered Species Act: Law, Policy, and Perspectives 317 (Donald C. Baur & Wm. Robert Irvin eds., 2010); Michael De Alessi, *Protecting Endangered Species at Home and Abroad: The International Conservation Effects of the Endangered Species Act and its Relationship to CITES, in* Rebuilding the Ark: New Perspectives on Endangered Species Act Reform 201 (Jonathan H. Adler ed., 2011).

of the significant aspects of CITES and the Western Hemisphere Convention,[22] with an emphasis on the role of the ESA as the implementing statute for each.

9.5.1   CITES

The idea of an international agreement arose in the 1960s and resulted in CITES, in force since 1975,[23] with a membership that now includes more than 170 parties.[24] CITES broadly proclaims the parties' recognition of the need to protect "wild fauna and flora in their many beautiful and varied forms"[25] and translates this lofty goal into more detailed requirements, creating an intricate regulatory scheme governing international trade in wildlife and plants. Section 8a of the ESA formally implements CITES for the United States.[26] In particular, CITES requires that each party designate a Management Authority and a Scientific Authority, and ESA section 8a(a) designates the Secretary of the Interior as both the Management Authority and the Scientific Authority.[27] Sections 8 and 8a of the ESA, moreover, create a multilayered approach to conserving listed species abroad, including committing the United States to the "worldwide" protection of listed species, authorizing financial assistance to foreign countries,[28] and directing the encouragement of foreign conservation efforts as well as bilateral or multilateral agreements with foreign nations.[29]

Similar to the ESA, CITES applies only to certain designated, or listed, species.[30] While the ESA creates two lists of covered species (endangered and threatened), CITES contains three separate lists, denoted simply as appendices I, II, and III.[31] Different

---

22. Convention on Natural Protection and Wildlife Preservation in the Western Hemisphere, Oct. 12, 1940, 56 Stat. 1354, T.S. No. 981.

23. *Id.* art. XXII, 27 U.S.T. at 1115. *See generally* WILLEM WIJNSTEKERS, THE EVOLUTION OF CITES (CITES Secretariat, 9th ed. 2011).

24. CITES, List of Contracting Parties, http://www.cites.org/eng/disc/parties/alphabet.php.

25. CITES, *supra* note 21, 27 U.S.T. at 1091.

26. 16 U.S.C. § 1537a(a)–(d) (establishing the Secretary of the Interior as the "Management Authority" and the "Scientific Authority" pursuant to CITES).

27. *See* 50 C.F.R. § 23.6.

28. 16 U.S.C. §1537a(a). This provision applies to species listed by the United States as endangered or threatened pursuant to section 4 of the ESA.

29. 16 U.S.C. §1537(b).

30. 16 U.S.C. § 1537. Section 8, as originally passed, applied only to fish and wildlife species; Congress authorized plant conservation efforts abroad in 1979. Pub. L. No. 96-159, § 5, 93 Stat. 1228 (1979).

31. *See* 50 C.F.R. § 23.4.

regulatory requirements apply to species listed in each appendix. CITES now protects several thousand species of animals, and many thousands of species of plants.[32]

Species are added to or removed from appendices I and II only by a two-thirds vote of the parties present and voting at a particular conference of the parties,[33] but any party may unilaterally add species to or remove species from appendix III.[34] Appendix I species are those threatened with extinction and that are or may be affected by trade; these species are subject to "particularly strict regulations."[35] Appendix II species are those that may not yet be threatened with extinction but that may become so without strict regulation of trade in those species.[36] Finally, appendix III species are any species identified by any convention party as being subject to regulation within its jurisdiction and for which the convention party needs the cooperation of other parties in the control of trade.[37] Because CITES emphasizes species threatened by trade, the ESA lists of endangered and threatened species do not perfectly overlap with the three CITES appendices. Also, "CITES allows for downlisting to Appendix II (and therefore, to trade of) threatened and endangered species if it can be shown that trade is *not detrimental* to the survival of the species," while the ESA "requires that permits to import threatened and endangered species will only be issued when it can be demonstrated that trade will result in *enhancing the survival* of the species."[38]

Any person engaging in international trade involving species listed under CITES must comply with detailed permitting

---

32. For CITES information and species, see http://www.cites.org/eng/disc/species.php; *see also* the checklist of CITES species at http://www.cites.org/eng/resources/pub/checklist11/index.html.

33. CITES, *supra* note 21, art. XV, 27 U.S.T. at 1110–12. When the FWS proposes changes to the appendices, it provides the public with notice and opportunity to comment on any proposed amendments at the next Conference of the Parties. *See, e.g.,* Conference of the Parties to the Convention on International Trade in Endangered Species of Wild Fauna and Flora (CITES); Sixteenth Regular Meeting: Taxa Being Considered for Amendments to the CITES Appendices, 77 Fed. Reg. 21,798 (Apr. 11, 2012).

34. CITES, *supra* note 21, art. XVI, 27 U.S.T. at 1113–14.

35. *Id.* art. 11(1), 27 U.S.T. at 1092.

36. *Id.* art. II(2)(a), 27 U.S.T. at 1092. In a provision analogous to the ESA's provision for listing species similar in appearance to endangered or threatened species, Appendix II may also include species that must be subject to regulation in order to control trade in other Appendix II species. *Id.* art. II(2)(b).

37. *Id.* art. 11(3), 27 U.S.T. at 1092.

38. De Alessi, *supra* note 21, at 206.

requirements.[39] ESA section 9(c) expressly makes unlawful any trade in, or possession of, any specimen of fish, wildlife, or plant in violation of CITES. Before the Management Authority will issue a permit for any appendix I or appendix II species, CITES requires that the Scientific Authority for the country of export make certain determinations, such as that such export will not be "detrimental to the survival of that species" (a nondetriment finding).[40] The Secretary's determination must be based upon the best available biological information derived from professionally accepted wildlife management practices, and estimates of population size are not required.[41] In the United States, the U.S. Department of Agriculture Animal Health Inspection Service inspects plants that are being imported or exported, sometimes inspecting over 50 million listed plants a year. Failure to secure the necessary and timely export permit may result in civil forfeiture in the United States when a party seeks to import the regulated specimen.[42] And export permits are to be granted only if the Management Authority has determined that the specimen was obtained in accordance with the laws of the country.[43]

A variety of special issues and rules apply to particular specimens being imported or exported. Captive breeding operations, for instance, for some specimens are treated separately.[44] In a highly publicized example, the Fish and Wildlife Service (FWS) had excluded certain specimens of U.S. captive-bred live wildlife and sport-hunted trophies of the scimitar-horned oryx, addax,

---

39. See 50 C.F.R. part 23 for permitting requirements for importing, exporting, reexporting, or possessing species listed under CITES. See also Revision of Regulations Implementing the Convention on International Trade in Endangered Species of Wild Fauna and Flora (CITES), 72 Fed. Reg. 48,402 (Aug. 23, 2007) (final rule). In 2012, the FWS proposed revisions to its permitting regulations, including removing obsolete requirements in part 17 and including certain requirements in part 23. Revisions of Regulations Implementing the Convention on International Trade in Endangered Species of Wild Fauna and Flora (CITES); Updates Following the Fifteenth Meeting of the Parties to CITES, 77 Fed. Reg. 14,200 (Mar. 8, 2012) (proposed rule). The program also may preempt inconsistent state laws. See Man Hing Ivory & Imps., Inc. v. Deukmejian, 702 F.2d 760 (9th Cir. 1983); H.J. Justin & Sons, Inc. v. Deukmejian, 702 F.2d 758 (9th Cir. 1983).
40. CITES, *supra* note 21, art. IV, 27 U.S.T. at 1095.
41. 16 U.S.C. § 1537a(c).
42. See Conservation Force v. Salazar, 646 F.3d 1240 (9th Cir. 2011) (challenging civil forfeiture of leopard skin and skull as violating the Civil Asset Forfeiture Reform Act of 2000).
43. See Castlewood Prods., LLC v. Norton, 365 F.3d 1076 (D.C. Cir. 2004).
44. See 50 C.F.R. § 17.21(g) (allowing take, trade, and commercial activity when the purpose of such activity is to enhance the propagation or survival of the affected species). See generally Young & Wheeler, *supra* note 21, at 323–24.

and dama gazelle from the take and export prohibitions under the ESA, but later had to remove this exclusion after a court held that the exclusion had been improperly adopted.[45] Imported sport trophies present another unique problem.[46] Species listed on appendix I and endangered under the ESA require an import permit, with exacting standards. For some specimens, the Secretary moreover will only allow the importation upon certain conditions and findings, such as upon an enhancement finding for importing specimens of sport-hunted African elephants.[47]

9.5.2   Western Hemisphere Convention

In addition to implementing CITES, section 8a of the ESA[48] implements the Western Hemisphere Convention. The Secretary of the Interior, in cooperation with the Secretary of State, acts on behalf of the United States in all issues respecting the Western Hemisphere Convention.[49] Though in place since 1940, the Western Hemisphere Convention has gone largely unnoticed until relatively recently.[50] Congress specifically directed the Secretary of the Interior to take such steps as are necessary to implement the Western Hemisphere Convention, including but not limited to:

---

45. *See* 77 Fed. Reg. 431 (Jan. 5, 2012); Friends of Animals v. Salazar, 626 F. Supp. 2d 102 (D.D.C. 2009). *Cf.* 50 C.F.R. § 17.21(h). After many years, the Service added the three African antelope species to the ESA list and included an exemption (allowing take, trade, transportation, and sale) for captive-bred populations undertaken in compliance with certain requirements. 70 Fed. Reg. 52,310, 52,319 (Sept. 2, 2005). The Service's rescission of its earlier rule is currently in litigation. *See* Safari Club Int'l v. Salazar, 11-CV-01564 (D.D.C. Mar. 16, 2012).
46. *See* Young & Wheeler, *supra* note 21, at 325–26 (discussing trade in hunting trophies). The FWS has been reluctant to issue section 10 permits for importing sport hunting trophies. *See* FWS, Draft Policy for Enhancement-of-Survival Permits for Foreign Species Listed Under the Endangered Species Act, 68 Fed. Reg. 49,512 (Aug. 18, 2003). *See also* Conservation Force v. Salazar, 2012 WL 1059732 (D.D.C. 2012) (noting delay in issuing wood bison trophies, and remanding back to Service decision to deny import permits); Conservation Force v. Salazar, 811 F. Supp. 2d 18 (D.D.C. 2011) (markhor importation permits).
47. *See, e.g.,* Franks v. Salazar, 816 F. Supp. 2d 49 (D.D.C. 2011). *See also* Marcum v. Salazar, 810 F. Supp. 2d 56 (D.D.C. 2011) (involving attempt to import hunted African elephants from Zambia, and concluding that challenges to permit denials may not be brought under the ESA citizen suit provision).
48. 16 U.S.C. § 1537a(e).
49. *Id.*
50. For a discussion of the Western Hemisphere Convention, see Mark C. Trexler & Laura H. Kosloff, *International Implementation: The Longest Arm of the Law?* 114–33, *in* BALANCING ON THE BRINK OF EXTINCTION: THE ENDANGERED SPECIES ACT AND LESSONS FOR THE FUTURE (Kathryn A. Kohm ed., 1993).

1. Cooperating with other parties and international organizations to develop personnel, resources, and programs to facilitate implementation of the convention;
2. Identifying species of birds that migrate between the United States and other contracting parties, and taking steps to conserve these species; and
3. Identifying measures necessary and appropriate to implement provisions of the convention addressing the protection of wild plants.[51]

Since 1983, the Secretary of the Interior, through FWS, has implemented the Western Hemisphere Program by supporting such programs as graduate student training, reserve manager training, and construction of biological documentation centers; and by supporting university environmental education and migratory bird conservation through small grants.[52] The parties to the program developed a broad initiative in 2003, although in the last few years, total leveraged funding amounts aggregated have been less than $1 million.

9.6   Prohibited Acts

Section 9 of the ESA limits the scope of prohibited take of listed species of fish or wildlife to the United States, its territorial seas, and the high seas.[53] But the Act also broadly prohibits certain other types of activities, such as the import, export, and "foreign commerce"[54] of listed species. ESA section 9(c) also makes unlawful and a violation of the ESA any trade or possession of species

---

51. 16 U.S.C. § 1537a(e)(2).
52. *See generally* FWS, Western Hemisphere Migratory Species Initiative, http://www.fws.gov/international/DIC/WHMSI/whmsi_eng.html. The Multinational Species Conservation Fund also often works in conjunction with CITES to fund conservation efforts. *See* Pervaze A. Sheikh & M. Lynee Corn, Cong. Res. Serv., International Species Conservation Funds (Mar. 5, 2010).
53. 16 U.S.C. § 1538(a)(1)(B), (C). *See* 18 U.S.C. § 5 (defining *United States* for purposes of criminal jurisdiction); 18 U.S.C. § 7 (defining *special maritime and territorial jurisdiction of the United States*).
54. *See generally* 16 U.S.C. § 1538(a), (b), (d). *See also* 16 U.S.C. § 1532(9) (defining *foreign commerce* very broadly to include transactions between persons in foreign countries).

in violation of CITES.[55] "A specimen that has been traded contrary to CITES becomes contraband at the time it enters the jurisdiction of the United States."[56] This does not, however, expand the reach of the Act beyond the United States, because it still only applies these prohibitions to "person[s] subject to the jurisdiction of the United States."[57] But if trade in the specimen is not prohibited under CITES, and the species is listed under the ESA, a party can import the specimen if they satisfy the requirements of section 10 or section 4(d) of the ESA.[58]

In addition, although the Secretary may, after consultation with the Secretary of State or the Secretary of Treasury, as appropriate, conduct law enforcement investigations in foreign countries,[59] jurisdictional realities limit the extent to which the Act's prohibitions apply.

55. 16 U.S.C. § 1538(c). See also 16 U.S.C. § 1540(a)(1), (2) (prescribing civil and criminal penalties for violation of ESA section 9(c)); United States v. Place, 2012 WL 3569712 (1st Cir. Aug. 21, 2012) (crime to violate CITES regulations).

56. 72 Fed. Reg. at 48,405.

57. 16 U.S.C. §§ 1538(a)(1), (2), 1538(g).

58. A section 4(d) rule, for instance, applies to some species of saltwater crocodiles listed under the ESA, allowing the import of body parts under the premise that it might enhance conservation programs in the species' native land. 61 Fed. Reg. 32,356 (June 24, 1996).

59. 16 U.S.C. § 1537a(d).

10 Experimental Populations

10.1   Overview

As discussed in chapter 3, section 7(a)(1)[1] of the Endangered Species Act (ESA) directs all federal agencies to carry out programs for the conservation of endangered species. The Act defines *conservation* to include "live trapping, and transplantation."[2] But early efforts to relocate endangered species were often plagued by staunch local opposition concerned with the strict take prohibitions applicable to the relocated species.[3]

In 1982, Congress amended the ESA to "relax certain restrictions" governing experimental populations, with the goal of encouraging private support for reintroduction efforts.[4] Through section 10(j) of the ESA,[5] Congress created a flexible approach for the reintroduction of endangered and threatened species. As discussed in this chapter, the degree of protection afforded an "experimental population" under section 10(j) can vary considerably, depending on whether the particular population is designated as "essential" or "nonessential." Also, because experimental

---

1.   16 U.S.C. § 1536(a)(1).

2.   *Id.* § 1532(3).

3.   *See* H.R. Rep. No. 97-567, at 17 (1982), *reprinted in* 1982 U.S.C.C.A.N. 2807, 2817 ("Another shortcoming of the Act is its tendency to discourage voluntary introduction of species in areas of their historic range. State F&W agencies had probed the feasibility of introducing such experimental populations, but they feared political opposition to reintroducing species unless some assurances were simultaneously extended to prevent the creation of Endangered Species Act problems."). *See generally* Mimi S. Wolok, *Experimenting with Experimental Populations,* 26 Envtl. L. Rep. 10,018 (1996).

4.   H.R. Rep. No. 97-567, *supra* note 3, at 33, 1982 U.S.C.C.A.N. at 2833. *See also* Wyo. Farm Bureau Fed'n v. Babbitt, 199 F.3d 1224, 1231 (10th Cir. 2000).

5.   16 U.S.C. § 1539(j).

populations are classified as "threatened"[6] rather than as "endangered" species, special regulations under section 4(d) (applicable to threatened species) may be tailored to address the needs of each particular species, as well as any concerns of the public. Since inception of the experimental population program, the Fish and Wildlife Service (FWS) has exercised its authority rather cautiously and to date has avoided designating essential experimental populations.[7]

10.2   Establishing an Experimental Population

Section 10(j) authorizes the Secretary to establish an experimental population of a listed species. An experimental population is defined as "any population (including any offspring arising solely therefrom) authorized by the Secretary for release . . . but only when, and at such times as, the population is wholly separate geographically from nonexperimental populations of the same species."[8] When establishing an experimental population, the Secretary may authorize the transportation and release of any

---

6.   16 U.S.C. § 1539(j)(2)(C).

7.   Congress expected that "in most cases experimental populations will not be essential." H.R. CONF. REP. NO. 97-835, at 34 (1982). The designations are in 50 C.F.R. §§ 17.84, 17.85. The NMFS has been less active in developing experimental populations, but recent efforts exist. *See, e.g.,* Omnibus Public Land Management Act of 2009, Pub. L. No. 111-11, § 10011 (Mar. 30, 2009) (re California Central Valley spring-run chinook salmon reintroduction into San Joaquin River); 76 Fed. Reg. 28,715 (May 18, 2011) (proposed rule for designation of nonessential experimental population for Middle Columbia River steelhead above the Pelton Round Butte Hydroelectric Project).

8.   16 U.S.C. § 1593(j)(2). The regulations further define an experimental population as

> an introduced and/or designated population (including any off-spring arising solely therefrom) that has been so designated in accordance with the procedures of this subpart but only when, and at such times as the population is wholly separate geographically from nonexperimental populations of the same species. Where part of an experimental population overlaps with natural populations of the same species on a particular occasion, but is wholly separate at other times, specimens of the experimental population will not be recognized as such while in the area of overlap. That is, experimental status will only be recognized outside the area of overlap. Thus, such a population shall be treated as experimental only when the times of geographic separation are reasonably predictable; e.g., fixed migration patterns, natural or man-made barriers. A population is not treated as experimental if total separation will occur solely as a result of random and unpredictable events.

50 C.F.R. § 17.80(a).

"population (including eggs, propagules, or individuals) of an endangered or threatened species outside its current range."[9] Before authorizing the release of any experimental population, however, the Secretary must employ the "best scientific and commercial data available," determine if the release will further the conservation of the species,[10] and consider

- the possible adverse affects on existing populations resulting from removal of individuals, eggs, or propagules for introduction elsewhere
- the likelihood that the experimental population will become established and survive in the foreseeable future
- the relative effects that the experimental population will have on the recovery of the species
- the effects of existing or anticipated federal, state, or private activities within or adjacent to the experimental population area[11]

The release area must be "suitable natural habitat" outside of the species' "current natural range" and yet within the "probable historic range" of the species, unless such habitat has been "unsuitably and irreversibly altered or destroyed," in which case a release may occur in areas not formerly occupied by the species.[12]

The Secretary must follow the informal rulemaking process under the Administrative Procedure Act (APA) when establishing an experimental population, and any such regulation must contain the following:

- appropriate means to identify the experimental population, its location, migration, numbers, and so forth
- management restrictions, protective measures, or other special management concerns
- a process for the periodic review and evaluation of the success or failure of the release and the effect of the release on the conservation and recovery of the species[13]

---

9.   16 U.S.C. § 1539(j)(2)(A).
10.   16 U.S.C. § 1539(j)(2)(A). See chapter 2, section 2.3 for a discussion of "best scientific and commercial data available."
11.   50 C.F.R. § 17.81(b)(1)–(4).
12.   50 C.F.R. § 17.81(a).
13.   50 C.F.R. § 17.81(c)(1), (3), (4).

And when developing and implementing an experimental population rule, the Secretary has committed to consulting with all affected stakeholders.[14] Also, the regulation may establish any applicable prohibitions,[15] as discussed later in this chapter.

Specimens collected for relocation may come from any existing population of the species, including populations not currently listed under the Act.[16] Section 10(a)(1)(A) research permits and "enhancement of survival" permits[17] are the vehicles used to authorize activities necessary to collect, relocate, establish, and maintain an experimental population, while avoiding inadvertent injury to the species as a whole.[18]

10.3   **Essential versus Nonessential Experimental Populations**

Prior to authorizing the release of any experimental population, the Secretary must determine whether the population is "essential to the continued existence of an endangered species or a threatened species."[19] An *essential experimental population* is one "whose loss would be likely to appreciably reduce the likelihood of the survival of the species in the wild"; all other experimental populations are to be classified as nonessential.[20] The two primary regulatory distinctions between essential and nonessential experimental populations are found in application of the Act's critical habitat and section 7 consultation provisions.

---

14. 50 C.F.R. § 17.81(d). The Secretary's decision to propose an experimental population triggers the National Environmental Policy Act, as well. *E.g.,* Forest Guardians v. U.S. Fish & Wildlife Serv., 611 F.3d 692, 700 (10th Cir. 2010).

15. 50 C.F.R. § 17.82.

16. United States v. McKittrick, 142 F.3d 1170, 1174 (9th Cir. 1998) (Secretary does not have to deplete endangered or threatened populations in order to gather individuals for creation of an experimental population).

17. *See* chapter 6, section 6.4 (discussing enhancement of survival permits).

18. 50 C.F.R. § 17.81. *See* 16 U.S.C. § 1539(d) (providing that no section 10 permit may be issued if doing so would operate to the disadvantage of the species).

19. 16 U.S.C. § 1539(j)(2)(B); 50 C.F.R. § 17.81(c)(II).

20. 50 C.F.R. § 17.80(b).

10.4   Geographic Separation

A population designated as experimental remains so only at such times as the population is "wholly separate geographically from non-experimental populations of the same species."[21] The issue of geographic overlap between experimental populations and natural populations of the same species was "carefully considered" by Congress when enacting the experimental population provision.[22] Congress was concerned about the need to "protect natural populations and . . . avoid potential complicated problems of law enforcement" triggered by experimental populations.[23] Congress noted that when such overlap occurs, the experimental population designation does not apply within the area of overlap, and thus the full protections afforded a listed, nonexperimental population apply to both the naturally occurring population and the reintroduced population. Conversely, when the sporadically overlapping populations are geographically separated, the reintroduced population is afforded the reduced level of protection of an experimental population, but only when the times of geographical separation are "reasonably predictable" and not a result of "random and [un]predictable events."[24]

The FWS interprets the geographic overlap concept as applying to populations, not individual members of the species, such as lone dispersers. This interpretation has been affirmed in two cases involving the reintroduction of gray wolves.[25] In 1994, FWS promulgated final rules authorizing the establishment of an experimental population of gray wolves in Yellowstone National Park, central Idaho, and southwestern Montana.[26] In *Wyoming Farm Bureau,* the U.S. Court of Appeals for the Tenth Circuit upheld FWS's determination that the ESA's geographic separation requirement applies only to "population" overlap and not to overlap with "lone dispersers" or individuals of a species.[27] The naturally occurring, individual wolves in the reintroduction area did not amount to

---

21.   16 U.S.C. § 1539(j)(1).

22.   H.R. Rep. No. 97-567, at 33–34 (1982), *reprinted in* 1982 U.S.C.C.A.N. 2833.

23.   *Id.*

24.   *Id. See also* 50 C.F.R. § 17.80 (largely mirroring H.R. Rep. No. 97-567).

25.   United States v. McKittrick, 142 F.3d 1170, 1175 (10th Cir. 1998); Wyo. Farm Bureau Fed'n v. Babbitt, 199 F.3d 1224, 1234–37 (10th Cir. 2000).

26.   59 Fed. Reg. 60,252 (1994) (codified at 50 C.F.R. § 17.84(1)).

27.   *Wyo. Farm Bureau,* 199 F.3d at 1233–36.

a population, and thus the reintroduced wolves remained "wholly separate geographically" from any known *population* of naturally occurring wolves. The Tenth Circuit again deferred to the Secretary's interpretation for the reintroduction of the northern Aplomado falcon.[28] The Ninth Circuit Court of Appeals reached the same conclusion in an ESA section 9 criminal case.[29] On appeal of his conviction for unlawfully taking, possessing, and transporting a gray wolf (a member of the same experimental population at issue in *Wyoming Farm Bureau),* defendant McKittrick challenged the validity of the experimental population designation. In upholding McKittrick's conviction, the appeals court deferred to FWS's interpretation that the "wholly separate geographically" requirement applies only to populations, not to individual animals.[30]

10.5   Critical Habitat

The Secretary may designate critical habitat for an essential experimental population[31] but not for nonessential experimental populations. Even for essential populations, critical habitat designation is slightly limited: When the essential experimental population overlaps with a natural population of the same species during certain periods of the year, no critical habitat should be designated in the area of overlap, unless the designation is done as a revision to the natural population's critical habitat.[32]

10.6   Section 7 Consultation

For purposes of the consultation provisions of section 7 of the ESA,[33] nonessential experimental populations are treated as species proposed to be listed, except for nonessential populations occurring within a national park or a national wildlife refuge.[34] Sections 7(a)(1)

---

28. Forest Guardians v. U.S. Fish & Wildlife Serv., 611 F.3d 692 (10th Cir. 2010).
29. *McKittrick,* 142 F.3d 1170.
30. *Id.* at 1175 ("sporadic sightings of isolated indigenous wolves in the release area, lone wolves, or 'dispersers,' do not constitute a population").
31. 16 U.S.C. § 1539(j)(2)(C)(ii); 50 C.F.R. § 17.81(f).
32. *Id.*
33. 16 U.S.C. 1536(a)(2). *See* chapter 5, section 5.4 (discussing ESA section 7 consultation).
34. 16 U.S.C. § 1539(j)(C)(i); 50 C.F.R. § 17.83(a).

and 7(a)(2) apply to populations inside units of a national park or wildlife refuge. For populations outside any national park or wildlife refuge, neither a section 7 consultation nor the section 7 prohibition against jeopardy is required for federal actions affecting nonessential experimental populations. Instead, the less stringent section 7(a)(4) "conferencing" requirement applies to proposed actions that are "likely to jeopardize" a nonessential population.[35] Section 7(a)(4) requires that federal agencies "confer" with the Service on proposed actions that are likely to jeopardize the continued existence of a species proposed for listing, but the results of this conference are advisory and do not prohibit agency actions. By contrast, experimental populations determined to be essential to the survival of a species are treated as any other threatened species for section 7 purposes.[36]

10.7   Special Rules with Respect to Experimental Populations

Each member of an experimental population, whether essential or nonessential, is treated as a threatened species.[37] In Congress's view, such a designation "grants the Secretary broad flexibility in promulgating regulations to protect such species," and these regulations "can even allow the taking of threatened animals."[38] For example, Congress noted that special regulations associated with experimental populations could allow for such activities as the inadvertent take of experimental fish species by fishermen seeking other species in the same body of water, or the taking of predators such as wolves, if depredations occur or if the release of a population would continue to be frustrated by public opposition.[39] In *Gibbs v. Babbitt*,[40] the U.S. Court of Appeals for the Fourth Circuit upheld a special regulation for the taking of the experimental population of red wolves.

---

35. 16 U.S.C. § 1536(a)(4). *See* chapter 5, section 5.7 (discussing ESA section 7 conferencing).
36. 50 C.F.R. § 17.83(b).
37. 16 U.S.C. § 1539(2)(C).
38. H.R. Rep. No. 97-567, *supra* note 3, 1982 U.S.C.C.A.N. at 2834 ("the committee fully expects that there will be instances where the regulations allow for the incidental take of experimental populations . . . [and] that, where appropriate, the regulations could allow for the directed taking of experimental populations").
39. *Id.*
40. 214 F.3d 483 (4th Cir. 2000).

11 Citizen Suits, Standing, and Procedure

11.1 Overview

Generally, the Secretaries of Interior, Commerce, Agriculture, Treasury, and the U.S. Coast Guard all enforce aspects of the Endangered Species Act (ESA).[1] But Congress also intended to facilitate enforcement by allowing private citizens to act as "private attorneys general."[2] ESA section 11(g)[3] allows "any person"[4] to bring suit in federal district court to enforce the Act.[5] This chapter discusses the statutory scope of ESA section 11(g), as well as its constitutional and procedural limitations. Although the ESA's citizen suit provision is premised on the belief that citizens can hold government enforcement agencies accountable, the process requires that citizens initiating such lawsuits have proper standing and give appropriate notice.

11.2 Scope of ESA Section 11(g)

The Act's citizen suit provision grants district courts jurisdiction over suits when the relevant agency has neglected a nondiscretionary duty.[6] Under section 11(g), any person may "commence a

---

1. 16 U.S.C. § 1540(e).
2. Bennett v. Spear, 520 U.S. 154, 165 (1997).
3. 16 U.S.C. § 1540(g).
4. *See* 16 U.S.C. § 1531(13) (defining *person* very broadly).
5. 16 U.S.C. § 1540(g)(3)(A). *See also* 16 U.S.C. § 1540(g)(1) (providing that the district court shall have jurisdiction, without regard to the amount in controversy or the citizenship of the parties).
6. 16 U.S.C. § 1540(g)(1)(c) (authorizing suit "where there is alleged a failure of the Secretary to perform any act or duty under section 1533 of this title which is not discretionary with the Secretary").

civil suit on his own behalf" to attempt to enjoin any entity alleged to be in violation of a 1533 duty.[7] The citizen suit provision specifically allows suits:

> (A) To enjoin any person, including the United States and any other governmental instrumentality or agency (to the extent permitted by the 11th Amendment to the Constitution) who is alleged to be in violation of any provision of [the ESA or its regulations]; or
> (B) To compel the Secretary to apply [section 4(d) or section 9 prohibitions] with respect to the taking of any resident endangered species or threatened species within any state; or
> (C) Against the Secretary where there is alleged a failure of the Secretary to perform any act or duty under [section 4 of the Act] which is not discretionary with the Secretary.[8]

Subsection (A) enables private parties to enforce the ESA against any party regulated by the Act, including private entities and government agencies.[9] Any violation of the Act or its regulations is actionable under subsection (A), except that for actions against the Secretaries of Interior or Commerce, citizen suits are generally limited under section 11(g) to the discrete subject matter outlined in subsections (B) and (C)—that is, section 9 and section 4(d) enforcement and nondiscretionary actions under section 4 of the Act.[10] Challenges to the Secretary's implementation or "administration"[11] of the Act are not reviewable under ESA section 11(g). In some circumstances, actions not reviewable under section 11(g) may be reviewed under the Administrative Procedure Act.

11.3   60-Day Notice Requirement

As a general rule, ESA section 11(g) citizen suits may not be commenced prior to 60 days after written notice has been given to the Secretary, and to any alleged violator intended to be a defendant

---

7. *Id.*
8. 16 U.S.C. § 1540(g)(1)(A)–(C).
9. *Id.*
10. *See, e.g.,* Bennett v. Spear, 520 U.S. 154, 172 (1997) (concluding that critical habitat designation under section 4(d)(2) of the Act is a nondiscretionary action reviewable under the citizen suit provision).
11. *Bennett,* 520 U.S. at 173–75 (concluding that allegations regarding the Secretary's failure to perform his duties as administrator of the Act are not reviewable under section 11(g)). *See also* Salmon Spawning and Recovery Alliance v. U.S. Customs and Border Prot., 550 F.3d 1121, 1129 (Fed. Cir. 2008) (citizen suit provision not available to challenge implementation and enforcement of the Act).

in the lawsuit.[12] A few exceptions exist to this 60-day statutory notice requirement. No notice, for instance, is required for actions challenging the grant of an exemption by the Endangered Species Committee.[13] Also, an action may be brought immediately after notification of the alleged violation when the violation would immediately affect a legal interest of the plaintiff.[14] This includes actions alleging that the Secretary has failed to perform a nondiscretionary duty under ESA section 4, which actions may proceed "immediately" after notification to the Secretary if there is an "emergency posing a significant risk to the well being of any species."[15] Potential litigants should be aware that the emergency exception to the 60-day notice requirement is strictly limited to alleged failures of the Secretary to perform *nondiscretionary* acts under section 4 (listing, critical habitat, recovery planning) of the ESA.[16]

The purpose of the 60-day notice requirement is to afford people advance notice of perceived violations of the statute and to ensure that they are given an opportunity to review their actions and take corrective measures if warranted.[17] The 60-day notice provision, therefore, establishes a "litigation-free window" allowing parties time to resolve disputes short of litigation.[18] Since the Supreme Court's discussion of notice requirements in

---

12. 16 U.S.C. § 1540(g)(2)(A), (B), (C). No action may be commenced under subsections 1540(g)(1)(A) or (B) if the Secretary has commenced action to impose a penalty or is diligently prosecuting the violator. Citizens must give the target a 60-day notice of intent to file an ESA suit. 16 U.S.C. § 1540(g)(2)(C). The "appropriate" Secretary must be provided notice. *See* Hawksbill Sea Turtle v. Federal Emergency Management Auth., 126 F.3d 461, 473 (3d Cir. 1997) (because the Departments of Interior and Commerce shared jurisdiction over sea turtles, notification of only the Secretary of the Interior, and not the Secretary of Commerce, was insufficient to meet the 60-day notice requirement).

13. 16 U.S.C. § 1536(m).

14. 43 U.S.C. § 1349(a)(3); *see also* Brown v. Offshore Specialty Fabricators, Inc., 663 F.3d 759, 768 (2011) (describing and rejecting plaintiff's claim that their rights are immediately affected by defendant's conduct); Pac. Nw. Venison Producers v. Smitch, 20 F.3d 1008 (9th Cir. 1994) (dismissal of plaintiffs' ESA claim for lack of notice would be unjust because it would have precluded timely relief to save breeding season).

15. 16 U.S.C. § 1540(g)(2)(C). *See* Me. Audubon Soc'y v. Purslow, 672 F. Supp. 528, 531 (D. Me. 1987) (dismissing suit against developer who was planning to subdivide property near bald eagle nest for failure to provide 60-day notice, and holding that Congress did not intend to "grant citizen plaintiffs immediate enforcement power").

16. *E.g.*, Salmon Spawning and Recovery Alliance v. U.S. Customs and Border Prot., 532 F.3d 1338 (Fed. Cir. 2008).

17. Water Keeper Alliance v. U.S. Dep't of Def., 271 F.3d 21, 29–30 (1st Cir. 2001); Sw. Ctr. for Biological Diversity v. Bureau of Reclamation, 143 F.3d 515, 521 (9th Cir. 1998).

18. *Sw. Ctr. for Biological Diversity*, 143 F.3d at 521.

Hallstrom v. Tillamook,[19] lower courts are increasingly demanding strict compliance with such statutory notice requirements.

A proper 60-day notice must sufficiently alert the recipient of the actual alleged violation so that the recipient may attempt to abate the violation.[20] (This is true as well for Clean Water Act cases that require a notice of intent to sue.) The notice must be "sufficiently specific to inform the alleged violator about what it [was] doing wrong" in order that the violator knows what corrective actions may be taken.[21] Courts typically require that letters give notice of the asserted violation and intent to sue.[22] Likewise, "comments" submitted in a formal rulemaking process do not meet the Act's notice requirement "no matter how vehemently it [the notice] may have conveyed the party's intention to go to court if the rule ultimately adopted were not to [the commentor's] liking."[23] Some courts even suggest that the particular plaintiffs must be identified in a required notice letter.[24] And an otherwise adequate notice that is provided less than 60 days prior to commencement of the lawsuit is generally insufficient to meet the requirements of the Act.[25] Failure to satisfy the substantive and timing requirements for a valid 60-day notice may result in dismissal of the suit, with some courts treating the issue as "jurisdictional."[26] Potential ESA citizen suit

---

19.   493 U.S. 1037 (1989) (in case involving RCRA's citizen suit provision, comparable to the ESA's citizen suit provision, Court held that failure to provide notice mandates dismissal of the case).

20.   *Id. See also* Ctr. for Biological Diversity v. Marina Point Dev., 535 F.3d 1026 (9th Cir. 2008) (CWA notice issue); Water Keeper Alliance v. U.S. Dep't of Def., 271 F.3d 21, 29–30 (1st Cir. 2001) (CWA notice).

21.   Nat. Res. Council of Me. v. Int'l Paper Co., 424 F. Supp. 2d 235, 249 (D. Me. 2006) (CWA case).

22.   Save the Yaak Comm. v. Block, 840 F.2d 714, 721 (9th Cir. 1988) (notice was also insufficient in that it was never sent to the Secretary). *But cf.* Marbled Murrelet v. Babbitt, 83 F.3d 1068, 1072–73 (9th Cir. 1996) (notice was adequate to support suit based on ESA section 7, even though the focus of the letter was on ESA section 9 violations and section 7 was mentioned in only one part of the letter).

23.   Humane Soc'y v. Lujan, 768 F. Supp. 360, 362 (D.D.C. 1991).

24.   *See* N.M. Citizens for Clean Air & Water v. Espanola Mercantile Co., 72 F.3d 830, 833 (10th Cir. 1996); Wash. Trout v. McCain Foods, Inc., 45 F.3d 1351, 1354–55 (9th Cir. 1995).

25.   *See* Me. Audubon Soc'y v. Purslow, 907 F.2d 265 (1st Cir. 1990) (filing suit one day after providing notice was clearly insufficient); Protect Our Eagles' Trees (POETS) v. City of Lawrence, 715 F. Supp. 996, 998 (D. Kan. 1989) (16 days' notice of lawsuit was insufficient). *But cf.* Sierra Club v. Block, 614 F. Supp. 488, 492 (D.D.C. 1985) (court allowed citizen suit to proceed in spite of only 35 days' notice because (1) the defendant agencies had responded to the notice of intent in writing, stating that they were not reconsidering their position; and (2) the defendants were not prejudiced).

26.   *See, e.g.,* Am. Rivers v. NMFS, 126 F.3d 1118, 1124 (9th Cir. 1997); Hawksbill Sea Turtle v. Federal Emergency Management Auth., 126 F.3d 461, 471 (3d Cir. 1997).

plaintiffs, therefore, should send a notice at least 60 days prior to commencing an action. The notice should (1) be clearly identified as a 60-day notice under ESA section 11(g), (2) clearly discuss all issues that the party believes could be the basis of a future lawsuit, and (3) be served upon the Secretary and the alleged ESA violator.

11.4   APA Review as an Alternative to an ESA Citizen Suit

The Administrative Procedure Act (APA) provides a right to judicial review of any "final agency action for which there is no other adequate remedy in a court."[27] Certain final actions of the Secretary that are not reviewable under ESA section 11(g)(B) or (C) are reviewable under the APA. For example, in *Bennett v. Spear,* the Supreme Court held that alleged deficiencies in a final biological opinion (BO) prepared by the Fish and Wildlife Service (FWS) were not reviewable under ESA section 11(g), but that the BO represented final agency action reviewable under the APA.[28]

One important aspect of APA review of secretarial decisions under the ESA is that, unlike citizen suit review, the APA does not require 60 days' notice prior to filing suit. In one informative post-*Bennett* case, the U.S. Court of Appeals for the Ninth Circuit held that an environmental plaintiff's challenge to the adequacy of a BO was an APA claim, and that therefore the ESA citizen suit 60-day notice requirement was inapplicable.[29] Conversely, the court also ruled that claims filed in the same lawsuit against two federal action agencies (the Bureau of Reclamation and the U.S. Army Corps of Engineers) were ESA citizen suit claims and subject to the 60-day notice requirement.[30]

27.   5 U.S.C. § 704.

28.   Bennett v. Spear, 520 U.S. 154, 174–79 (1997). *See generally* Sam Kalen, *Standing on Its Last Legs:* Bennett v. Spear *and the Past and Future of Standing in Environmental Cases*, 13 J. Land Use & Envtl. L. 1 (1997).

29.   Am. Rivers v. NMFS, 126 F.3d 1118, 1124–25 (9th Cir. 1997). *See also* Earth Island Inst. v. Albright, 147 F.3d 1352, 1357–58 (Fed. Cir. 1998) (discussing that "maladministration" of the ESA is not reviewable under ESA section 11(g), but rather under the APA).

30.   *Am. Rivers*, 126 F.3d at 1125. Whether under ESA section 11(g) or the APA, parties should ensure that a court of appeals does not otherwise have exclusive jurisdiction over particular agency decisions. *See* Am. Bird Conservancy v. FCC, 545 F.3d 1190 (9th Cir. 2008) (ESA citizen suit case could not be brought in district court, when court of appeals exercised exclusive jurisdiction over actions of the FCC).

Plaintiffs, however, should be cautious if they presume that they have a choice between APA or ESA citizen suit review. If an action may proceed pursuant to ESA section 11(g), a plaintiff should proceed in compliance with section 11(g) and, indeed, may prefer to do so. And little is likely to be accomplished if plaintiffs attempt to circumvent the notice requirements of the ESA by merely "re-styling their claims to fit within the APA."[31] Likewise, for actions not reviewable as section 11(g) citizen suits, plaintiffs must satisfy the APA's requirement that the "action" being challenged is "final" and therefore otherwise reviewable.[32] Yet it has become common practice even in APA-styled claims for plaintiffs to comply with the section 11(g) notice requirements, possibly with the goal of securing attorneys' fees under the citizen suit provision.[33]

11.5   Standing

Article III of the Constitution requires that a party satisfy the "irreducible constitutional minimum" of standing to ensure that there is a proper case or controversy, and the ESA does not otherwise relax the constitutionally minimum standing requirements.[34] In addition to constitutional standing, the federal courts also have created "self-imposed" limits on the exercise of federal jurisdiction, referred to collectively as "prudential" standing requirements.[35] One particular element of prudential standing, the so-called zone-of-interest test, has until fairly recently limited standing in ESA cases to persons seeking to further the environmental and

---

31. Citizens Interested in Bow Run, Inc. v. Edrington, 781 F. Supp. 1502 (D. Or. 1991).

32. *Bennett*, 520 U.S. at 175. Challenges to import permit decisions by the Service have been held to be improper citizen suit cases and must be brought under the APA. *E.g.*, Conservation Force v. Salazar, 2012 WL 1059732 (D.D.C. 2012).

33. And the Ninth Circuit has suggested that distinguishing between the two types of cases is not all that significant. W. Watersheds Project v. Kraayenbrink, 632 F.3d 472, 481 (9th Cir. 2011). *But cf.* Coos Cnty. Bd. of Cnty. Comm'rs v. Kempthorne, 531 F.3d 792, 801–12 (9th Cir. 2008) (discussing both the citizen suit provision and the APA on a claim involving a failure to delist a species).

34. Lujan v. Defenders of Wildlife, 504 U.S. 555, 560 (1992) (reaffirming the applicability of Article III standing requirements and denying standing to environmental plaintiffs seeking to challenge FWS/NMFS rule excluding agency actions carried out abroad from ESA section 7 consultation).

35. *Bennett*, 520 U.S. at 163.

conservation goals of the Act. Since the Supreme Court's decision in *Bennett v. Spear*,[36] however, the zone-of-interest test generally no longer inhibits ESA citizen suits.

11.5.1   Article III Standing

In a 1992 case challenging the Services' regulations excluding agency actions carried out abroad from ESA section 7 consultation requirements, the Supreme Court reiterated the Article III requirements for standing.[37] Article III standing requires satisfying three elements:

1. The plaintiff must have suffered an "injury in fact."
2. There must be a causal connection between the injury and the conduct complained of.
3. It must be likely that the injury will be redressed by a decision favorable to the plaintiffs.[38]

More than one court has observed that "standing is not a concept that can be defined by strict metes and bounds and is not susceptible to facile application; so litigation about standing often results in a close call."[39] Although a detailed discussion of Article III standing is beyond the scope of this book,[40] any person filing or defending against an ESA citizen suit must have at least a general understanding of the three-prong test for Article III standing articulated in *Defenders of Wildlife*. And parties should appreciate that questions of Article III standing can be raised at any time during a proceeding.[41]

---

36. *Id.*
37. *Defenders of Wildlife*, 504 U.S. at 560.
38. *Id.*
39. Pac. N.W. Generating Coop. v. Brown, 38 F.3d 1058, 1066 (9th Cir. 1994) (citations omitted).
40. *See generally* Robin Kundis Craig, *Removing "The Cloak of Standing Inquiry": Pollution Regulation, Public Health, and Private Risk in the Injury-in-Fact Analysis*, 29 Cardozo L. Rev. 149 (2007); Cass R. Sunstein, *What's Standing After Lujan? Of Citizen Suits, "Injuries," and Article III*, 91 Mich. L. Rev. 163 (1992).
41. Pac. Rivers Council v. U.S. Forest Serv., 2012 WL 336133 (9th Cir. Feb. 3, 2012) (standing challenged for the first time on appeal); Ctr. for Biological Diversity v. Kempthorne, 588 F.3d 701, 707 (9th Cir. 2009). *See also* W. Watersheds Project v. Kraayenbrink, 632 F.3d 472, 482 (9th Cir. 2011).

11.5.1.1   Prong 1: "Injury in Fact"

To have an injury in fact, a plaintiff must have suffered an inva-
sion of a legally protected interest that is both (1) concrete and
particularized and (2) actual or imminent, as opposed to merely
"conjectural" or "hypothetical."[42] Even though "purely aesthetic"
interests are legally cognizable for purposes of standing,[43] plaintiffs must show some actual and imminent injury to their aesthetic
(or other) interests.[44] For example, in *Defenders of Wildlife,* the
plaintiffs alleged that the Secretaries' failure to apply ESA section
7 consultation requirements abroad would injure members who
had visited, and planned to return to, Sri Lanka and Egypt (the
sites of two proposed federal projects) to observe endangered
wildlife.[45] The Court, however, noted that the mere fact that the
plaintiffs had visited those locations in the past to observe endangered animals, and planned to return "someday," was simply

42. *Defenders of Wildlife,* 504 U.S. at 560. Even State plaintiffs alleging special solicitude for standing purposes must establish a concrete injury. *See* Wyoming v. U.S. Dep't of the Interior, 674 F.3d 1220 (10th Cir. 2012); Del. Dep't of
Nat. Res. & Envtl Control v. FERC, 558 F.3d 575, 579 n.6 (D.C. Cir. 2009).
43. *Defenders of Wildlife,* 504 U.S. at 563–64 (citing Sierra Club v. Morton,
405 U.S. 727 (1972)). *See also* Summers v. Earth Island Inst., 555 U.S. 488, 494
(2009). An injury-in-fact may be aesthetic and/or psychological. Animal Legal Def.
Fund v. Glickman, 154 F.3d 426, 430–31 (D.C. Cir. 1998) (en banc) ("Because
USDA regulations permit the nonhuman primates in zoos, such as the Long Island
Game Farm and Zoological Park to be housed in isolation, Marc Jurnove was
exposed to and will be exposed in the future to behaviors exhibited by these animals which indicate the psychological debilitation caused by social deprivation.
Observing these behaviors caused and will cause Marc Jurnove personal distress
and aesthetic and emotional injury"). But visits without evidence of aesthetic
injury may not suffice. *See* Am. Soc'y for Prevention of Cruelty to Animals v. Feld
Entm't, Inc., 659 F.3d 13 (D.C. Cir. 2011); *see also* Wilderness Soc'y v. Rey, 622
F.3d 1251 (9th Cir. 2010).
44. *See, e.g.,* Humane Soc'y v. Hodel, 840 F.2d 45, 52 (D.C. Cir. 1988) (plaintiffs adequately alleged injury based upon FWS decision to open wildlife refuges
to hunting, thereby "forcing members to witness animal corpses and environmental degradation . . . [and] depleting the supply of animals and birds refuge visitors
seek to view"). The Supreme Court has indicated that even when a party invokes
standing based on a procedural injury, it must still have some concrete interest.
See Summers v. Earth Island Inst., 555 U.S. 488, 496 (2009). This is often satisfied
with a proximity to the area. *E.g.,* Sierra Club v. U.S. Army Corps of Eng'rs, 645
F.3d 978 (8th Cir. 2011) (proximity and engagement in bird watching and other
activities).
45. An organization or association has standing to bring suit on behalf of its
members when (1) its members would otherwise have standing to sue in their own
right; (2) the interests it seeks to protect are germane to the organization's purpose;
and (3) neither the claim asserted nor the relief requested requires the participation
of individual members in the lawsuit. Friends of the Earth, Inc. v. Laidlaw Envtl.
Serv., 528 U.S. 167, 181 (2000); Hunt v. Wash. State Apple Advertising Comm'n,
432 U.S. 333, 343 (1977).

not sufficient to show actual or imminent injury.[46] Likewise, the Court rejected the plaintiffs' purportedly novel "animal nexus" or "vocational nexus" theories, holding that injury cannot be shown merely because one has an interest—even a professional interest—in observing an animal.[47]

Since the Court's decision in *Defenders of Wildlife*, plaintiffs in ESA cases arguably have become adept at successfully articulating the necessary Article III injury to establish standing. Examples of such injuries include injury to the ability to observe and study wolves;[48] injury to economic interests, such as receipt of a water supply from Bureau of Reclamation reservoirs;[49] and injury to property, based upon a showing of past flooding and an increased threat of future flooding.[50] Yet in *Summers v. Earth Island Institute*,[51] the Court recently reaffirmed the importance of establishing a temporal or geographic nexus by the plaintiff to the area arguably adversely affected by the defendant's alleged conduct.

11.5.1.2   Prong 2: "Causation"

Plaintiffs must show a causal connection between their injury and the conduct complained of.[52] An "attenuated chain of conjecture"

---

46. *Defenders of Wildlife*, 504 U.S. at 564. Had the plaintiffs demonstrated "concrete" plans to visit Sri Lanka or Egypt (by establishing travel dates, for example), the Court might have determined that an imminent injury existed. *Id.*

47. *Id.* at 566 n.3.

48. Wyo. Farm Bureau Fed'n v. Babbitt, 987 F. Supp. 1349, 1359 (D. Wyo. 1997) (holding that plaintiffs who demonstrated actual plans to use specific areas of Idaho had standing to challenge the government's reintroduction of wolves into those areas), *rev'd on other grounds*, 199 F.3d 1224 (10th Cir. 2010). *See also* Strahan v. Coxe, 939 F. Supp. 963, 978 (D. Mass. 1996), *aff'd in part, vacated in part*, 127 F.3d 155 (1st Cir. 1997) (holding that plaintiff, a conservation biologist engaged in whale research, would be injured by harm to whales in Massachusetts waters, where he regularly observed whales).

49. Bennett v. Spear, 520 U.S. 154 (1997).

50. Glover River Org. v. U.S. Dep't of Interior, 675 F.2d 251, 254 (10th Cir. 1982) (standing ultimately denied on causation and redressability grounds). *See also* Bldg. Indus. Ass'n v. Babbitt, 979 F. Supp. 893, 899 (D.D.C. 1997) (plaintiffs presented adequate evidence that listing of fairy shrimp had depressed land values and had halted or impeded development, thereby causing injury).

51. 555 U.S. 488, 494–95 (2009). *See generally* Bradford Mank, *Revisiting the Lyons Den: Summers v. Earth Island Institute's Misuse of Lyons's "Realistic Threat" of Harm Standing Test*, 42 ARIZ. ST. L.J. 837 (2010).

52. *Defenders of Wildlife*, 504 U.S. at 560 (Court did not rule on whether plaintiffs met the requirement for causation, instead dismissing the action for failure to show injury and redressability).

is not enough;[53] the injury suffered must be "fairly traceable to the challenged action of the defendant, and not the result of the independent action of some third party not before the court."[54] Courts, for instance, may reject causation where plaintiffs appear to rely on "speculation" about what future parties not before the court will do, particularly when subsequent actions by those parties will otherwise trigger federal involvement.[55]

Causation may be absent when the injury is the result of the independent action of a third party; however, the "fairly traceable" requirement does not mean that the defendant's actions that caused the injury must be the very last step in a chain of causation.[56] For example, even though a BO issued under section 7 is "advisory" and does not mandate particular action agency activity,[57] the fact that a BO has a "powerful coercive effect on the action agency"[58] is generally sufficient to support an allegation that its issuance causes injury. Similarly, industry plaintiffs have successfully argued that the Secretary's decision to list a species had a "determinative or coercive effect" on other agencies (the Army Corps of Engineers, for example), which in turn forced the plaintiff to incur costs and delays or injury.[59] When the actions of a third party cause an injury, and those actions would not occur but for the actions of the defendant, sufficient causation exists to support standing.[60] Assuming that the actions of the defendant can fairly be said to have caused the plaintiff's injury, a plaintiff must still meet the third prong of Article III standing: redressability.

---

53. Salmon Spawning & Recovery Alliance v. Gutierrez, 545 F.3d 1220, 1228 (9th Cir. 2008) (citing Ecological Rights Found. v. Pac. Lumber Co., 230 F.3d 1141, 1152 (9th Cir. 2000)).

54. *Id.*

55. Ctr. for Biological Diversity v. U.S. Dep't of Interior, 563 F.3d 466, 479 (D.C. Cir. 2009).

56. Bennett v. Spear, 520 U.S. 154, 168–69 (1997).

57. *See* chapter 5, section 5.4 (discussing section 7 consultation and biological opinions).

58. *Bennett,* 520 U.S. at 169.

59. Bldg. Indus. Ass'n v. Babbitt, 979 F. Supp. 893, 899 (D.D.C. 1997). *But cf.* Glover River Org. v. U.S. Dep't of Interior, 675 F.2d 251, 255 (10th Cir. 1982) (holding that the causal link between listing of the leopard darter and the loss of federal funding for proposed dam projects was "far too speculative to support standing").

60. Strahan v. Coxe, 939 F. Supp. 963, 978–79 (D. Mass. 1996) (operations of licensed commercial fishing and whale-watching vessels, which injure whales, are fairly traceable to the defendant issuing licenses for such activity).

11.5.1.3 Prong 3: "Redressability"

Courts will adjudicate a case only if the plaintiff's injury can be redressed by a favorable decision of the court.[61] The legal standard for redressability is that it be "likely," as opposed to merely "speculative," that a favorable decision will redress the plaintiff's asserted injury.[62] *Bennett v. Spear* and *Defenders of Wildlife* provide two examples of the Supreme Court's treatment of redressability in ESA cases. In *Bennett,* the plaintiff ranchers and irrigation districts challenged the validity of a BO, which had concluded that operation of the Klamath Irrigation Project by the Bureau of Reclamation would jeopardize the continued existence of two listed species.[63] The government argued that the proximate cause of any harm to the plaintiffs (through reductions in water deliveries) would be a decision by the Bureau of Reclamation regarding water allocations, and not the BO itself.[64] Although the Court agreed that an action agency is technically free to disregard a BO and proceed with its own proposed action, the Court noted the "virtually determinative effect" of BOs on agency actions, as well as the fact that the BO at issue contained an incidental take statement, a violation of which would be a violation of section 9 of the ESA.[65] Given that the Bureau of Reclamation had operated the Klamath Project in the same manner throughout the 20th century, until receipt of the BO, the Court held that without the BO, the Bureau would not likely impose water level restrictions; and if the plaintiffs were to succeed in having the BO overturned, their injuries "likely" would be redressed.[66]

In *Defenders of Wildlife,* conversely, the plaintiffs mounted a programmatic challenge to the Services' regulation rendering the section 7 consultation process inapplicable to federal agency actions in foreign countries. The Supreme Court held that invalidation of the regulation would not redress the plaintiffs' claimed injuries to environmental interests in Sri Lanka and Egypt.[67] The Court concluded that even if the plaintiffs prevailed on the merits and the Secretary was ordered to promulgate new regulations applying section 7 consultation abroad, redress of the

---

61. Lujan v. Defenders of Wildlife, 504 U.S. 555, 561 (1992).
62. *Id.*
63. Bennett v. Spear, 520 U.S. 154 (1997).
64. *Id.* at 168.
65. *Id.* at 169–71.
66. *Id.*
67. *Defenders of Wildlife*, 504 U.S. at 568–69.

respondents' injuries would require other, nonparty agencies to take action (i.e., to terminate funding of foreign projects pending consultation).[68] Because the nonparty agencies would not have been bound by the new regulation, and because the agencies had provided only a fraction (10 percent) of the funding for the foreign projects in question, the Court held that it was "entirely conjectural" whether the activity that affected the respondents would be altered or affected by the promulgation of new section 7 regulations.[69]

Together, *Bennett* and *Defenders of Wildlife* serve as useful preliminary guides for any party wishing to establish, or refute, standing in any ESA lawsuit.[70] In some situations, however, a lack of redressability also might suggest that the case is no longer ripe, or possibly that it has become moot.[71]

11.5.2   Prudential Standing

In addition to Article III standing requirements, courts often impose additional jurisdictional limitations, referred to as "prudential" standing principles.[72] Notable among these requirements is a doctrine that requires a plaintiff's grievance to fall within the "zone of interests" of the particular statutory or constitutional provision at issue.[73] Because the ESA's focus is on conservation or preservation of species, some courts initially held that suits based upon economic or nonenvironmental interests were not within the zone of interest of the ESA.[74] In *Bennett v. Spear,* the Supreme Court effectively permitted anyone to file a citizen suit under section 11(g) of the ESA.[75] For ESA claims brought under the APA, the Court presumed a slightly more demanding application of the zone-of-interest test, but nonetheless held that economic interests

---

68. *Id.* at 571.
69. *Id.*
70. *See also* Glover River Org. v. U.S. Dep't of Interior, 675 F.2d 251, 255 (10th Cir. 1982) (plaintiffs could not show that, absent the listing of the leopard darter, certain flood control projects would be undertaken; thus, delisting of the darter would not redress plaintiffs' injuries).
71. *See* Marcum v. Salazar, 810 F. Supp. 2d 56 (D.D.C. 2011); Rio Grande Silvery Minnow v. Bureau of Reclamation, 601 F.3d 1096 (10th Cir. 2010).
72. Bennett v. Spear, 520 U.S. 154, 161–65 (1997).
73. *Id.*
74. *See* Bennett v. Plenert, 63 F.3d 915, 918 n.3 (9th Cir. 1995), *rev'd sub nom.* Bennett v. Spear, 520 U.S. 154 (1997).
75. *Bennett,* 520 U.S. at 165–66.

were within the zone of interests protected by ESA's section 7(a)(2), the particular provision at issue in *Bennett*.[76] Although every plaintiff must still satisfy Article III standing requirements, the zone-of-interest test no longer excludes those with an economic interest from filing suits under ESA section 11(g). The Court also clarified that at least some claims (such as claims challenging BOs developed under ESA section 7(a)(2)) brought pursuant to the APA may be grounded in alleged economic injury.

---

76. *Id.*

A   Frequently Asked Questions

Listing

1. Where do I find the official list of endangered and threatened species?

The complete list of all species listed as threatened or endangered under the ESA, including species under both FWS and NMFS jurisdiction, is published in the Code of Federal Regulations. 50 C.F.R. §§ 17.11 (wildlife), 17.12 (plants). Species under NMFS jurisdiction are also listed separately at 50 C.F.R. §§ 223.102 and 224.101. However, because the Code of Federal Regulations is generally published just once a year, species may have been listed since its last publication. New listings are agency rules, and therefore are published individually in the *Federal Register.* Thus, the most accurate way to compile an official, up-to-the-minute list of threatened and endangered species is to check every *Federal Register* volume (using available cumulative indexes) published since the date of the most current Code of Federal Regulations. In addition, FWS's list of all threatened and listed species, at http://www.fws.gov/endangered/species/us-species.html, is updated daily.

2. What is a "species" for purposes of the ESA?

Any members of the plant or animal kingdoms (except for certain insects that are classified as "pests") are potentially eligible for listing under the ESA. The ESA defines the term *species* more broadly than the scientific community, and uses traditional scientific nomenclature only as a starting point. Individual subspecies of fish or wildlife or plants are also eligible for listing as separate "species" under the ESA. Moreover, the ESA also provides for listing (as separate species) so-called distinct population segments (DPSs) of vertebrate fish or wildlife. The Act does not allow listing of DPSs of plants or invertebrates—only vertebrate fish or wildlife that "interbreed when mature." The ability to separately list subspecies and distinct population segments under the ESA explains why a particular plant or animal might be very common in one location but protected as an endangered species in another.

3. What criteria are used to determine whether a species should be listed?

The following five criteria are the only criteria relevant to any ESA listing decision:

- present or threatened destruction, modification, or curtailment of a species' habitat or range
- overutilization of the species for commercial, recreational, scientific, or educational purposes
- disease or predation
- inadequacy of existing regulatory mechanisms
- other natural or man-made factors affecting the species' continued existence

The Secretary must use only the "best scientific and commercial data available," and may not consider the potential economic impact of the proposed listing determination.

4. What are the criteria for identifying distinct population segments for listing purposes?

For species of salmonids native to the Pacific, NMFS policy provides that a distinct population segment (DPS) exists only if a particular stock of salmon represents an "evolutionarily significant unit" (ESU) of the biological species at issue. A stock must meet two tests to qualify as an ESU: (1) it must be substantially reproductively isolated from other nonspecific population units; and (2) it must represent an important component in the evolutionary legacy of the species.

For all other species of vertebrates, FWS and NMFS have promulgated joint policy guidance that outlines the following three principles for determining whether a DPS exists: (1) the discreteness of the population segment in relation to the remainder of the species to which it belongs; (2) the significance of the population segment to the species to which it belongs; and (3) the conservation status of the population segment. 61 Fed. Reg. 4721 (1996).

5. What is the difference between an "endangered" and a "threatened" species?

An endangered species is temporally more imperiled than a threatened species. The ESA defines an *endangered species* as one that is actually "in danger of extinction" throughout all or a portion of its range. A *threatened species* is by definition not yet in danger of extinction, but is likely to become endangered within the foreseeable future. In some cases, endangered and threatened species are afforded different protections under the Act.

6. **How are species added to or removed from the endangered and threatened species list?**

The Secretary initiates the listing process, either on his or her own initiative or in response to a petition submitted by any interested person. Except for emergency listings, any other listing, delisting, or reclassification (collectively "listing") action requires the Secretary to follow the formal rulemaking process set out in section 4 of the ESA. The Secretary begins the listing process by publishing a notice of any proposed listing and the listing's complete text in the *Federal Register*. This proposed rule contains, among other information, a summary of the data upon which the proposed listing is based and a summary of factors affecting the species in question. The Secretary must provide actual notice of the proposed listing to certain federal, state, local, and private individuals and entities. For at least 60 days following publication of the proposed listing, the Secretary must take public comment on the proposed rule, and must hold at least one public hearing if timely requested. Within 12 months of publication of the proposed listing, the Secretary must either

- publish a final rule implementing the proposed rule,
- publish a notice withdrawing the proposed rule, upon a finding that the evidence does not justify the action proposed, or
- extend the deadline for a final decision on the proposed listing by no more than six months.

The final rule listing, delisting, or reclassifying a species becomes effective 30 days after publication of the final rule in the *Federal Register*.

7. **How do I get a species added to or removed from the endangered and threatened species list?**

Any interested person can formally request that FWS or NMFS list, delist, or reclassify a particular species. A person initiates this process by submitting a written petition to the appropriate Secretary. A valid petition must be clearly identified as a petition, must be dated, and must include the name, signature, address, telephone number, and business or other affiliation of the petitioner. The aim of a particular petition is to present substantial scientific or commercial information to lead a reasonable person to believe that the petitioned-for action may be warranted. A petition should

- clearly indicate the administrative measure (delisting, listing, reclassification) sought;
- give the scientific and common names of the species involved;
- contain a detailed narrative justification for the recommended measure based upon available information, past and present numbers and distribution of the species, and any threats to the species;

- provide information regarding the status of the species overall or throughout a significant portion of its range;
- provide supporting documentation in the form of scientific publications, letters, reports, and the like.

8. How must the Secretary respond to my listing petition?

Within 30 days of receiving a listing petition (including petitions to list, delist, or reclassify a species), the Secretary must notify you that he or she has received your petition. Within 90 days of receiving an otherwise valid petition, the Secretary must determine whether the petition presents information indicating that the petitioned-for action "may be warranted." The Secretary may delay this 90-day finding on your petition only by demonstrating that it would be "impracticable" to make the 90-day finding because staff resources are devoted to listing other species in greater need of protection. Within 12 months of receiving your petition, the Secretary must make one of the following three findings:

- The petitioned action is warranted.
- The petitioned action is not warranted.
- The petitioned action is warranted but that promulgation of a rule to implement the action is precluded because of other pending proposals to list, delist, or reclassify, and that expeditious progress is being made to list, delist, or reclassify qualified species.

If the Secretary determines that any petitioned action is "warranted but precluded," the original petition is considered automatically resubmitted every 12 months.

9. What is an "emergency listing" and when is it appropriate?

Under certain limited conditions, section 4(b)(7) of the ESA allows the Secretary to avoid the lengthy rulemaking process normally required to list any species as threatened or endangered. The Secretary may respond to an "emergency posing a significant risk to the well-being of any species" by publishing an emergency listing in the *Federal Register*. The listing is effective immediately upon publication and remains in effect for up to 240 days.

Prohibitions and Penalties

10. Can I harm or kill a listed species that is threatening me? My family? My property?

A person may legally harm or kill any listed species based upon a good-faith belief that he or she is acting to protect himself or herself, a member of his or her family, or any other individual from bodily harm from any listed species. However, absent some special rule (such as those applicable to some threatened species or experimental populations), a person may not harm or kill a listed species in order to protect livestock, pets, or any other type of property.

11. Have I committed an ESA violation if I accidentally shoot an endangered or threatened species?

If you knew you were shooting at an animal, and you knowingly pulled the trigger, you have violated the ESA whether or not you knew the animal you shot was an endangered species. For example, if you shoot an endangered wolf, honestly believing it to be a coyote, you are still guilty of a section 9 violation. ESA section 9 violations require only that a person "knowingly" commit an act in violation of the ESA; Congress stated that the term *knowingly* is intended to make ESA violations general-intent crimes, not specific-intent crimes.

12. Have I committed an ESA violation if I modify habitat in a manner that harms listed fish or wildlife species?

Yes. Habitat modification or degradation that "harms" listed fish or wildlife species is a violation of ESA section 9. The term *harm* means any act (including habitat modification) that actually kills or injures wildlife by significantly impairing essential behavioral patterns. However, courts appear likely to apply ordinary principles of causation and foreseeability in cases involving application of the ESA's prohibition on harm. The resulting harm to a listed species, therefore, most likely must be at least minimally foreseeable before section 9 liability should attach.

13. Are endangered species and threatened species subject to the same section 9 protections?

Usually, but not always. To fully answer this question, one must first determine whether the particular threatened species at issues is under FWS or NMFS jurisdiction; the two agencies treat threatened species differently. FWS has promulgated a blanket rule affording full ESA section 9 protection to all threatened species under FWS jurisdiction, except for those species subject to a separate rule applying lesser or differing protections to a particular threatened species. NMFS, in contrast, has not published a blanket rule extending section 9 protections to threatened species. Therefore, unless and until NMFS publishes an individual section 4(d) rule for a particular threatened species (which it typically does), that species is not subject to ESA section 9 protections.

14. How do I find out whether a particular threatened species is covered by its own special rules?

Both Services publish threatened species rules in the Code of Federal Regulations. FWS rules respecting threatened species are published in 50 C.F.R. part 17; NMFS rules respecting threatened species are published in 50 C.F.R. part 223.

15.   What protection does the ESA provide to threatened and endangered plants?

Section 9 of the ESA provides special protections to endangered plants. Specifically, it is unlawful to

> remove and reduce to possession any such species from areas under Federal jurisdiction; maliciously damage or destroy any such species on any such area; or remove, cut, dig up, or damage or destroy any such species on any other area in knowing violation of any law or regulation of any state or in the course of any violation of a state criminal trespass law.

In addition, section 9 also prohibits the import, export, and sale of endangered plants.

Threatened plants are somewhat less protected than endangered plants. The statutory prohibitions against maliciously damaging or destroying endangered species on federal land, as well as the statutory prohibition against certain acts committed in violation of state law, are omitted from the regulations protecting threatened plants.

16.   Do ESA section 9 prohibitions apply to everyone?

Section 9 prohibitions apply to any "person" subject to the jurisdiction of the United States. A person, for ESA section 9 purposes, includes any individual, corporation, partnership, trust, association, or any other private entity; or any officer, employee, agent, department, or instrumentality of the federal government, of any state, municipality, or political subdivision of a state, or of any foreign government; any state, municipality, or political subdivision of a state; or any other entity subject to the jurisdiction of the United States.

Section 7 Consultation

17.   What activities are subject to ESA section 7 consultation?

All discretionary federal agency "actions" are subject to ESA section 7 consultation requirements. An activity is an *action* for section 7 purposes only when there is some discretionary federal involvement or control. The term *action* is defined very broadly to include all activities or programs of any kind authorized, funded, or carried out in whole or in part by federal agencies. Examples of federal actions include

- actions intended to conserve listed species or their habitat
- promulgation of regulations
- granting of licenses, contracts, leases, or grants-in-aid
- actions directly or indirectly causing modifications to the land, water, or air

Ongoing actions are also subject to section 7 consultation require-ments, provided that a federal agency has retained some discretionary involvement or control over some aspect of the activity. Federal agency activities carried out in foreign countries are not subject to section 7 consultation.

18.   Can an agency proceed with a proposed action before consulting under section 7?

If a proposed action will have no effect on a listed species, no section 7 consultation is required and the agency may proceed with the action. In instances when consultation is required, ESA section 7(d) prohibits an agency from proceeding with any activity that amounts to an "irreversible or irretrievable commitment of resources which would foreclose the formu-lation or implementation of any reasonable and prudent alternative [RPA]." An activity is prohibited by this section only if it is both "irreversible or irre-trievable" and also would have the effect of foreclosing RPAs. The corollary to this qualified prohibition is that certain agency activities may proceed prior to the completion of section 7 consultation, provided the activities do not violate the section 7(d) prohibition. At least one court determined that an agency must at least initiate section 7 consultation before it can proceed with any activity at all; agencies that do not take great care in complying with section 7 consultation requirements are subject to having their activi-ties enjoined by federal courts. Agencies also should take note of the fact that section 7(d) does not sanction incidental take. Therefore, if a proposed action may result in prohibited take of listed species, the agency should not proceed with the action until it obtains a biological opinion (BO) with an incidental take statement allowing such take.

19.   Where can I find detailed guidance as to how federal agencies conduct section 7 consultation?

There are two primary sources of information regarding the consulta-tion process: the official consultation regulations and the *Consultation Handbook*. NMFS and FWS promulgated joint consultation regulations in 1986, and these regulations are published at 50 C.F.R. part 402. In 1998, NMFS and FWS finalized the *Consultation Handbook,* intended primarily to aid biologists and other agency personnel engaged in section 7 consultation. The *Handbook* is available (on the FWS website) to the public and provides detailed analysis, discussion, and examples of liter-ally every aspect of the consultation process.

20.   What are ESA section 7 "applicants" and what are their rights?

An *applicant* for section 7 purposes is defined broadly to include any per-son who requires formal approval or authorization from a federal agency as a prerequisite to conducting the action. Anyone seeking a permit, license, lease, letter of authorization, or any other form of approval before carrying out an action may be an applicant in any section 7 consultation on that action. The action agency, and not the Service, is responsible for determining whether applicants exist for a particular section 7 consultation. Any person determined by the action agency to be an applicant may serve as the designated nonfederal representative for purposes of preparing a biological assessment (BA). In addition, an applicant is entitled to

- be informed by the action agency, in writing, of the estimated length of any delay in preparing a BA, and the reasons for the delay
- refuse to grant more than a 60-day extension to NMFS or FWS of the 90-day time limit for preparation of a biological opinion (BO)
- review the draft BO and provide comments on the draft through the action agency
- discuss with NMFS or FWS the basis of the biological determinations in the draft BO, and assist in the development of RPAs (in the case of a draft "jeopardy opinion")
- receive a copy of the final BO
- request "early consultation" prior to actually applying for a federal license or permit
- apply for an exemption if the BO concludes that the proposed action will jeopardize the continued existence of a listed species or adversely modify critical habitat, and that there are no RPAs

21. What is the "environmental baseline" for section 7 consultation purposes?

The *environmental baseline* is a current (as of the consultation) measurement of the status of listed species or their critical habitat, as well as the status of the present environment in which the species or critical habitat exist. This present set of conditions serves as a floor upon which the potential future effects of any proposed action will be measured. The environmental baseline includes the past and present impacts of all federal, state, or private actions and any other human activities in the action area. The environmental baseline also includes the anticipated future effects of proposed federal projects that have already undergone formal or early section 7 consultation, as well as the impact of state or private actions that are contemporaneous with the consultation in progress.

22. What is the difference between an incidental take statement and an incidental take permit?

An incidental take statement (ITS) is part of the biological opinion (BO) provided to a federal action agency by the Service as a consequence of an

ESA section 7 consultation on a proposed federal action. Once a federal agency receives a BO containing an ITS, the agency may proceed with its proposed action, even if some "take" of listed species will occur, so long as the action agency complies with the terms and conditions of the ITS. Private parties also may avail themselves of the protections of an ITS issued to an agency, provided that the private actions are clearly contemplated by and consistent with the ITS.

An incidental take permit (ITP) may be obtained by a private party pursuant to ESA section 10, to allow purely private activities to proceed that result in some "take" of members of a listed species. The take must, however, be incidental to, and not the purpose of, an otherwise lawful activity. A section 10 ITP requires the private applicant first to prepare an acceptable habitat conservation plan, which, among other requirements, adequately mitigates and minimizes the impact of the anticipated incidental take.

23. What is the difference between a reasonable and prudent alternative and a reasonable and prudent measure?

A reasonable and prudent alternative (RPA) is an alternative or change to a proposed federal agency action, developed through formal section 7 consultation. If a biological opinion (BO) concludes that a proposed agency action will jeopardize listed species or modify designated critical habitat, the BO must contain RPAs, if any exist. By definition, an RPA is an alternative that (1) can be implemented consistent with the purpose of the action; (2) can be implemented consistent with the scope of the action agency's legal authority and jurisdiction; (3) is economically and technologically feasible; and (4) will actually avoid jeopardy to listed species and adverse modification of critical habitat. The action agency is responsible for determining whether a particular alternative is, or is not, reasonable and prudent.

A reasonable and prudent measure (RPM) is included only in BOs that contain an incidental take statement. RPMs represent those measures that NMFS or FWS consider necessary or appropriate to minimize the impact of the taking. RPMs are mandatory, in that any agency that fails to implement them runs the risk of violating ESA section 9.

24. When is a biological assessment required?

A federal agency must prepare a biological assessment (BA) before engaging in any "major construction activity" when a listed species or designated critical habitat may be present in the action area. *Major construction activities* are construction projects, or activities having similar physical impacts, that rise to the level of a major federal action significantly affecting the human environment (as defined by NEPA). But agencies generally prepare a BA for other, nonconstruction activities that may affect listed species; in such cases, a BA represents a convenient and widely accepted vehicle for documenting vital agency findings during consultation.

25. Are federal action agencies required to comply with biological opinions?

Technically, no. After consultation, the action agency (and not the Service) is responsible for determining how to proceed. Yet, because BOs carry considerable weight with courts, an action agency ignores a BO at its peril. Any decision to deviate from a BO should be scientifically based and thoroughly documented for the administrative record. In addition, federal agencies should be cautioned that failure to implement the terms of any incidental take statement contained in a BO may result in an ESA section 9 violation.

Permits

26. Is my HCP-based incidental take permit a firm deal, or might my obligations change in the future?

The no surprises policy gives the holder of an incidental take permit a regulatory assurance that no additional land-use restrictions or financial compensation beyond the level agreed to in the habitat conservation plan (HCP) will be required of any permittee in order to address future unforeseen circumstances. An *unforeseen circumstance* is one that results in a substantial and adverse change to a species covered by an HCP, but that could not have been reasonably anticipated by the Service and the plan developers at the time the HCP was negotiated and developed. FWS or NMFS will use their own authorities to address any unforeseen circumstances that arise. The no surprises policy applies only to species adequately covered by the permit, and only if the HCP is being properly implemented.

27. What is the difference between a safe harbor agreement and a habitat conservation plan?

A safe harbor agreement (SHA) is an agreement to implement a set of conservation measures that will have a "net conservation benefit" to one or more listed species. In exchange for carrying out the habitat-enhancing activities called for in the SHA, the landowner is issued an ESA section 10(a)(1)(A) "enhancement of survival" permit. The enhancement of survival permit assures the landowner/permittee that he or she may subsequently engage in activities that may incidentally take species covered by the SHA, or degrade the species' habitat back down to an agreed-upon baseline. The SHA is appropriate for persons considering future land use or development, but who are willing to improve habitat in the short term.

A habitat conservation plan (HCP) is appropriate for persons with immediate plans to engage in activities that will result in incidental take of listed species. The key components of an HCP are the steps the permittee will take to minimize and mitigate the impacts of the expected incidental take. A successful HCP leads to issuance of an ESA section 10(a)(1)(B) incidental take permit.

28. What information is required for a valid habitat conservation plan?

All HCPs are required to contain the following four elements: (1) an assessment of the impacts of the taking; (2) the steps the applicant will take to "minimize and mitigate" the impacts of the taking, and the funding that will be available to implement these steps; (3) alternative actions to the taking that the applicant has considered, and the reasons why the alternatives are not being utilized; and (4) other measures that the Secretary may require as necessary or appropriate for purposes of the plan.

29. Are habitat conservation plans widely used, or are they rare?

HCPs are becoming quite common, but this was not always so. Between 1982 and 1992, only 14 HCPs were approved. Today, almost 700 HCPs have been approved.

30. Where can I find detailed guidance as to how federal agencies consider habitat conservation plans and process incidental take permit applications?

There are two primary sources of information regarding HCPs and incidental take permits: (1) regulations promulgated by NMFS and FWS, and (2) the *Habitat Conservation Planning Handbook.* Unlike the ESA section 7 consultation process, where NMFS and FWS promulgated joint regulations, the two agencies have separate (but similar) regulations for incidental take permits. *See* 50 C.F.R. pts. 13 & 17 (FWS); 50 C.F.R. pts. 220 & 222 (NMFS). In 1996, the Services finalized the *Joint Habitat Conservation Planning Handbook,* which is invaluable for any person attempting to prepare an HCP and apply for a section 10 permit. The *Habitat Conservation Planning Handbook* is available to the public on the Services' websites.

31. Do I need a permit to take unlisted or candidate species?

No permit is needed to take candidate species, because ESA section 9 prohibitions apply only to listed species. However, because candidate species may ultimately become listed species, landowners should seriously consider the potential future impacts of such listings on proposed land-use activities. A nonfederal landowner who is willing to implement immediate measures that benefit candidate species may develop a candidate conservation agreement with assurances (CCAA), and obtain a section 10(a)(1)(A) enhancement of survival permit. Similar to a safe harbor agreement for listed species, a CCAA provides a landowner with certain assurances that additional conservation measures will not be required of the landowner should covered candidate species become listed species.

Miscellaneous Issues

32. Where can I find descriptions of a particular species' critical habitat?

Whenever NMFS or FWS designate critical habitat for any species, the agency must delineate the habitat on a map. Descriptions and maps of designated critical habitat for species under FWS jurisdiction are published in 50 C.F.R. part 17. Descriptions, and some maps, of designated critical habitat for species under NMFS jurisdiction are published at 50 C.F.R. part 225; maps and charts not provided in part 225 may be obtained upon request to the Office of Protected Resources, F/PR, National Marine Fisheries Service, NOAA, 1315 East-West Highway, Silver Spring, MD 20910. The Services in May 2012 decided to avoid the costly process of publishing textual descriptions of designated critical habitat in the Code of Federal Regulations.

33. Are recovery plans legally binding on federal agencies or the public?

No. Courts and the Services to date do not treat recovery plans as having the force of law. A recovery plan merely sets guidelines and goals, and does not mandate any particular action. This does not mean that an agency's decision deviating from a recovery will not be held to be arbitrary or capricious if it fails to explain the deviation.

34. What is the "God Squad"?

God Squad is a nickname for the Endangered Species Committee (ESC), an entity created by Congress as an administrative court of last resort to resolve conflicts between the needs of listed species and proposed federal projects. The ESC is composed of six high-ranking federal officials: the Secretary of Agriculture, the Secretary of the Army, the Chairman of the Council of Economic Advisors, the administrator of the Environmental Protection Agency, the Secretary of the Interior, and the administrator of the National Oceanic and Atmospheric Administration, as well as one individual from each state affected by the particular federal project at issue. Convened only rarely, the ESC follows highly structured substantive and procedural guidelines to determine whether a federal project should be exempted from the requirements of the ESA. In the most extreme scenario, the ESC could legally sanction the extinction of a species. It is generally believed that the *God Squad* scenario is not likely to be employed anymore.

35. Can an experimental population be established in an area that already contains some individuals of the species to be released?

Yes, as long as there are not enough naturally occurring individuals to constitute a "population" of the species at issue. A population requires the presence of a group of individuals that interbreed when mature.

Isolated or sporadic occurrence of individual animals is not enough to establish a population. Thus, experimental populations may overlap with isolated, naturally occurring individuals of the same species without losing experimental population status.

36. What is the difference between an "essential" and a "nonessential" experimental population?

An *essential experimental population* is one whose loss would be likely to appreciably reduce the likelihood of the survival of the species in the wild. All other experimental populations are considered nonessential. There are two key differences in management of essential and nonessential populations. First, FWS and NMFS may designate critical habitat for essential experimental populations, but not for nonessential populations. Second, section 7 consultation requirements are relaxed for nonessential populations; consultation is required only for federal actions affecting nonessential populations occurring on National Park Service or FWS refuge lands. Standard section 7 consultation requirements apply to essential experimental populations.

37. Is 60 days' advance notice always required before filing a lawsuit under the ESA?

For most lawsuits filed pursuant to the citizen suit provision of ESA section 11, 60 days' notice must always be given prior to filing suit. This even includes situations in which take of a listed species may be imminent; the only emergency exception to the 60-day notice requirement is for suits alleging that the Secretary has failed to perform nondiscretionary duties under section 4 of the Act. In contrast, no prior notice is required for lawsuits challenging final agency actions under the Administrative Procedure Act (APA). However, plaintiffs may not pick and choose between ESA section 11 and the APA. Instead, potential plaintiffs must closely examine ESA section 11 to determine if their claims fit within that section; if so, the plaintiffs must provide 60 days' notice and proceed under section 11. To the contrary, if a particular claim involves a final agency action not within the purview of ESA section 11, which is otherwise reviewable under the APA, plaintiffs may file an APA-based suit immediately.

38. Does the Supreme Court's decision in *Bennett v. Spear* abolish all standing requirements for ESA litigants?

No. All plaintiffs in ESA cases must still meet the standing requirements of Article III of the U.S. Constitution. These requirements are that (1) the plaintiffs have suffered an "injury in fact"; (2) there is a causal connection between the injury and the conduct complained of; and (3) it is likely that the injury will be redressed by a decision favorable to the plaintiffs. However, the Supreme Court held in *Bennett v. Spear* that the common law "zone of interest" test no longer denies standing to ESA citizen suit litigants asserting economic interests or injury.

B Key Cases

Alabama Tombigbee Rivers Coalition v. U.S. Department of Interior, 26 F.3d 1103 (11th Cir. 1994) (in case involving FWS listing of sturgeon, court enjoined use of scientific report prepared in violation of the Federal Advisory Committee Act), *rejected by Cargill v. United States,* 173 F.3d 323 (5th Cir. 1999).

Aluminum Co. of America v. Administrator of EPA, 175 F.3d 1156 (9th Cir. 1999) (after receipt of a biological opinion (BO), it is action agency's decision as to how to proceed, and even when a BO concludes that the proposed action will not jeopardize a listed species or adversely modify critical habitat, an action agency may not simply rubber-stamp the Service's analysis).

American Bald Eagle v. Bhatti, 9 F.3d 163 (1st Cir. 1993) (court refused to enjoin deer hunt that allegedly created risk to eagles because they might ingest carrion containing lead slugs; court considered low likelihood of lead ingestion by eagles, as well as fact that plaintiffs had not introduced any evidence that any eagle had ever ingested lead in such a fashion).

American Forest & Paper Ass'n v. EPA, 137 F.3d 291 (5th Cir. 1998) (EPA cannot, pursuant to Clean Water Act, require delegee state to engage in section 7 consultation as a precursor to state issuance of a discharge permit).

Arizona Cattle Growers Ass'n v. U.S. Fish & Wildlife Service, 273 F.3d 1229 (9th Cir. 2001) (reviewing the specified level of take in an incidental take statement).

Arizona Cattle Growers' Ass'n v. Salazar, 606 F.3d 1160 (9th Cir. 2010) (applying baseline approach in economic consideration for designating critical habitat; discussing when a species "occupies" an area for purpose of critical habitat designation).

Babbitt v. Sweet Home Chapter of Communities for a Great Oregon, 515 U.S. 687 (1995) (landmark case holding that Secretary of Interior reasonably construed intent of Congress when he defined *harm* to include "significant habitat modification or degradation that actually kills or injures wildlife").

Bay's Legal Fund v. Brown, 828 F. Supp. 102 (D. Mass. 1993) (investment of more than $100 million prior to completion of consultation was held not to violate section 7(d), because project proponents retained sufficient flexibility to alter project's design if necessary to protect endangered whales).

Biodiversity Legal Foundation v. Babbitt, 146 F.3d 1249 (10th Cir. 1998) (rejecting claim that FWS's listing priority guidance violates ESA section 4 listing criteria).

Butte Environmental Council v. U.S. Army Corps of Engineers, 620 F.3d 936 (9th Cir. 2010) (some loss of critical habitat may be acceptable).

Carlton v. Babbitt, 26 F. Supp. 2d 102 (D.D.C. 1998) (ESA listing case holding that FWS failed to present defensible case that 26–36 grizzly bears was 'minimal, viable, population size" for bears, but also holding that FWS had "provided adequate support for their application of the [listing priority] guidelines to rank the Cabinet/Yaak Grizzly").

Carson-Truckee Water Conservancy District v. Clark, 741 F.2d 257 (9th Cir. 1984), *cert. denied,* 470 U.S. 1083 (1985) (upholding Bureau of Reclamation decision to refuse, pursuant to ESA section 7(a)(1), request for new water contract, even though bureau possessed discretion to execute such contract).

Center for Biological Diversity v. Salazar, 2012 WL 3570667 (9th Cir. Aug. 21, 2012) (incidental take statement required in a biological opinion even if no section 9 take liability).

Center for Biological Diversity v. U.S. Department of Interior, 563 F.3d 466 (D.C. Cir. 2009) (ESA claim not ripe at five-year leasing stage under the Outer Continental Shelf Lands Act).

Christy v. Hodel, 857 F.2d 1324 (9th Cir.), *cert. denied,* 490 U.S. 1114 (1989) (upholding fine imposed against rancher who shot endangered grizzly bear that was killing rancher's sheep).

City of Las Vegas v. Lujan. See Las Vegas, City of.

Conner v. Burford, 848 F.2d 1441 (9th Cir. 1982), *cert. denied,* 489 U.S. 1012 (1989) (holding that Minerals Leasing Act, unlike Outer Continental Shelf Land Act, did not contemplate incremental step activities, and thus section 7 consultation may not occur incrementally).

Defenders of Wildlife v. Babbitt, 958 F. Supp. 670 (D.D.C. 1997) (holding that for ESA section 4 listing decisions, "best available" data requirement does not mean that FWS must have "conclusive evidence").

Defenders of Wildlife v. EPA, 882 F.2d 1294 (8th Cir. 1989) (holding that EPA's decision to register strychnine as a pesticide "was critical to the resulting poisonings" of listed species, thus establishing requisite ESA section 9 causation).

Dow AgroSciences v. NMFS, 450 F.3d 930 (4th Cir. 2011) (biological opinion is reviewable under APA section 704, for registration of pesticides).

Earth Island Institute v. Albright, 147 F.3d 1352 (Fed. Cir. 1998) (holding that Secretary of State's and Secretary of Commerce's "maladministration" of ESA section 8 was not reviewable under ESA section 11(g), but rather was an APA review case).

Forest Conservation Council v. Rosboro Lumber Co., 50 F.3d 781 (9th Cir. 1995) (holding that "historic injury" is not required to show an ESA section 9 violation and that "reasonably certain" and "imminent" threat of harm to listed species is sufficient to find violation of section 9).

Forest Guardians v. Babbitt, 174 F.3d 1178 (10th Cir. 1999), *amending Forest Guardians v. Babbitt,* 164 F.3d 1261 (10th Cir. 1998) (holding that designation of critical habitat is nondiscretionary, and that Secretary's duty to act cannot be excused by "generalized claim of inadequate resources").

Friends of Blackwater v. Salazar, 2012 WL 3538236 (D.C. Cir. Aug. 17, 2012) (holding that the recovery plans are nonbinding).

Friends of Endangered Species v. Jantzen, 760 F.2d 976 (9th Cir. 1985) (upholding San Bruno Habitat Conservation Plan allowing take of endangered butterflies, in part due to Congress's reliance on plan as model for incidental take permit program).

Friends of the Wild Swan v. Babbitt, 12 F. Supp. 2d 1121 (D. Or. 1997) (holding that FWS arbitrarily and capriciously made finding with respect to five distinct population segments of bull trout, when petitioner had specifically requested that entire range of bull trout be listed).

Gifford Pinchot Task Force v. U.S. Fish & Wildlife Service, 378 F.3d 1059 (9th Cir. 2004) (rejecting regulatory definition of adverse modification or destruction and holding that prohibition applies to either survival or recovery).

Glover River Organization v. U.S. Department of Interior, 675 F.2d 251 (10th Cir. 1982) (for standing purposes, holding that although plaintiffs had shown requisite Article III injury to property, based upon evidence of past flooding and increased threat of future flooding, plaintiffs could not meet Article III causation and redressability criteria to have standing to challenge listing of leopard darter).

Grand Canyon Trust v. U.S. Bureau of Reclamation, 2012 WL 326499 (9th Cir. Aug. 13, 2012) (annual operating plans not trigger section 7(a)(2)).

Idaho Farm Bureau Federation v. Babbitt, 58 F.3d 1392 (9th Cir. 1995) (holding that Secretary's failure to make listing decision within statutory time frames did not render final listing invalid; statutory time frames of ESA section 4 are impetus to act rather than prohibition on action taken after time expires).

Karuk Tribe of California v. U.S. Forest Service, 681 F.3d 1006 (9th Cir. 2012) (en banc) (ESA applied to notice of intent to conduct mining activities on national forest lands).

Klamath Water Users Protective Ass'n v. Patterson, 191 F.3d 1115 (9th Cir. 1999) (Bureau of Reclamation ownership of dam and its retention of management discretion respecting dam was held to trigger ESA section 7 consultation requirement).

Las Vegas, City of v. Lujan, 891 F.2d 927 (D.C. Cir. 1989) (holding that something less than "substantial evidence" is required to support emergency listing, and that ESA contemplates "somewhat less rigorous process of investigation and explanation for emergency rules than for normal rulemaking").

Loggerhead Turtle v. County Council of Volusia County, 148 F.3d 1231 (11th Cir. 1998) (holding that county caused prohibited harm to listed turtles through inadequate regulation of beachfront lighting).

Lujan v. Defenders of Wildlife, 504 U.S. 555, 558–59 (1992) (applying Article III standing requirements to deny standing to environmental plaintiffs seeking to challenge FWS/NMFS rule excluding federal agency actions carried out abroad from consultation requirements of ESA section 7).

Maine Audubon Society v. Purslow, 907 F.2d 265 (1st Cir. 1990) (holding that plaintiffs who filed suit one day after providing notice had clearly failed to meet ESA's 60-day notice requirement).

Marbled Murrelet v. Babbitt, 83 F.3d 1068 (9th Cir. 1996) (holding that FWS advice to lumber company, as to how to avoid take of listed species during logging operation, did not represent discretionary involvement or control for purposes of ESA section 7, and also holding that plaintiffs' 60-day notice was adequate to support suit based on section 7 even though focus of notice letter was on section 9 violations and section 7 was mentioned in only one part of letter).

Modesto Irrigation District v. Gutierrez, 619 F.3d 1024 (9th Cir. 2010) (discussing the designation of distinct population segments).

National Ass'n of Home Builders v. Defenders of Wildlife, 551 U.S. 644 (2007) (section 7(a)(2) applies only to discretionary agency actions, and the Environmental Protection Agency's delegation of the Clean Water Act section 402 permitting program to the state of Arizona did not afford the agency discretion to consider endangered or threatened species).

National Ass'n of Home Builders v. Babbitt, 130 F.3d 1041 (D.C. Cir. 1997), *cert. denied,* 524 U.S. 937 (1998) (upholding ESA protection of species of fly that exists only in California as valid exercise of Congress's commerce clause authority).

National Wildlife Federation v. Coleman, 529 F.2d 359 (5th Cir. 1976) (holding that mere proposed actions by others do not ensure that project will not jeopardize listed species, and holding that residential and commercial development "that can be expected to result from the construction of the highway" must be considered as indirect effect of highway construction).

National Wildlife Federation v. NMFS, 481 F.3d 1224 (9th Cir. 2007) (jeopardy analysis requires considering both the likely effect on survival of the species as well as the likely effect on recovery), *amended and superseded by* 524 F.3d 917 (9th Cir. 2008) (same).

Natural Resources Defense Council v. Salazar, 686 F.3d 1092 (9th Cir. 2012) (settlement contracts not subject to section 7(a)(2)).

Natural Resources Defense Council v. Houston, 146 F.3d 1118 (9th Cir. 1998) (holding that ESA definition of agency "action" includes renewal of existing water service contracts, and that certain Bureau of Reclamation contracts executed prior to conclusion of consultation were not adequately conditioned to allow for future needs of endangered species).

Natural Resources Defense Council v. U.S. Department of Interior, 1133 F.3d 1121 (9th Cir. 1997) (holding that FWS's refusal to designate critical habitat for coastal California gnatcatcher was not supported, and that FWS's conclusory statements with regard to increased threats associated with such designation were unsupported by record; finding unpersuasive FWS's contention that designation of critical habitat on private lands would not benefit species).

New Mexico Cattle Growers' Ass'n v. U.S. Fish & Wildlife Service, 248 F.3d 1277 (10th Cir. 2001) (applying coextensive approach in economic consideration when designating critical habitat).

North Slope Borough v. Andrus, 642 F.2d 589 (D.C. Cir. 1980) (holding that segmented consultation was appropriate for offshore leasing activities in light of "checks and balances" provided by Outer Continental Shelf Land Act).

Northern Spotted Owl v. Hodel, 716 F. Supp. 479 (W.D. Wash. 1988) (holding that FWS had disregarded expert opinions of its own biologists, and had failed to provide its own or any other expert analysis supporting its decision not to list spotted owl).

O'Neil v. United States, 50 F.3d 677 (9th Cir. 1995) (holding that section 7 consultation requirement was triggered with respect to existing contracts because Bureau of Reclamation must act annually to deliver water pursuant to such existing contracts).

Oregon Natural Resources Council v. Daley, 6 F. Supp. 2d 1139 (D. Or. 1998) (holding that NMFS failed to correctly apply "within the foreseeable future" standard of ESA section 4, and that NMFS had wrongly based its listing determination on finding that coho would not likely become endangered in interval between NMFS's "not warranted" finding and adoption of habitat protection measures by state of Oregon).

Otay Messa Property, L.P. v. U.S. Department of Interior, 646 F.3d 914 (9th Cir. 2011) (addressing what constitutes "occupied" for purposes of designating critical habitat).

Pacific Rivers Council v. Robertson, 854 F. Supp. 713 (D. Or. 1993), *aff'd in part, rev'd in part sub nom. Pacific Rivers Council v. Thomas,* 30 F.3d 1050 (9th Cir. 1994) (holding that procedural violations of ESA, such as not initiating section 7 consultation when required, mandate that underlying action be enjoined).

Pacific Rivers Council v. Thomas, 30 F.3d 1050 (9th Cir. 1994) (holding that Forest Service is required to consult on its existing land and resource management plans whenever a species is listed that might be affected by ongoing and future forest management projects).

Palila v. Hawaii Department of Land & Natural Resources (Palila I), 639 F.2d 495 (9th Cir. 1981), *aff'g* 471 F. Supp. 985 (D. Haw. 1979) (watershed section 9 case holding that habitat modification alone may amount to a prohibited "take").

Palila v. Hawaii Department of Land & Natural Resources (Palila II), 649 F. Supp. 1070 (D. Haw. 1986), *aff'd,* 852 F.2d 1106 (9th Cir. 1988) (holding that 1981 change to ESA definition of *harm* "did not embody a substantial change" to definition, and that activities that significantly degrade habitat and cause actual injury to the palila bird remain prohibited under new rule).

Platte River Whooping Crane Trust v. FERC, 962 F.2d 27 (D.C. Cir. 1992) (holding that no "action" existed, for ESA section 7 purposes, when FERC was required to issue annual operation license "under the terms and conditions of the existing license").

Portland Audubon Society v. Endangered Species Committee, 984 F.2d 1534 (9th Cir. 1992) (holding that Endangered Species Committee's hearings must be open to public, and that such hearings are governed by provisions of APA applicable to formal adjudications, including prohibition against ex parte communications).

Pyramid Lake Paiute Tribe of Indians v. U.S. Department of Navy, 898 F.2d 1410 (9th Cir. 1990) (holding that agencies have "affirmative obligations" under section 7(a)(1) and also holding that one year's diversion of water to lands leased by U.S. Navy did not cause harm to endangered cui-ui fish).

Riverside Irrigation District v. Andrews, 752 F.2d 508 (10th Cir. 1985) (holding that issuance of nationwide permit under section 404 of the Clean Water Act by the Army Corps of Engineers is "action" pursuant to ESA).

Riverside Irrigation District v. Andrews, 758 F.3d 508 (10th Cir. 1985) (holding that Army Corps of Engineers, in considering whether to grant Clean Water Act permit necessary to construct dam, must consider future effects of increased consumptive use of water that will result from darn and affect whooping cranes 150 miles away).

Sierra Club v. Babbitt, 15 F. Supp. 2d 1274 (S.D. Ala. 1998) (overturning issuance of section 10 incidental take permit because, among other reasons, FWS had inconsistently applied mitigation standards regarding Alabama beach mouse to developments along Alabama coast).

Sierra Club v. Babbitt, 65 F.3d 1502 (9th Cir. 1995) (holding that Bureau of Land Management (BLM) issuance of reciprocal right-of-way agreement was not "action," because agreement did not give BLM authority to affect road construction by private parties).

Sierra Club v. Glickman, 156 F.3d 606 (5th Cir. 1998) (ordering USDA, pursuant to ESA section 7(a)(1), to consult with FWS to develop programs for conservation of species dependent upon Edwards Aquifer in central Texas).

Sierra Club v. Lyng, 694 F. Supp. 1260 (E.D. Tex. 1988), *aff'd in part, vacated in part sub nom. Sierra Club v. Yeuter,* 926 F.2d 437 (5th Cir. 1991) (holding that USFS logging practices harmed red-cockaded woodpeckers).

Sierra Club v. Marsh, 816 F.2d 1376 (9th Cir. 1987) (holding that Army Corps of Engineers violated section 7 of ESA by failing to ensure implementation of mitigation actions prior to allowing destruction or adverse modification of two endangered species' habitat).

Southwest Center for Biological Diversity v. Babbitt, 980 F. Supp. 1080 (D. Ariz. 1997) (holding that NMFS's and FWS's Joint Policy on Distinct Population Segments, to the extent it limited the DPS to one subspecies, was arbitrary and capricious).

Southwest Center for Biological Diversity v. Babbitt, 215 F.3d 58 (D.C. Cir. 2000) (holding that Secretary of Interior is not obligated to conduct actual counts of Queen Charlotte goshawks, and may base listing determination on population estimates).

Southwest Center for Biological Diversity v. Bureau of Reclamation, 143 F.3d 515 (9th Cir. 1998) (holding that ESA section 7 action agency is not required to select first reasonable and prudent alternative (RPA) developed, nor must action agency select RPA that might be "best" alternative; also holding that proper ESA 60-day notice of intent must sufficiently alert recipient of actual alleged violation, so that recipient may attempt to abate violation).

Strahan v. Coxe, 127 F.3d 155 (1st Cir. 1997), *cert. denied,* 525 U.S. 830 (1998) (in case involving state licensing of fishing and lobstering equipment and subsequent entanglement of whales in the equipment, court held that "a governmental third party pursuant to whose authority an actor directly exacts a taking of an endangered species may be deemed to have violated the provisions of the ESA").

Sweet Home Chapter of Communities for a Great Oregon v. Babbitt, 1 F.3d 1 (D.C. Cir. 1993), *rev'd on other grounds,* 515 U.S. 687 (1995) (upholding Secretary of Interior's blanket application of section 9 prohibitions to all threatened species).

Tennessee Valley Authority v. Hill, 437 U.S. 153, 180 (1978) (landmark case holding that Congress intended to afford species the highest of priorities, and that section 7 demanded that nearly complete dam project be halted to protect listed fish, the snail darter).

Tribal Village of Akutan v. Hodel, 869 F.2d 1185 (9th Cir. 1988) (holding that action agency's deviations from BO do not constitute violation of ESA if action agency implements adequate alternative measures to meet ESA's substantive requirements).

Trout Unlimited v. Lohn, 559 F.3d 946 (9th Cir. 2009) (addressing the role of hatchery fish in the designation of an evolutionary significant unit).

United States v. Guthrie, 50 F.3d 936 (11th Cir. 1995) (section 9 criminal case; court held that criminal defendant's failure to avail himself of opportunity to comment on proposed listing of red-bellied turtle precluded him from collaterally attacking validity of listing at his later section 9 criminal trial).

United States v. McKittrick, 142 F.3d 1170 (9th Cir. 1998) (holding that Secretary does not have to deplete endangered or threatened populations in order to gather individuals for creation of an experimental population; also upholding Secretary's definition of geographic separation for purposes of section 10 experimental populations).

Wyoming Farm Bureau Federation v. Babbitt, 199 F.3d 1224 (10th Cir. 2000) (upholding FWS's determination that geographic separation requirement for "experimental populations" applies only to "population" overlap, and not to overlap with "lone dispersers" or individuals of species).

Glossary

Act: "the Endangered Species Act of 1973, as amended, 16 U.S.C. 1531 *et seq.*" 50 C.F.R. § 402.02.

action: "all activities or programs of any kind authorized, funded, or carried out, in whole or in part, by Federal agencies in the United States or upon the high seas. Examples include, but are not limited to:

> (a) actions intended to conserve listed species or their habitat;
> (b) the promulgation of regulations;
> (c) the granting of licenses, contracts, leases, easements, rights-of-way, permits, or grants-in-aid; or
> (d) actions directly or indirectly causing modifications to the land, water, or air."

50 C.F.R. § 402.02.

action area: "all areas to be affected directly or indirectly by the Federal action and not merely the immediate area involved in the action." 50 C.F.R. § 402.02.

adequately covered: "means with respect to species listed pursuant to section 4 of the ESA, that a proposed conservation plan has satisfied the permit issuance criteria under section 10(a)(2)(B) of the ESA for the species covered by the plan, and, with respect to unlisted species, that a proposed conservation plan has satisfied the permit issuance criteria under section 10(a)(2)(B) of the ESA that would otherwise apply if the unlisted species covered by the plan were actually listed. For the Services to cover a species under a conservation plan, [the species] must be listed on the section 10(a)(1)(B) permit." 50 C.F.R. § 17.3.

Alaskan Native: "a person defined in the Alaska Native Claims Settlement Act (43 U.S.C. 1603(b)) (85 Stat. 588) as a citizen of the United States who is of one-fourth degree or more Alaskan Indian (including Tsimshian Indians enrolled or not enrolled in the Metlaktla Indian Community), Eskimo, or Aleut blood, or combination thereof. The term includes any Native, as so defined, either or both of whose adoptive parents are not Natives. It also includes, in the absence of proof of a minimum blood quantum, any citizen of the

United States who is regarded as an Alaska Native by the Native village or town of which he claims to be a member and whose father or mother is (or, if deceased, was) regarded as Native by any Native village or Native town. Any citizen enrolled by the Secretary pursuant to section 5 of the Alaska Native Claims Settlement Act shall be conclusively presumed to be an Alaskan Native for purposes of this part." 50 C.F.R. § 17.3.

alternative courses of action: with respect to the Endangered Species Exemption Process, "means all reasonable and prudent alternatives, including both no action and alternatives extending beyond original project objectives and acting agency jurisdiction." 50 C.F.R. § 450.01.

applicant: "any person, as defined in section 3(13) of the Act, who requires formal approval or authorization from a Federal agency as a prerequisite to conducting the action." 50 C.F.R. § 402.02.

best scientific and commercial data available: undefined, but the Services explain the term as "to assure the quality of the biological, ecological, and other information used in the implementation of the Act, it is the policy of the Services to: (1) evaluate all scientific and commercial data available; (2) gather and impartially evaluate biological, ecological, and other information disputing official positions, decisions, and actions proposed or taken by the Services; (3) document their evaluation of comprehensive, technical information regarding the status and habitat requirements for a species throughout its range, whether it supports or does not support a position being proposed as an official agency position; (4) use primary and original sources of information as the basis for recommendations; (5) retain these sources referenced in the official document as part of the administrative record supporting an action; (6) collect, evaluate, and complete all reviews of biological, ecological, and other relevant information within the schedules established by the Act, appropriate regulations, and applicable policies; and (7) require management-level review of documents developed and drafted by Service biologists to verify and assure the quality of the science used to establish official positions, decisions, and actions taken by the Services during their implementation of the Act." U.S. FISH & WILDLIFE SERVICE & NAT'L MARINE FISHERIES SERVICE, ENDANGERED SPECIES CONSULTATION HANDBOOK, at xi (March 1998) [hereinafter NMFS/FWS CONSULTATION HANDBOOK].

biological assessment: "the information prepared by or under the direction of the Federal agency concerning listed and proposed species and designated and proposed critical habitat that may be present in the action area and the evaluation [sic] potential effects of the action on such species and habitat." 50 C.F.R. § 402.02.

biological opinion: "the document that states the opinion of the Service as to whether or not the Federal action is likely to jeopardize the continued existence of listed species or result in the destruction or adverse modification of critical habitat." 50 C.F.R. § 402.02.

candidate species: species "for which the Service has sufficient information on their biological status and threats to propose them as endangered or threatened under the [ESA], but for which development of a proposed listing regulation is precluded by other higher priority listing activities." *See* U.S. Fish & Wildlife Service, Candidate Species, http://www.fws.gov/endangered/esa-library/pdf/candidate_species.pdf. For species under the jurisdiction of NMFS, *candidate species* means "species for which concerns remain regarding their status, but for which more information is needed before they can be proposed for listing." U.S. FISH & WILDLIFE SERVICE & NATIONAL MARINE FISHERIES SERVICE, JOINT ENDANGERED SPECIES HABITAT CONSERVATION PLANNING HANDBOOK 8-1 (November 1996) [hereinafter HCP HANDBOOK].

Chairman: "the Chairman of the Endangered Species Committee, who is the Secretary of the Interior." 50 C.F.R. § 450.01.

changed circumstances: "changes in circumstances affecting a species or geographic area covered by a conservation plan that can reasonably be anticipated by plan developers and the Service and that can be planned for (e.g., the listing of new species, or a fire or other natural catastrophic event in areas prone to such events)." 50 C.F.R. § 17.3.

commercial activity: "all activities of industry and trade, including, but not limited to, the buying or selling of commodities and activities conducted for the purpose of facilitating such buying and selling: *Provided, however,* That it does not include exhibition of commodities by museums or similar cultural or historical organizations." ESA section 3, 16 U.S.C. § 1532.

Committee: "the Endangered Species Committee established pursuant to section 7(e) of the Act, 16 U.S.C. 1536(e)." 50 C.F.R. § 450.01.

complete application package: "Section 10 permit application package presented by the permit applicant to the Field Office or Regional Office for processing. It contains an application form, fee (if required), HCP, EA, or EIS. In order to begin processing, the package must be accompanied by a certification by the Field Office that it has reviewed the application documents and finds them to be statutorily complete." HCP HANDBOOK 8-1.

conference: "a process which involves informal discussions between a Federal agency and the Service under section 7(a)(4) of the Act regarding the impact of an action on proposed species or proposed critical habitat and recommendations to minimize or avoid adverse effects." 50 C.F.R. § 402.02.

conservation measures: "actions to benefit or promote the recovery of listed species that are included by the Federal agency as an integral part of the proposed action. These actions will be taken by the Federal agency or applicant, and serve to minimize or compensate for, project effects on the species under review. These may include prior to the initiation of consultation, or actions which the Federal agency or applicant have committed to complete in a biological assessment or similar document." NMFS/FWS Consultation Handbook, at xii.

conservation plan: "the plan required by section 10(a)(2)(A) of the ESA that an applicant must submit when applying for an incidental take permit. Conservation plans also are known as 'habitat conservation plans' or 'HCPs.'" 50 C.F.R. § 17.3.

conservation plan area: "lands and other areas encompassed by specific boundaries which are affected by the conservation plan and incidental take permit." HCP Handbook 8-1.

conservation recommendations: "suggestions of the Service regarding discretionary measures to minimize or avoid adverse effects of a proposed action on listed species or critical habitat or regarding the development of information." 50 C.F.R. § 402.02.

conserve, conserving, conservation: "to use and the use of all methods and procedures which are necessary to bring any endangered species or threatened species to the point at which the measures provided pursuant to [the ESA[are no longer necessary. Such methods and procedures include, but are not limited to, all activities associated with scientific resources management such as research, census, law enforcement, habitat acquisition and maintenance, propagation, live trapping, and transplantation, and, in the extraordinary case where population pressures within a given ecosystem cannot be otherwise relieved, may include regulated taking." ESA section 3, 16 U.S.C. § 1532.

conserved habitat areas: "areas explicitly designated for habitat restoration, acquisition, protection, or other conservation purposes under a conservation plan." 50 C.F.R. § 17.3.

Convention: "the Convention on International Trade in Endangered Species of Wild Fauna and Flora, signed on March 3, 1973, and the appendices thereto." ESA section 3, 16 U.S.C. § 1532.

covered species: "Unlisted species that have been adequately addressed in an HCP as though they were listed, and therefore included on the permit or, alternately, for which assurances are provided to the permittee that such species will be added to the permit if listed under certain circumstances. 'Covered species' are also subject to the assurances of the 'No Surprises' policy." HCP Handbook 8-1.

critical habitat: "(A) for a threatened or endangered species means

> (a) the specific areas within the geographical area occupied by the species, at the time it is listed . . . , on which are found those physical or biological features (I) essential to the conservation of the species and (II) which may require special management considerations or protection; and
> (b) specific areas outside the geographical area occupied by the species at the time it is listed . . . , upon a determination by the Secretary that such areas are essential for the conservation of the species.
> (c) Critical habitat may be established for those species now listed as threatened or endangered species for which no critical habitat has heretofore been established as set forth in subparagraph (A) of this paragraph.
> (d) Except in those circumstances determined by the Secretary, critical habitat shall not include the entire geographical area which can be occupied by the threatened or endangered species."

ESA section 3, 16 U.S.C. § 1532.

cumulative effects: "those effects of future State or private activities, not involving Federal activities, that are reasonably certain to occur within the action area of the Federal action subject to consultation." 50 C.F.R. § 402.02.

designated nonfederal representative: "a person designated by the Federal agency as its representative to conduct informal consultation and/or to prepare any biological assessment." 50 C.F.R. § 402.02.

destruction or adverse modification: "a direct or indirect alteration that appreciably diminishes the value of critical habitat for both the survival and recovery of a listed species. Such alterations include, but are not limited to, alterations adversely modifying any of the physical or biological features that were the basis for determining the habitat to be critical." 50 C.F.R. § 402.02. *But cf.* Gifford Pinchot Task Force v. U.S. Fish & Wildlife Serv., 378 F.3d 1059 (9th Cir. 2004) (rejecting regulatory definition).

development or land use area: "those portions of the conservation plan area that are proposed for development or land use or are anticipated to be developed or utilized." HCP HANDBOOK 8-2.

distinct population segment: a term with specific meaning "when used for listing, delisting, and reclassification purposes to describe a discrete vertebrate stock that may be added or deleted from the list of endangered and threatened species. The use of the term 'distinct population segment' will be consistent with the Services' popula-tion policy." NMFS/FWS CONSULTATION HANDBOOK, at xiii.

downlist: "to reclassify an endangered species to a threatened species based on alleviation of any of the five listing factors provided under section 4(a)(1) of the ESA." HCP HANDBOOK 8-2.

early consultation: "a process requested by a Federal agency on behalf of a prospective applicant under section 7(a)(3) of the Act." 50 C.F.R. § 402.02.

effects of the action: "the direct and indirect effects of an action on the species or critical habitat, together with the effects of other activi-ties that are interrelated or interdependent with that action, that will be added to the environmental baseline. The environmental baseline includes the past and present impacts of all Federal, State, or private actions and other human activities in the action area, the anticipated impacts of all proposed Federal projects in the action area that have already undergone formal or early section 7 consultation, and the impact of State or private actions which are contemporaneous with the consultation in process. Indirect effects are those that are caused by the proposed action and are later in time, but still are reasonably certain to occur. Interrelated actions are those that are part of a larger action and depend on the larger action for their justification. Interdependent actions are those that have no independent utility apart from the action under consider-ation." 50 C.F.R. § 402.02.

endangered species: "any species which is in danger of extinction throughout all or a significant portion of its range other than a spe-cies of the Class Insecta determined by the Secretary to constitute a pest whose protection under the provisions of [the ESA] would pres-ent an overwhelming and overriding risk to man." ESA section 3, 16 U.S.C. § 1532.

enhance the propagation or survival: "when used in reference to wildlife in captivity, includes but is not limited to the following activities when it can be shown that such activities would not be detrimen-tal to the survival of wild or captive populations of the affected species:

(a) Provision of health care, management of populations by culling, contraception, euthanasia, grouping or handling of wildlife to control survivorship and reproduction, and similar normal practices of animal husbandry needed to maintain captive populations that are self-sustaining and that possess as much genetic vitality as possible;
(b) Accumulation and holding of living wildlife that is not immediately needed or suitable for propagative or scientific purposes, and the transfer of such wildlife between persons in order to relieve crowding or other problems hindering

the propagation or survival of the captive population at the location from which the wildlife would be removed; and

(c) Exhibition of living wildlife in a manner designed to educate the public about the ecological role and conservation needs of the affected species."

50 C.F.R. § 17.3.

environmental baseline: for ESA section 7 consultation purposes, includes "the past and present impacts of all Federal, State, or private actions and other human activities in the action area, the anticipated impacts of all proposed Federal projects in the action area that have already undergone formal or early section 7 consultation, and the impact of State or private actions which are contemporaneous with the consultation in process." 50 C.F.R. § 402.02 (contained within the definition of *effects of the action*).

federal agency: "any department, agency, or instrumentality of the United States." ESA section 3, 16 U.S.C. § 1532.

fish or wildlife: "any member of the animal kingdom, including without limitation any mammal, fish, bird (including any migratory, non-migratory, or endangered bird for which protection is also afforded by treaty or other international agreement), amphibian, reptile, mollusk, crustacean, arthropod or other invertebrate, and includes any part, product, egg, or offspring thereof, or the dead body or parts thereof." ESA section 3, 16 U.S.C. § 1532.

foreign commerce: "includes, among other things, any transaction

(a) between persons within one foreign country;

(b) between persons in two or more foreign countries;

(c) between a person within the United States and a person in a foreign country; or

(d) between persons within the United States, where the fish and wildlife in question are moving in any country or countries outside the United States."

ESA section 3, 16 U.S.C. § 1532.

formal consultation: "a process between the Service and the Federal agency that commences with the Federal agency's written request for consultation under section 7(a)(2) of the Act and concludes with the Service's issuance of the biological opinion under section 7(b)(3) of the Act." 50 C.F.R. § 402.02.

formal permit application phase: "the phase of the section 10 process that begins when the Regional Office receives a 'complete application package' and ends when a decision on permit issuance is finalized." HCP HANDBOOK 8-3.

habitat: "the location where a particular taxon of plant or animal lives and its surroundings, both living and non-living; the term includes the presence of a group of particular environmental conditions surrounding an organism including air, water, soil, mineral elements, moisture, temperature, and topography." HCP Handbook 8-3.

harass: "in the definition of 'take' in the Act means an intentional or negligent act or omission which creates the likelihood of injury to wildlife by annoying it to such an extent as to significantly disrupt normal behavioral patterns which include, but are not limited to, breeding, feeding, or sheltering. This definition, when applied to captive wildlife, does not include generally accepted:

> (a) Animal husbandry practices that meet or exceed the minimum standards for facilities and care under the Animal Welfare Act,
> (b) Breeding procedures, or
> (c) Provisions of veterinary care for confining, tranquilizing, or anesthetizing, when such practices, procedures, or provisions are not likely to result in injury to the wildlife."

50 C.F.R. § 17.3.

harm: "in the definition of 'take' in the Act means an act which actually kills or injures wildlife. Such act may include significant habitat modification or degradation where it actually kills or injures wildlife by significantly impairing essential behavioral patterns, including breeding, feeding, or sheltering." 50 C.F.R. § 17.3.

implementing agreement: "an agreement that legally binds the permittee to the requirements and responsibilities of a conservation plan and section 10 permit. It may assign the responsibility for planning, approving, and implementing the mitigation measures under the HCP." HCP Handbook 8-3.

import: "to land on, bring into, or introduce into, or attempt to land on, bring into, or introduce into, any place subject to the jurisdiction of the United States, whether or not such landing, bringing, or introduction constitutes an importation within the meaning of the customs laws of the United States." ESA section 3, 16 U.S.C. § 1532.

incidental take: "takings that result from, but are not the purpose of, carrying out an otherwise lawful activity conducted by the Federal agency or applicant." 50 C.F.R. § 402.02.

incidental take permit: "a permit that exempts a permittee from the take prohibition of section 9 of the ESA issued by the FWS or NMFS pursuant to section 10(a)(1)(B) of the ESA." HCP Handbook 8-4.

indirect effects: for ESA section 7 consultation purposes, "[i]ndirect effects are those that are caused by the proposed action and are later in time, but still are reasonably certain to occur." 50 C.F.R. § 402.02 (contained within the definition of *effects of the action*).

industry or trade: "in the definition of 'commercial activity' in the Act means the actual or intended transfer of wildlife or plants from one person to another person in the pursuit of gain or profit." 50 C.F.R. § 17.3.

informal consultation: "an optional process that includes all discussions, correspondence, etc., between the Service and the Federal agency or the designated non-Federal representative prior to formal consultation, if required." 50 C.F.R. § 402.02.

interdependent actions: for ESA section 7 consultation purposes, "those [actions] that have no independent utility apart from the action under consideration." 50 C.F.R. § 402.02 (contained within the definition of *effects of the action*).

interrelated actions: for ESA section 7 consultation purposes, actions "that are part of a larger action and depend on the larger action for their justification." 50 C.F.R. § 402.02 (contained within the definition of *effects of the action*).

is likely to adversely affect: "the appropriate finding in a biological assessment (or conclusion during informal consultation) if any adverse effect to listed species may occur as a direct or indirect result of the proposed action or its interrelated or interdependent actions, and the effect is not: discountable, insignificant, or beneficial [see *is not likely to adversely affect*]. In the event the overall effect of the proposed action is beneficial to the listed species, but is also likely to cause some adverse effects, then the proposed action 'is likely to adversely affect' the listed species. If incidental take is anticipated to occur as a result of the proposed action, an 'is likely to adversely affect' determination should be made. An 'is likely to adversely affect' determination requires the initiation of formal section 7 consultation." NMFS/FWS CONSULTATION HANDBOOK, at xv.

is not likely to adversely affect: "the appropriate conclusion when effects on listed species are expected to be discountable, insignificant, or completely beneficial. Beneficial effects are contemporaneous positive effects without any adverse effects to the species. Insignificant effects relate to the size of the impact and should never reach the scale where take occurs. Discountable effects are those extremely unlikely to occur. Based on best judgment, a person would not: (1) be able to meaningfully measure, detect, or evaluate insignificant effects; or (2) expect discountable effects to occur." NMFS/FWS CONSULTATION HANDBOOK, at xvi.

jeopardize the continued existence of: "to engage in an action that reasonably would be expected, directly or indirectly, to reduce appreciably the likelihood of both the survival and recovery of a listed species in the wild by reducing the reproduction, numbers, or distribution of that species." 50 C.F.R. § 402.02.

listed species: "any species of fish, wildlife, or plant which has been determined to be endangered or threatened under section 4 of the Act. Listed species are found in 50 C.F.R. 17.11–17.12." 50 C.F.R. § 402.02.

major construction activity: "a construction project (or other undertaking having similar physical impacts) which is a major Federal action significantly affecting the quality of the human environment as referred to in the National Environmental Policy Act [NEPA, 42 U.S.C. § 4332(2)(C)]." 50 C.F.R. § 402.02.

may affect: "the appropriate conclusion when a proposed action may pose any effects on listed species or designated critical habitat. When the Federal agency proposing the action determines that a 'may affect' situation exists, then they must either initiate formal consultation or seek written concurrence from the Services that the action 'is not likely to adversely affect' [see *is not likely to adversely affect*] listed species." NMFS/FWS CONSULTATION HANDBOOK, at xvi.

mitigation and enhancement measures: with respect to the Endangered Species Exemption process, means "measures, including live propagation, transplantation, and habitat acquisition and improvement, necessary and appropriate (a) to minimize the adverse effects of a proposed action on listed species or their critical habitats and/ or (b) to improve the conservation status of the species beyond that which would occur without the action. The measures must be likely to protect the listed species or the critical habitat, and be reasonable in their cost, the availability of the technology required to make them effective, and other considerations deemed relevant by the Committee." 50 C.F.R. § 450.01.

no effect: "the appropriate conclusion when the action agency determines its proposed action will not affect a listed species or designated critical habitat." NMFS/FWS CONSULTATION HANDBOOK, at xvi.

Office of Enforcement: "the national fisheries enforcement office of the National Marine Fisheries Service. Mail sent to the Office of Enforcement should be addressed: Office of Enforcement, F/EN, National Marine Fisheries Service, NOAA, 8484 Suite 415, Georgia Ave., Silver Springs, MD 20910." 50 C.F.R. § 222.102.

Office of Protected Resources: "the national program office of the endangered species and marine mammal programs of the National Marine Fisheries Service. Mail sent to the Office of Protected Resources should be addressed: Office of Protected Resources, F/PR, National Marine Fisheries Service, NOAA, 1315 East-West Highway, Silver Spring, MD 20910." 50 C.F.R. § 222.102.

permit or license applicant: "when used with respect to an action of a Federal agency for which exemption is sought under section 1536 of [the ESA], any person whose application to such agency for a permit or license has been denied primarily because of the application of section 1536(a) of [the ESA] to such agency action." ESA section 3, 16 U.S.C. § 1532.

person: "an individual, corporation, partnership, trust, association, or any other private entity; or any officer, employee, agent, department, or instrumentality of the Federal Government, of any State, municipality, or political subdivision of a State; or any other entity subject to the jurisdiction of the United States." ESA section 3, 16 U.S.C. § 1532.

plant: "any member of the plant kingdom, including seeds, roots and other parts thereof." ESA section 3, 16 U.S.C. § 1532.

population: "a group of fish or wildlife in the same taxon below the subspecific level, in common spatial arrangement that interbreed when mature." 50 C.F.R. § 17.3.

pre-Act endangered species part: "any sperm whale oil, including derivatives and products thereof, which was lawfully held within the United States on December 28, 1973, in the course of a commercial activity; or any finished scrimshaw product, if such product or the raw material for such product was lawfully held within the United States on December 28, 1973, in the course of a commercial activity." 50 C.F.R. § 222.102.

preliminary biological opinion: "an opinion issued as a result of early consultation." 50 C.F.R. § 402.02.

programmatic consultation: "consultation addressing an agency's multiple actions on a program, regional or other basis." NMFS/FWS CONSULTATION HANDBOOK, at xvii.

properly implemented conservation plan: "any conservation plan, Implementing Agreement and permit whose commitments and provisions have been or are being fully implemented by the permittee." 50 C.F.R. § 17.3.

proposed critical habitat: "habitat proposed in the *Federal Register* to be designated or revised as critical habitat under section 4 of the Act for any listed or proposed species." 50 C.F.R. § 402.02.

proposed species: "any species of fish, wildlife, or plant that is proposed in the *Federal Register* to be listed under section 4 of the Act." 50 C.F.R. § 402.02.

reasonable and prudent alternatives: "alternative actions identified during formal consultation that can be implemented in a manner consistent with the intended purpose of the action, that can be implemented consistent with the scope of the Federal agency's legal authority and jurisdiction, that is economically and technologically feasible, and the Director believes would avoid the likelihood of jeopardizing the continued existence of listed species or resulting in the destruction or adverse modification of critical habitat." 50 C.F.R. § 402.02.

reasonable and prudent measures: "those actions the Director believes necessary or appropriate to minimize the impacts, i.e., amount or extent, of incidental take." 50 C.F.R. § 402.02.

recovery: "improvement in the status of listed species to the point at which listing is no longer appropriate under the criteria set out in section 4(a)(1) of the Act." 50 C.F.R. § 402.02.

resident species: "for purposes of entering into cooperative agreements with any state pursuant to section 6(c) of the Act, a species that exists in the wild in that state during any part of its life." 50 C.F.R. § 222.102.

scrimshaw product: "any art form which involves the substantial etching or engraving of designs upon, or the substantial carving of figures, patterns, or designs from any bone or tooth of any marine mammal of the order Cetacea. For purposes of this part, polishing or the adding of minor superficial markings does not constitute substantial etching, engraving, or carving." 50 C.F.R. § 222.102.

Secretary: "except as otherwise herein provided, the Secretary of the Interior or the Secretary of Commerce as program responsibilities are vested pursuant to the provisions of Reorganization Plan Numbered 4 of 1970; except that with respect to the enforcement of the provisions of [the ESA] and the Convention which pertain to the importation or exportation of terrestrial plants, the term also means the Secretary of Agriculture." ESA section 3, 16 U.S.C. § 1532.

Service: "the U.S. Fish and Wildlife Service or the National Marine Fisheries Service, as appropriate." 50 C.F.R. § 402.02.

species: "includes any subspecies of fish or wildlife or plants, and any distinct population segment of any species of vertebrate fish or wildlife which interbreeds when mature." ESA section 3, 16 U.S.C. § 1532.

specimen: "any animal or plant, or any part, product, egg, seed or root of any animal or plant." 50 C.F.R. § 17.3.

State: "any of the several States, the District of Columbia, the Commonwealth of Puerto Rico, American Samoa, the Virgin Islands, Guam, and the Trust Territory of the Pacific Islands." ESA section 3, 16 U.S.C. § 1532.

State agency: "any State agency, department, board, commission, or other governmental entity which is responsible for the management and conservation of fish, plant, or wildlife resources with a State." ESA section 3, 16 U.S.C. § 1532.

steering committee: "group or panel of individuals representing affected interests or stakeholders in a conservation planning program, the private sector, and the interested public, which may be formed by the applicant to guide development of the HCP, recommend appropriate development, land use, and mitigation strategies, and to communicate progress to their larger constituencies. FWS and NMFS representatives may participate to provide information on procedures, statutory requirements, and other technical information." HCP HANDBOOK 8-5.

subsistence: "the use of endangered or threatened wildlife for food, clothing, shelter, heating, transportation and other uses necessary to maintain the life of the taker of the wildlife, or those who depend upon the taker to provide them with such subsistence, and includes selling any edible portions of such wildlife in native villages and towns in Alaska for native consumption within native villages and towns." 50 C.F.R. § 17.3.

survival: "for determination of jeopardy/adverse modification: the species' persistence as listed or as a recovery unit, beyond the conditions leading to its endangerment, with sufficient resilience to allow for the potential recovery from endangerment. Said another way, survival is the condition in which a species continues to exist into the future while retaining the potential for recovery. This condition is characterized by a species with a sufficient population, represented by all necessary age classes, genetic heterogeneity, and number of sexually mature individuals producing viable offspring, which exists in an environment providing all requirements for completion of the species' entire life cycle, including reproduction, sustenance, and shelter." HCP HANDBOOK, at xviii.

take: "to harass, harm, pursue, hunt, shoot, wound, kill, trap, capture, or collect, or to attempt to engage in any such conduct." ESA section 3, 16 U.S.C. § 1532.

threatened species: "any species which is likely to become an endangered species within the foreseeable future throughout all or a significant portion of its range." ESA section 3, 16 U.S.C. § 1532.

transportation: "to ship, convey, carry or transport by any means whatever, and deliver or receive for such shipment, conveyance, carriage, or transportation." 50 C.F.R. § 222.102.

unforeseen circumstances: "changes in circumstances affecting a species or geographic area covered by a conservation plan that could not reasonably have been anticipated by plan developers and the Service at the time of the conservation plan's negotiation and development, and that result in a substantial and adverse change in the status of the covered species." 50 C.F.R. § 17.3.

United States: "when used in a geographical context, includes all States." ESA section 3, 16 U.S.C. § 1532.

Bibliography

Adler, Jonathan H., ed. *Rebuilding the Ark: New Perspectives on Endangered Species Act Reform* (2011).

Baur, Donald C., and Wm. Robert Irvin, eds. *Endangered Species Act: Law, Policy, and Perspectives* (2010).

Bean, Michael J., and Melanie J. Rowland. *The Evolution of National Wildlife Law* (1997).

Bean, Michael J., et al. *Reconciling Conflicts under the Endangered Species Act: The Habitat Conservation Planning Experience* (World Wildlife Fund 1991).

Beatley, Timothy. *Habitat Conservation Planning: Endangered Species and Urban Growth* (1994).

Blumm, Michael C., et al. "Practiced in the Art of Deception: The Failure of Columbia Basin Salmon Recovery under the Endangered Species Act." 36 Envtl. L. 709 (2006).

Bosselman, Fred. "What Lawmakers Can Learn from Large-Scale Ecology." 17 J. Land Use & Envtl. L. 207 (2002).

Brennan, Michael J., David E. Roth, Murray D. Feldman, and Andrew Robert Greene. "Square Pegs and Round Holes: Application of the 'Best Scientific Data Available' Standard in the Endangered Species Act." 16 Tul. Envtl. L.J. 387 (2003).

Cheever, Federico. "An Introduction to the Prohibition against Takings in Section 9 of the Endangered Species Act of 1973: Learning to Live with a Powerful Species Preservation Law." 62 U. Colo. L. Rev. 109 (1991).

Coggins, George Cameron, and Irma S. Russell. "Beyond Shooting Snail Darters in Pork Barrels: Endangered Species and Land Use in America." 70 Geo. L.J. 1433 (1982).

Corn, M. Lynne. *The Convention on International Trade in Endangered Species: Its Past and Future* (Congressional Research Service, Aug. 24, 1994).

Corn, M. Lynne, and Pamela Baldwin. *Endangered Species Act: The Listing and Exemption Processes* (Congressional Research Service, May 8, 1990).

Craig, Robin Kundis. "Removing the 'Cloud of Standing Inquiry': Pollution Regulation, Public Health, and Private Risk in the Injury-in-Fact Analysis." 29 Cardozo L. Rev. 149 (2007).

Davison, Steven. "The Aftermath of *Sweet Home Chapter:* Modification of Wildlife Habitat as a Prohibited Taking in Violation of the Endangered Species Act." 27 Wm. & Mary Envtl. L. & Pol'y Rev. 541 (2003).

Derry, Amy C. Note, "No Surprises after *Winstar:* Contractual Certainty and Habitat Conservation Planning under the ESA." 17 Va. Envtl. L.J. 357 (Spring 1998).

des Rosiers, Jared. Note, "The Exemption Process under the Endangered Species Act: How the 'God Squad' Works and Why." 66 Notre Dame L. Rev. 825 (1991).

Doremus, Holly. "Listing Decisions under the Endangered Species Act: Why Better Science Isn't Always Better Policy." 75 Wash. U. L.Q. 1029 (1997).

Duggan, Patrick. "Incidental Extinction: How the Endangered Species Act's Incidental Take Permits Fail to Account for Population Loss." 41 Envtl. L. Rep. 10,628 (2011).

Feldman, Murray D., and Michael J. Brennan. "The Growing Importance of Critical Habitat for Species Conservation." 16 Nat. Res. & Env't 88 (2001).

Galbraith, Hector, and Jeff Price. *A Framework for Categorizing the Relative Vulnerability of Threatened and Endangered Species to Climate Change* (Global Research Program 2009).

Gleaves, Karl, et al. "The Meaning of 'Species' under the Endangered Species Act." 13 Pub. Land L. Rev. 25 (1992).

Houck, Oliver. "The Endangered Species Act and Its Implementation by the U.S. Departments of the Interior and Commerce." 64 U. Colo. L. Rev. 277 (1993).

Jeffers, Jennifer. "Reversing the Trend towards Species Extinction or Merely Halting It?: Incorporating the Recovery Standard into ESA Section 7 Jeopardy Analyses." 35 Ecology L. Q. 455 (2008).

_____. Note, "Habitat Conservation Plans under Section 10 of the Endangered Species Act: The Alabama Beach Mouse and the Unfulfilled Mandate of Species Recovery." 26 B.C. Envtl. Aff. L. Rev. 131 (Fall 1998).

Kalen, Sam. "Standing on Its Last Legs: *Bennett v. Spear* and the Past and Future of Standing in Environmental Cases." 13 J. Land Use & Envtl. L. 1 (1997).

Karkkainen, Bradley C. "Collaborative Ecosystem Governance: Scale, Complexity, and Dynamism." 21 Va. Envtl. L.J. 189 (2002).

Kilbourne, James C. "The Endangered Species Act under the Microscope: A Closeup Look from a Litigator's Perspective." 21 Envtl. L. 499 (1991).

Kohm, Kathryn A., ed. *Balancing on the Brink of Extinction: The Endangered Species Act and Lessons for the Future* (1991).

Liebesman, Lawrence R., and Steven G. Davison. "Takings of Wildlife under the Endangered Species Act after *Babbitt v. Sweet Home Chapter of Communities for a Great Oregon*." 5 U. Balt. J. Envtl. L. 137 (1997).

Mank, Bradford. "Revisiting the *Lyons* Den: *Summers v. Earth Island Institute*'s Misuse of *Lyons*'s 'Realistic Threat' of Harm Standing Test." 42 Ariz. St. L.J. 837 (2010).

Murchison, Kenneth M. *The Snail Darter Case: TVA versus the Endangered Species Act* (2007).

Regenstein, Lewis. *The Politics of Extinction: The Shocking Story of the World's Endangered Wildlife* (1975).

Reimer, Hadassah M., and Murray D. Feldman. "Give PECE a Chance: Evaluating Conservation Programs to Avoid Endangered Species Act Listings." 56 Rocky Mtn. Min. L. Inst. 21-1 (2010).

Rohlf, Daniel J. *The Endangered Species Act: A Guide to Its Protections and Implementation* (1989).

_____. "Section 4 of the Endangered Species Act: Top Ten Issues for the Next Thirty Years." 34 Envtl. L. 483 (2004).

Ruhl, J.B. "Regional Habitat Conservation Planning under the Endangered Species Act; Pushing the Legal and Practical Limits of Species Protection." 44 Sw. L.J. 1393 (1991).

_____. "Section 7(a)(1) of the 'New' Endangered Species Act: Rediscovering and Redefining the Untapped Power of Federal Agencies' Duty to Conserve Species." 25 Envtl. L. 1107 (1995).

_____. "How to Kill Endangered Species, Legally: The Nuts and Bolts of Endangered Species Act 'HCP' Permits for Real Estate Development." 6 Envtl. L. 345 (1999).

Ruhl, J.B., and James Salzman. "Gaming the Past: The Theory and Practice of Historic Baselines in the Administrative State." 64 Vand. L. Rev. 1 (2011).

Rylander, Jason C. "Recovering Endangered Species in Difficult Times: Can the ESA Go Beyond Mere Salvage?," 42 Envtl. L. Rep. 10017 (2012).

Sanders, Marren. *Implementing the Federal Endangered Species Act in Indian Country: The Promise and Reality of Secretarial Order 3206* (Joint Occasional Papers on Native Aff. 2007).

Sheikh, Pervaze A., and M. Lynne Corn. *The Convention on International Trade in Endangered Species of Wild Fauna and Flora (CITES): Background and Issues* (Congressional Research Service, Feb. 5, 2008).

Smith, Molly K. "Abuse of the Warranted but Precluded Designation: A Real or Imagined Purgatory?" 19 Southeastern Envtl. L.J. 119 (2010).

Stanford Environmental Law Society. *The Endangered Species Act* (2001).

Sunstein, Cass R. "What's Standing after *Lujan?* Of Citizen Suits, 'Injuries,' and Article III." 91 Mich. L. Rev. 163 (1992).

Tarlock, Dan. "Ecosystem Services in the Klamath Basin: Battlefield Casualties or the Future." 22 J. Land Use & Envtl. L. 207 (2007).

Thorton, Robert D. "Searching for Consensus and Predictability: Habitat Conservation Planning under the Endangered Species Act of 1973." 21 Envtl. L. 605 (1991).

Thompson, Barton H. Jr. "The Endangered Species Act: A Case Study in Takings and Incentives." 49 Stan. L. Rev. 305 (1997).

Trexler, Mark C., and Laura H. Kosloff. "International Implementation: The Longest Arm of the Law?" In *Balancing on the Brink of Extinction: The Endangered Species Act and Lessons for the Future* (Kathryn A. Kohm ed., 1993).

Wilkinson, Charles F. "The Role of Bilateralism in Fulfilling the Federal-Tribal Relationship: The Tribal Rights-Endangered Species Secretarial Order." 72 Wash. L. Rev. 1063 (1997).

Table of Cases

Index